THE TRANSCENDENCE
OF GOD

THE TRANSCENDENCE OF GOD

A Study in Contemporary Philosophical Theology

by
EDWARD FARLEY

WIPF & STOCK · Eugene, Oregon

Wipf and Stock Publishers
199 W 8th Ave, Suite 3
Eugene, OR 97401

The Transcendence of God
A Study in Contemporary Philosophical Theology
By Farley, Edward
Copyright©1962 Methodist Publishing - Epworth Press
ISBN 13: 978-1-5326-3177-1
Publication date 4/6/2017
Previously published by Epworth Press, 1962

Every effort has been made to trace the current copyright
owner of this publication but without success. If you have
any information or interest in the copyright, please contact the publishers.

To my wife
Doris

Contents

PREFACE	9
I. THE NEW TEMPER AND ITS BACKGROUND	13
1. The Location of God	13
2. The Age of Immanence	16
3. The Liberal Theology	20
4. The Coming of the "Realistic" Temper	25
5. The Problem of Transcendence: The "Kerygmatic" Side	36
6. The Problem of Transcendence: The Metaphysical Side	40
II. GOD AS TRANSCENDENT SELF AND SOURCE: REINHOLD NIEBUHR	42
1. God as Transcendent Self ("Biblical Faith")	42
2. God as Transcendent Source ("Ontological Analysis")	51
3. The Apprehension and Expression of the Transcendent	73
III. GOD AS TRANSCENDENT GROUND: PAUL TILLICH	75
1. The Religious Socialist Years: Transcendence in the Early Tillich	75
2. The Doctrine of God: Transcendence in the Developed System	82
3. The Principle of Correlation: Transcendence and Theological Method	97

CONTENTS

IV. Transcendence in a Dimensional Metaphor: Karl Heim ... 103
  1. The Metaphysical Problem ... 104
  2. The I-Thou-It World (Intramundane Transcendence) ... 111
  3. The Suprapolar World (Supramundane Transcendence) ... 121

V. God as Dynamic Whole: Charles Hartshorne ... 130
  1. Polemics and the Problem ... 131
  2. Hartshorne's Cosmological Metaphysics ... 138
  3. God Absolute and Relative ... 146
  4. Transcendence as Unrivaled Superiority ... 153

VI. God as Suprahuman Event: Henry Nelson Wieman ... 162
  1. The Immediate Background ... 162
  2. The Problem: Cultural and Philosophical ... 165
  3. The Philosophy of Henry Nelson Wieman ... 167
  4. Wieman's Philosophy of Religion ... 176
  5. God's Transcendence: Metaphysical and Functional ... 182

VII. The Transcendence of God ... 192
  1. The Transcendent as Limit ... 193
  2. The Transcendent as God ... 202
  3. The Analogy of Grace ... 211

Notes ... 223

Some Suggestions for Further Reading ... 245

Index ... 251

PREFACE

In the recent past a number of studies have been made of various "motifs" in contemporary theology, motifs such as history and faith, the hiddenness of God, and subject and object. This, too, is such a "motif" study. Why was the particular motif, the transcendence of God, chosen? Actually, a larger and more general problem began the matter, the problem of the natural and the supernatural. A brief glance at theological literature in the last half century finds that "natural" and "supernatural" are terms rarely and infrequently used. The exception to this would be Roman Catholic theologians (and Neo-Thomists) and conservative Protestant theologians (and fundamentalists). Hesitation to approach theological problems by means of this distinction hails from nineteenth-century critiques of "supernaturalism," critiques that both liberal and neo-reformation theologies seem to have accepted.

Yet, these theologians, regardless of their theological party line, were neither naturalists nor idealists. They not only spoke of God in more or less traditional terms, they employed distinctions and spoke of realities that sounded very much like the "supernatural." None of them would have affirmed that God was another word for human values or nature as a whole. A line, a very pronounced and black line, is thus drawn between God and everything else. Thus for Tillich, identifying *anything* (any word, polarity, entity, or value) with being-itself is a terrible idolatry. Hence, in the 1930's some American naturalists labeled theologies like Tillich's (much to Tillich's horror) " neo-supernaturalism."

What was the issue between theologians such as Tillich, Reinhold Niebuhr, and Barth and the " old supernaturalism " ? What troubled many about the cruder types of supernaturalism was its cosmological overtones. The " unenlightened " supernaturalist actually seemed to picture another world or realm, analogous to this one, *somewhere* in or beyond the cosmos. Supernaturalism in this sense constantly approached the precipice of obscurantism. But criticism was also addressed to the " enlightened " (nonobscurantist) supernaturalist. " Natural-supernatural " is the language of a dualism that calls up the image of the one and the many, the time and eternity of Hellenistic thought. In short, what troubled many about traditional supernaturalism was the precise way it related God and the world.

But how can God and the " not-God " be related in a way that will avoid cosmology, obscurantism, and a simple dualism? This was the general problem, and the method of narrowing it was to study the doctrine of God's transcendence. Furthermore, it seemed that the hidden issues might better be exposed if quite different approaches to " time and eternity " were looked at: neo-naturalist, process philosophy, dialogic philosophy, etc.

I should say here that for initial inspirations and guidance in the early stages of this project, I am in debt to Profs. Daniel Day Williams, Robert McAfee Brown, and Wilhelm Pauck, of Union Theological Seminary, and also Prof. John Hutchinson, of Claremont College. I must also express gratitude to Prof. Robert C. Johnson, of Pittsburgh Theological Seminary, and to Prof. Arnold Hearn, of Bangor Theological Seminary, who made valuable suggestions for the final stages of the manuscript.

E. F.

I
THE NEW TEMPER AND ITS BACKGROUND

Daniel Day Williams has described the "theological renaissance" in our time in terms of a "reality at the base of all Christian living which gives us our reason for being and the final test for all our decisions."[1] This underlying Reality, unidentifiable with anything other than itself, is the subject of this study in contemporary theology, namely, the transcendence of God. The "transcendence of God," however, like many theological phrases, carries many connotations and usages. Yet in spite of such variations, we can speak of a general "climate of opinion" that serves as a background for renewed concern about transcendence. The purpose of this introduction is simply to describe that background. Such a description will inevitably be general in nature; thus we lay no claim to writing a "history" of transcendence in recent theology.

1. The Location of God

The child's question, "Where is God?" is not, of course, just a child's question. Job's despairing cry, "Oh, that I knew where I might find him!" is neither childish nor irrelevant. The question of the "place" of God is another way of asking, Can God be known? Furthermore, if the philosophies and religions of the world are our context, God's "places" are legion, for they are many. His place may be nature in both its creative and destructive aspects. Or nature may be his sphere at the level of "all things," in which case God would be the all-inclusive reality within which nature's particular powers have their being. Or God's place may not be in the sphere of nature or existence at all, but "beyond" it. In this sense he may not have a "place," or even a function. He would be the "Beyond" itself; remote, distinctionless, and contentless. Or God may be located primarily in the sphere of the human. To look for God, examine man. His place may thus be the human cultus, human values, or human mystical experiences. Such is the history of religion, and Feuerbach may be right. These "places" of God may tell us more about man than they do about God.

In the Hebraic-Christian tradition the paradoxical claim arose that God was both placeless yet had a "place." He could never be assigned a "place." The mountain, the Ark, the temple, even the heavens and the earth, could not contain him. Yet this God who had no "place" chose to "place" himself, first in the events of the history of a particular people, and finally in the Event that ended (fulfilled) that history and began a new history, the Event of Jesus Christ. Thus God placed himself where no one would have thought to look, or even dared to look, namely, in a Galilean peasant who doubled as miracle worker and rabbi.

However, the Hebraic-Christian tradition has never been an unmixed stream of pure revelation. The kerygma, or essential proclamation of the saving message, has always been proclaimed in terms of, and received by means of, many historical backgrounds. While that kerygma itself is essentially not a world view attempting merely to replace other world views, it has never existed apart from such earthen vessels as Platonism, Aristotelianism, Scholasticism, Kantianism, or existentialism. We should not be surprised, then, to find the patristic, medieval, or Reformation expressions of the Christian proclamation systematizing themselves within the framework of a pre-Renaissance world view. Thus for Dante, God was "located" not merely in the Event of Jesus Christ but also in terms of that outer region toward which the Ptolemaic spheres were stepping-stones. In so far as his place was in Jesus Christ, this was to be found *also* and *in terms of* a sacramental and hierarchical extension of that Event.

At this point came the Renaissance, cutting in two directions. With Copernicus and Bruno, a new *Weltbild* (picture of the cosmos) arose, and like a thief in the night it stole away the Ptolemaic spheres. With Boccaccio, Montaigne, and Erasmus, came a new *Weltanschauung* (view of reality) that was neither hierarchical nor sacramental but nominalistic and humanistic. Further, the Reformation added to this breakup of the "medieval synthesis" by its principle of *sola scriptura,* recognizing the priority of the Bible over hierarchy and tradition.[2]

However, what was decisive in the formation of postmedieval Western culture was not so much the Reformation as the Renaissance. With the victory of Renaissance humanism and Newtonian cosmology, God became more or less homeless, not in the sense that he was beyond every "place," but in the sense that the very notion, God, became inconceivable. To be sure, some of the Renaissance scientists like Galileo, Newton, and Bruno found a temporary home for God in space (the divine sensorium). Others, anticipating the deists, admitted God might be the force that switched on the world machine and occasionally stepped in to repair it. All this, of course, was a halfway house between theism and humanism, with humanism gradually getting the upper hand, since God is now conveniently removed as a disturber of human history. It was thus only a short step from this to the simpler solution of the eighteenth-century Encyclopedists who could get along perfectly well without the hypothesis "God."

2. THE AGE OF IMMANENCE [3]

Various fluctuations between humanism, deism, and skepticism reigned throughout the Renaissance. When God was "placed," his place turned out to be at a safe distance, such as 'way off at the beginning of things. Then the mechanistic and rationalistic climate of opinion disintegrated before a new and vital way of looking at things, the romantic movement. When this happened, it was time to remember what had previously been thought to be a dead end, the philosophy of Spinoza. "Immanence," of course, is without explicit definition a vague concept. Two major types can be distinguished according to that with which God is associated or identified. The first is a cosmological immanence in which nature or some part thereof is God's location. The second is a humanistic immanence in which human powers, plans, causes, ideals, etc., are the dwelling place of God. Historically, the second seems to follow the first; or to put it another way, in the age of immanence the stress on continuity preceded the stress on autonomy.

a. *Continuity*. It has been said that the one great "unit-idea" (Lovejoy) that characterizes the nineteenth century is that of continuity.[4] If so, it is the work of many forces and movements rather than any single one. Romanticism certainly played an important part. The first generation of romantics in Germany inherited the religious skepticism in which the Enlightenment had culminated, and " positive religion " was something to be derided. However, far from seeing the universe as the grinding and pounding of a giant mechanism, possibly holding within it an alien substance called " mind," they reveled in a living universe, the proper object of a poet's praises. Within this circle arose the " father of modern theology," Friedrich Schleiermacher, siding with the criticisms of rationalistic and moralistic deism and the wooden creedalism of Protestant orthodoxy, yet insisting that the romantics' praise of and response to the living universe was the very essence of religion itself. Therefore according to Schleiermacher: " The usual conception of God as a single being outside of the world and behind the world is not essential to religion. . . . The true essence of religion is neither this idea nor any other, but the immediate consciousness of Deity as we find him in ourselves as well as in the world."[5] Response to the whole of things thus became a way of conceiving religion. God again had a location, and the age of immanence had begun.[6]

The romantics were not, however, the only opponents of the Enlightenment. The religious version of this revolt had already come in pietism, and this laid important groundwork for continuity by bridging the gap between the mind and external doctrines with feeling. The " strangely warmed " heart of John Wesley reflected an antideist mood, for he found that God was continuous enough with his world to be personally experienced. The romantic vision of " the everlasting universe of things " (Shelley) was reflected philosophically in the German idealists' reconstruction of the bifurcated world bequeathed to them by Kant. Naturalism and the whole scientific-empirical tradition, which had been accumulating since the early Renaissance, also furthered and reflected such continuity, especially in the negative sense of opposing supernaturalism. In this sense both naturalism and idealism are one in the contemporary "revolt against dualism," and thus in providing a framework for immanentist doctrines. Evolution became popular as early as the German humanists of the last half of the eighteenth century, and Darwin's role later was to establish the idea by biological documentation. Darwin thus was not so much a cause as a reflection of a temper that had begun long before.

Thus we have the background and major expressions of the nineteenth-century doctrine of continuity in which the world of gaps and gulfs was turned into a vast intuited spectrum of shades and degrees. This background includes the romantic reaction, pietism, idealism, naturalism, and evolution. All of this laid the ideological and cultural foundation of a mood that was theologically expressed in the doctrine of divine immanence, a doctrine that has been called the most characteristic theological doctrine of the nineteenth century.

b. *Autonomy.* However, to limit the background of the doctrine of immanence to the monistic mood of continuity is to tell only half the story. The five men in this study all advance their reconstructions against an opponent, yet that opponent is never simply the mood of continuity just described. The second half of the story comprises what happened culturally in addition to and possibly as a result of the above doctrine of continuity. We previously described eighteenth-century deism in terms of a dualism and externalism against which the romantics and others reacted. This seems to correlate the Enlightenment at least in its theological dimension with transcendence and the nineteenth century with immanence. But this would be terribly misleading. In spite of the presence of a rather wooden type of supernaturalism in the eighteenth century, the final mood of the Enlightenment was one of immanence in an important respect. Carl Becker has eloquently portrayed the "faith" of the eighteenth century in terms of human autonomy. In this period a new "heavenly city" was erected around such notions as "men of virtue," "posterity," and "man." Deism accordingly was the expected manifestation of this spirit, for there God "ceased to be personal and inconvenient, no longer demanding propitiatory sacrifices, he could be regarded merely as that Omniscience or Beneficence which men of sense could serenely contemplate with respect untempered with fear or adoration."[7] When the romantic temper did arise, its notion of God was like that of the eighteenth century in one important aspect. For the new World-Spirit was like the old remote God in that neither was he "personal or inconvenient." Rather, at this point the nineteenth century proved to be one step closer to autonomy than the eighteenth century. In the eighteenth century, man could go his own way by positing a remote and therefore irrelevant deity. In the nineteenth century, man could go his own way by bringing deity down into his own sphere and identifying him with man's own power and wisdom. For if God is all-pervasive, or even a name symbolizing human goods and values, there is no longer ground for these values to be challenged. In this sense there is strong continuity between eighteenth-century deism and nineteenth-century immanentism, for both represent stages toward human autonomy.

Culturally speaking, what we are describing in the eighteenth and nineteenth centuries is that flowering of the Renaissance and Enlightenment called "bourgeois culture." Probably the most thorough study of the nineteenth century as a century of the rise of autonomy is Tillich's *The Religious Situation*. Here we find the description of the emancipation from all criticism of sphere after sphere of human culture: science, art, education, and religion. When such autonomy is coupled with the notion of immanence, especially the immanence of God in man, we have the religious sanctification of some particular cause, goal, ideal, or enterprise. Immanence then, as it worked itself out culturally, can be seen in the " religious " claims for unqualified allegiance such as we find in modern nationalism and fascism. Sometimes these are made overtly religious by such forces as the German Faith Movement of the 1930's. In America the bridge between nineteenth-century doctrines of evolution and continuity, and bourgeois culture, can be documented in the way Spencer's sociological elaboration of evolution was spelled out by the Social Darwinians, producing the age of laissez-faire sociology and economics. " Immanentism " is this fusion of bourgeois autonomy, or as Tillich would have it, " self-sufficient finitude," with the notion of the continuity of God with human enterprises. It was against this " immanentism " that at least most of the men in this study arose in reaction.

3. THE LIBERAL THEOLOGY [5]

The theological movement reflecting various degrees of the temper of continuity is commonly known as liberalism. " Liberalism," like other " isms," is a loose and amorphous term denoting a certain spirit of openness, a historical movement and period, a circumscribed ideology that includes a wide variety of expressions. As a movement its broadest characteristic is a negative one, namely, the attempt to eschew all obscurantism in religious thought. For this reason, " modernism," however mild or radical, is always a feature of liberalism. Because of this fear of obscurantism, liberalism attempted to be open to various currents of thought in scientific and learned circles, including such areas as the study of other religions, historical method, the consequences and methods of the various sciences, and new philosophical currents. In contrast to humanism, however, liberalism has never been willing to forsake entirely the content of its inherited religious tradition, therefore the liberal's self-identification is always in a twofold direction. One is toward the past, the period of the genesis of Christianity and subsequent ages such as the Reformation. The other direction is toward the present in whatever age the liberal finds himself. And this provides us with the broadest positive characteristic of liberalism, namely, the mood and method of adaptation. This twofold orientation not only explains why liberalism is attacked from both progressive and conservative sides but also why as a movement it tends to be somewhat unstable. Liberals are willing to regard neither tradition and sources in tradition nor contemporary movements as wholly normative in relation to each other. Hence, there is in liberalism always an unresolved tension on the problem of authority.

This characteristic of semi but not total adaptation helps to explain the way in which liberalism reflected the immanentism described above. Because of this adaptive method, liberal theology was rarely immanental in any "pure" sense. The stress on immanence in liberal theology was derived from a continuity metaphysics; thus liberalism placed itself against any supernaturalism that carried cosmological connotations. The only instances where liberal theology capitulated to autonomy were certain crude versions of the social gospel in America where God's Kingdom and American history appeared to be synonyms, and the German Faith Movement where God's Kingdom and the Third Reich were identified.

Generally speaking, however, the total mood of liberalism

was one of continuity rather than discontinuity, and one dominated by immanence rather than transcendence. "Within" was the direction in which liberalism attempted to locate God rather than "without." This can be documented in Continental, English, and American theologies. On the Continent, in the nineteenth century, post-Hegelian philosophy was developing its various "wings," with some such as Fechner, Lotze, and Hartmann attempting to synthesize science and philosophy, and others such as Cohen and his successors making the epistemological problem central.[9] In spite of the many attacks on Hegel (Schelling, Kierkegaard, Feuerbach, Nietzsche, Marx, Trendelenburg, etc.), the dominant tone of the nineteenth century was pre-existentialist, with post-Kantian and post-Hegelian movements reigning. Theologically, this was reflected in the triumph of the Ritschlian school, especially in Hermann and Harnack.

In England the great period of immanence was the one immediately dominated by the neo-Hegelians, Bradley, and Bosanquet. *Lux Mundi* (1889) reflected this in Anglican circles. The "New Theology" controversy (1907–1910), centering around R. J. Campbell, marked the height of the immanentist movement in Free Church Britain. There was an immediate reaction against Campbell in behalf of transcendence on the part of P. T. Forsyth, Bishop Gore, J. R. Illingworth, and Baron von Hügel. In philosophical theology, idealism began to take a more personalistic bent in the work of Pringle-Pattison, C. C. J. Webb, and W. H. Moberly. Nevertheless, studies of the Gifford Lectures up to 1920 reveal that immanence remained the dominant tone in England, and it continued so until the 1930's.[10]

In America,[11] Drummond, Fiske, and Abbott marked the victory of immanence by appropriating the framework of evolution for the doctrine of God more or less before the turn of the century. Also before the turn of the century theological schools such as Oberlin, Union, Chicago, Yale, and Colgate joined the already liberal Andover because of the coming of such men as H. C. King (Oberlin), Shailer Mathews (Chicago), and W. N. Clarke (Colgate). Nor did this early generation of liberals arise *in vacuo* apart from long-standing forces before them; especially three: (1) a tradition of American liberalism hailing from Bushnell and also from the unitarian liberalism of Channing and Parker; (2) Continental influences such as Schleiermacher and Ritschl, which had been coming in as early as Bushnell; (3) American idealism, which from the 1870's on was being forged in local philosophical clubs such as the St. Louis Philosophical Society led by two Hegelians, W. T. Harris and H. Brokmeyer. After 1900 the doctrine of God became the central subject matter of a full-fledged program of immanence proclaimed under a caption reminiscent of R. J. Campbell, " the New Theology." Negatively, the program included a violent attack on supernaturalism and orthodox theism, which were misleadingly but frequently expounded as deism and spatialism. One of the baldest of these " spatialist " accusations is the following: " The fundamental view of God arises out of the imagery of a spatial gulf, fixed between man and God. God's coming to man is from somewhere. His abode is yonder, or up there. He is one among many beings albeit the highest, the supreme — within a spatial universe." [12]

In contrast to this, the New Theology claimed that God's location is " within." For the most part, " within " referred to nature which was now a fitting receptacle for the divine since the rise of idealist and evolutionary views of nature. However, in the 1920's a humanistic wing developed in liberalism in which the " within " referred to human goals and values, at least for those, such as Ames, who were still willing to use the word " God." Such immanentism soon began to be reflected far beyond mere books stressing the immanence of God.[13] The Gospel of Social Christianity waxed strong, driven by the hope that the Kingdom can come in and through America, reforming individuals and groups by means of a sermon-on-the-mount ethic. When World War I did come, it was looked upon in America, in contrast to the Continent, as the pain preceding the beautiful child, a necessary dark step toward better things. Hence, the 1920's in America were marked by classical liberal works on the immanence of God,[14] and there seemed to be no awareness whatever of the theological earthquake shaking the Continent in the same decade.

Hence, the first three decades in Britain and America, and the first two in Germany, are marked by the culmination and triumph of the theism of divine continuity and pervasiveness which already had been anticipated so much earlier. Furthermore, God's continuity with man and the world served as the presupposition for a methodological immanentism proceeding on the basis of a view of man as *homo religiosus*. God thus was continuous enough with man to be discovered within or by experience, reason, values, and social reconstructions. This methodological immanentism had many corollaries: the " easy conscience of modern man " (Niebuhr), various oversimplified doctrines of progress, and optimism concerning the possibility of realizing the aims of individual and social ethics.[15] In the light of these corollaries it is not surprising that when social catastrophes forced more realistic appraisals on the generation of the 1920's and 1930's, a question mark was placed over the whole temper of immanence.

4. The Coming of the "Realistic" Temper

If books and articles on theology written in the last three decades were compared with those written in the first three decades of this century, a change of climate would be quite apparent. The fact of this change is overt enough not to need documentation. However, its cause, nature, and permanence are more elusive matters. Whatever our conclusions may be, this "change of temper" is something more basic than a single movement or school such as "neo-supernaturalism," "neo-orthodoxy," or "realistic theology."

But can this temper or change of climate be designated under one all-inclusive term? If so, I know of no such term in general use and agreement. However, for want of anything better, "realism" in the broadest possible sense will have to serve. There is a correlation between realism and transcendence even in the medieval use of the term, for there it denotes the doctrine that universals are transcendental realities in relation to spatial-temporal objects. Also in more recent epistemological usages realism retains the element of transcendence, for it is the doctrine that in the knowledge process existing things transcend the knower as objects outside his own being and knowing. And it is within this context that "New Realism" and "Critical Realism" derive their names. Thus R. B. Perry defined the realist as one who "believes reality to be a datum, a somewhat that is given independently of whatever ideas may be found about it." Accordingly, it is the notion of "independence" that seems to be the common element in realism, and this is carried over to "religious realism" and "realistic theology." The former is characterized by "a common interest in maintaining the independent reality of the religious objects."[16] The latter, "realistic theology," is centered in the attempt to recognize frankly the radicality and extent of human evil that constantly undercuts the romances and rationalizations man tends to project.[17] The realism in which all of these participate is a culture-wide movement reflected in literature, aesthetics, philosophy, and religion. Five important strands serve as the background (and sometimes underground) for the change of temper from continuity and autonomy to realism.

a. *Persisting Protestant Orthodoxy.* This brief account of how theism fared through the age of immanence has totally omitted a strand that was relatively unaffected throughout, namely, continuing Protestant orthodoxy. Nor was this strand without its own periods of vitality. Pietism, although its doctrinal minimalism and its stress on experience opposed the emphases of Protestant Scholasticism, comprised an orthodoxy of a type. On the Continent, especially in the state church, orthodoxy continued strong and unabated throughout the age of immanence. With this in mind, Brunner lists as one of the five factors behind the rise of the dialectical theology a continuing stream of Confessional Lutherans such as Vilmar and Loehe, plus other conservatives such as Tholuk, Beck, Cremer, Kaehler, and Schlatter.[18] Furthermore, both the Continental theologians in this study, Heim and Tillich, have recognized such influences.

In England continuing orthodoxy is present even during the New Theology controversy. Both Anglican and Free Churches supported a strong though not necessarily narrow orthodoxy in Bishop Gore and P. T. Forsyth. In America orthodox vigor was manifested in the various waves of fundamentalism which covered a spectrum from the obscurantism of R. A. Torrey to the scholarly Calvinism of Charles Hodge and Benjamin B. Warfield.[19] Nor were fundamentalist criticisms of liberalism completely beside the point. However, the polemics orthodoxy offered for the most part failed to come to grips with the problems that bothered the liberals. Rather, the significance of orthodoxy consisted in its continuing witness to and seriousness about not only the Bible but the theologies of the sixteenth century, thus keeping available an indispensable, even if uncritically used, source of theological construction.

b. *Nineteenth- and Twentieth-Century Criticisms of Bourgeois Culture.* " Immanentism " in the sense we have used it comes about when the notion that God is continuous with man and his world is taken over by the various autonomies of bourgeois culture. Hence, any attacks on the foundations of such a culture will indirectly and perhaps unwittingly create the background for new affirmations of a God who transcends that culture. Such " cultural " critics have tended to be for the most part lonely prophets, yet they anticipated the moods of mass disillusionment that came later. The economic analyses of Marx and Engels comprise an important part of the picture, for they crumbled the myth of the disinterested goodness of political and economic groups that propagated a morality and a religion aimed at securing their own power and privilege. Freud's depth analyses dug up the incests and other unthinkabilities of an inner world that tore away the myth of moral autonomy and control. The implication for divine-human continuity seems only too clear, for the question then comes: Can *this* be identified with the divine?[20] Literature and the arts also had their prophets of disillusionment. Tillich, for instance, sees Nietzsche, Strindberg, and van Gogh as early prophets of revolt against the " capitalistic spirit." Among such critics should also be counted Sören Kierkegaard. Both his early "aesthetic" writings with their portrayals of bourgeois types, such as the Seducer, and his later " religious " writings, such as *Training in Christianity* and *Attack Upon Christendom,* should be listed. The early writings " indirectly," and the later writings " directly," attack the presuppositions of the nineteenth-century Burgher.

America too had its literary critics of bourgeois culture. In the nineteenth century both Herman Melville and Samuel Clemens struck deep at the roots of optimism about human nature. And in the early part of the twentieth century came such men as Dreiser, Mencken (who had read Nietzsche), and Sinclair Lewis, blasting away at the very foundations of American bourgeois morality and religion in the same decades when theologians were approvingly saying, " Man is recognized as himself divine." [21] These early criticisms should be stressed if for no other reason than to balance the attempts to write off the new temper as merely the expected psychological aftermath of world wars. Rather, men sensed something in life itself, in culture itself, that was shaky if not rotten, of which the wars are more reflections than causes.

c. *New Currents in Philosophy and Metaphysics.* There are a number of rather dissimilar philosophical currents, which nevertheless participate in a widespread " realistic " temper. Negatively, most of them are revolts against Hegel and some phase of idealism and the " identity principle."

Existentialism.[22] On the Continent, existentialism is perhaps the strongest reflection of the new temper. In the sense of a contemporary movement in philosophy, it arose out of early criticisms of Hegel. Both Kierkegaard and Schelling (in his last period) leveled existentialist analyses against Hegel, and the place of Kierkegaard behind the early Barth, and Schelling behind Tillich, is well known. Existentialism is a "realism" in the sense that it calls for openness to existence whatever existence proves to be. When this occurs the blinders are taken off and the radicality of the threats inherent in existence such as death, guilt, and shipwreck are recognized. Furthermore, it calls for a participation in existence that will be a permanent guard against identifying verbal statements and systems about existence with existence itself. The theological ramifications of existentialism are two in particular. There is a strong discontentment with merely God-ideas, and the refusal to confuse such ideas, even ideas of God's transcendence, with the reality of God himself. In the *ordo cognoscendi* at least, the *existence* of God precedes and transcends his *essence* and essential statements about it.

Secondly, existentialist analyses of *finitude* are relevant to transcendence. Some have pushed their way to the limits of finitude and have thus seen it surrounded. Finitude is finite because something "finitizes" it, be it the Encompassing (*das Umgreifende*) of Jaspers' analysis or the Ground of the later Heidegger.[23] Also, the phenomenological description of the estranged, alienated, distorted nature of *Existenz* makes it difficult to see finitude as in unambiguous continuity with the divine.

The Rediscovery of the "Other Person."[24] It would be foolish to deny that Hegel knew about individuals. However, the individual is in Hegel in the sense of a moment within a wider, more all-embracing scheme. We know the individual because of a rational dialectic that preceded and produced the individual. It was against this assumption that both Kierkegaard and Nietzsche protested. Both felt that the *existing* individual was ontologically and epistemologically prior to the logical schemes we derive from or impose upon the world. Thus we "know" the individual primarily by being individuals. For Nietzsche this meant asserting one's own individuality against bourgeois attempts to reduce that individuality to the least common denominator. Precisely because "morality" would force men to conform to one great average, Nietzsche's thought can be seen basically as an attack on morality and all its fellow travelers: nationalism, religion, and traditional philosophy.

In the twentieth century both Nicolas Berdyaev and Martin Buber wove these insights into decisive religious categories. Buber, especially, is important for his analysis of the Single One, and the relation between the Single One and the Other has been a classic description of transcendence. Thus the givenness, the mystery, the relative independence, and the threat of the Other Person is portrayed. When this is applied to God's transcendence, we find a framework for aserting God as the unreducible and unique Other. Of the men in this study both Karl Heim and Reinhold Niebuhr (in his later writings) reflect important influence from Buber.

The Movement Toward the Objective. On the face of it a movement toward the Objective seems the opposite of the dialogic philosophy mentioned above. That it may be, yet there is one feature of similarity between the two. Both are willing to break up reality to a degree and deal with what is "given" there. This too is an anti-idealist and anti-monist tendency, expressed classically in Arthur Lovejoy's *The Revolt Against Dualism* (1930). The relevance of such a "critical realism" for transcendence is illustrated in Robert L. Calhoun, who since the 1930's has attempted a reconstruction of his own.[25] Calhoun is a self-styled critical realist who draws on Lovejoy epistemologically and defends the doctrine of a "semidetached" knowing mind. The corollary to this in the understanding of God is the rejection of God as a mere " datum in human experience," and the insistence that "each man stands over against God as a real other self." [26] This, of course, does not mean that American philosophical realism necessarily results in reconstructions of the transcendence of God. Rather, it is only part of a general background, and Calhoun's attempt to use critical realism in just that way illustrates the relationship between the two. The temper such realism creates is the common-sense refusal to negate the environment in the name of self-sufficient mind. "Environment" (and for the religious realist, God) is over against us in some sense, even if not totally separated. Accordingly, religious realism in America participated with the Barthian theology in this attempt to transcend subjectivism in religion, although the norms guiding their methodologies were, of course, different. For Wieman scientific method is the only guarantee of objective self-criticism, while for Barth it is God speaking in revelation.

Trends in Cosmological Metaphysics.[27] When T. E. Hulme in 1924 attempted to re-establish "the temper or disposition of mind which can look at a gap or chasm without shuddering," [28] he was reflecting a mood fostered in part by a new metaphysics. In his attempt to outline regions of discontinuity (inorganic, organic, and ethicoreligious), he approximated Lloyd Morgan's *Emergent Evolution,* published one year earlier, which outlined a theory of emerging levels of reality with new levels not reducible to or explainable by earlier ones. In the 1930's in both England and America theists used Morgan's framework to establish cases for transcendence. H. P. Van Dusen argued that God was the "primordial and unchanging" condition for emergence as well as the indwelling nisus giving evolution its direction.[29] William Temple attempted to show that the emergence of mind is accounted for only by a primordial indwelling Mind on which all emergences depend.[30] The new physics, with its notions of finite (spherical) space and time as well as the relativity of mathematical and nomistic systems by which the world is a *uni*-verse, helped defeat all simple monisms. Related to this is the empirically oriented "new naturalism," which leans in the direction of cosmological pluralism. It was hesitant to posit any entity that could serve as the unifying and synthesizing factor. There is, of course, no easy step from such metaphysics to transcendence. The relation comes in the fact that these pluralisms encouraged the temper of relative discontinuity rather than continuity and monism.

d. *The Rise of New Disciplines in Religious Studies.* The "theological renaissance" of late is in part the result of the slow accumulation of new fields of study. The results of such studies have provided in many instances fertile ground for new stresses on God's transcendence.

One such discipline concerns the *nature of religion* itself. Hence in some circles, at least, primitivism as the key to the nature of religion has been strongly qualified by the work of Rudolf Otto. Professor Otto attempted to isolate an underlying, perennial element in religion, ancient and modern, which carried a distinctiveness deeper than moral, doctrinal, or sociological interpretations. Thus Otto stands in the line of Schleiermacher, in that the experience of the Holy finds strong parallels in Schleiermacher's "feeling (*Gefühl*) of absolute dependence." Otto's work is significant for transcendence because he finds in religion an element of awe and fascination before an Other which can never be completely understood in categories not generated by itself.[31] Related to Otto's studies is the revival of mysticism, which began at the turn of the century. In England it centered in Dean Inge, Evelyn Underhill, and Baron von Hügel. Otto played a similar role in Germany as did Rufus Jones in America.[32] This revival is also seen in the growth of new translations and studies of the classical mystics such as Boehme and Eckhart.

Historical theology is another discipline whose fruits contributed to the change of temper. Actually it was the eighteenth and nineteenth centuries that produced the rise of contemporary historical concerns and the "problem of history" itself. Such could not occur without new vistas being opened concerning historical figures and movements in the past. The discoveries most directly related to the new temper are those surrounding the Luther renaissance and the general reworking of the Reformation period. John Dillenberger's masterful study of one motif of Luther's thought, the hidden God, has shown how out of the Luther studies of the Ritschlian school (especially Holl and Kattenbusch) grew the Luther renaissance, the rediscoveries of which provided important background for the work of Barth and Brunner. For it was the Luther research that bequeathed to the Word of God theology the problem of Luther's understanding of "God hidden and revealed." They attempted to solve the problem by *correlating* hiddenness and revelation, which, according to Dillenberger, is the keystone in the structure of the Barthian theology.[33] Brunner has pointed out that Holl's *Luther* dispelled the nineteenth-century picture of Luther and his theology, thus comprising an important root of his and Barth's revolt.[34]

Thirdly, new work in the *Biblical field* is an important part of the theological change of scenery under consideration here. The rise of "Biblical theology," with its attempts to go behind the *Historisch* to the motifs that make up *Heilsgeschichte* (covenant, law, cult, salvation, God, etc.), has helped point out by more careful historical study the impossibility of many of the syntheses that were attempted in the liberal period. Furthermore, God as Lord, as King, as Holy, has become the basis of several Old Testament theologies such as those of Sellin (1933) and Köhler (1936). Walther Eichrodt has written an immensely important monograph in which covenant, law, and the understanding of man in the Old Testament are shown to be rooted in the encounter with a transcendent God manifested as an unconditional Ought.[35] Historical studies such as Eichrodt's broke down many of the parallelisms that were popular in the History of Religions School on the basis of which the Hebrew deity could be seen merely as a national or tribal deity. In addition, a distinction arose between the ancient world view in its details and more perennial elements. In short, the Scriptures had a theological content that could be neither dispelled nor expounded merely at the level of "ancient supernaturalism." Today the distinction between the *Weltbild* comprising the background, setting, or even medium of the revelatory event, and the kerygma itself, is quite sharply marked out in the whole program of demythologizing.

Thus, studies revealing the distinctiveness of religion, including its mystical elements, and also the distinctiveness of Biblical and Reformed faiths, all provided important background for the change that did come. To the degree that such studies were guided by historical documentation, they too add to the "realism" of the time, which is the willingness to receive whatever is given, even if there is no "purely given" entity, or no purely objective receiver.

e. *The Precipitating Factor: National and International Catastrophes.* So far we have limited our description of the strands making up the fabric of realism to "academic" movements. Many of these arose in and even because of the nineteenth century. However, not until the twentieth century did the few falling stones become a landslide. And this in the last analysis was directly due not to the above strands but to catastrophes that produced a culture-wide change of mood. In Europe it was of course World War I that marked the formal ending of the age of immanence. This does not hold, however, for America. The temper in America, at least in religious thought, was little changed after 1914. The reason for the earlier arrival of realism in Europe was due only in part to the fact that Europe's land and people directly experienced the ravages of war. Important also was the fact that the political and economic stresses and strains that led to war far exceeded anything America knew before 1929. The resulting disillusionment in Europe became then the "precipitating factor" by which the long-hovering clouds described above poured down the realist deluge. In America the cultural catastrophe that played a similar role was not the war but the depression of 1929 and subsequent years. However, to explain the various movements of these years (Theology of Crisis, Religious Realism, etc.) merely as the reflection of postcatastrophe pessimism is far too simple. The new temper had been gathering for a long time. A new climate of opinion had been gradually replacing the old, and the role of war and depression was that of midwife for what seemed to be a sudden birth.

The basic characteristic, then, of the "realistic" temper was the willingness to embrace reality, be it divine, human, or otherwise, in all its givenness. This did not mean a return to the myth of the objective spectator, for the notion was retained concerning the subjective element in every reception or exposition of reality. Nevertheless, reality, to use Calhoun's phrase, was " semidetached." If it was in part always colored by human projection, it nevertheless had its element of over-againstness; hence, its " givenness." Thus the historian, the epistemologist, and even the artist, all worked with material that they did not completely mold or control. Deity therefore is not reducible to ideas and projections about it. This is the " temper " behind the five reconstructions considered in this study.

5. The Problem of Transcendence: The " Kerygmatic " Side

a. *The Kerygmatic Revolt.* The story of the actual theological transition must now be told in more detail. Such detail is important because the early " revolts " against liberalism are of such a nature that they provide a clue to the *problem* of transcendence. The story of the theological revolution on the Continent is too well known to be repeated. Suffice it to say that Barth is the key figure, and that Barth's discovery of the " strange new world " in the Bible, his studies in the strange new world of Kierkegaard, and his experience of the bankruptcy of the gospel of Hermann as a wartime pastor, all led to the *Epistle of the Romans* of 1918. The controversies that ensued, the founding of the journal *Zwischen den Zeiten,* the writings of Gogarten, Brunner, and even Bultmann, are all events in a movement that changed the theological face of Europe in the 1920's.

In America and Britain we find a similar story although a decade later. The years 1929 to 1934 were the crucial years of change in both countries; hence, the 1930's marked the first decade of theological realism. Brunner had come to America in 1928 to lecture, the same year that Barth's *The Word of God and the Word of Man* was translated into English. Between 1929 and 1934 a flood of secondary sources on the "theology of crisis" appeared. At the same time articles began appearing in American journals bewailing the sickness of liberalism.[36] In 1932, Niebuhr's great critique of the cultural presuppositions of liberalism was made in *Moral Man and Immoral Society*. Shortly afterward, the "theological discussion group" was formed, and in 1933, Tillich came to America supplementing the crisis mood of this theological revolution. Thus by 1936 Wieman and Meland could describe "neo-supernaturalism" as the basic alternative to their own "neo-naturalism."

b. *The Nature of "Kerygmatic" Transcendence*. The kerygmatic revolt was essentially an attempt to return to a theological method based primarily on the revelatory events and redemptive acts recorded in the Bible. It thus would be expected that transcendence would be treated within this revelational reference. What, then, is "kerygmatic" transcendence? Kerygmatic transcendence refers to a transcendence established and known primarily in terms of the kerygma. The kerygma technically is that central message of good news preached by apostles and evangelists in New Testament times. We are using it here in a sense more or less synonymous with "gospel." Kerygmatic transcendence thus is a transcendence known primarily in and from that gospel. In so far as the gospel is more than a message, but in some sense resides in the person of the Word made flesh, transcendence would be known and characterized primarily in that Word. Such transcendence thus is not so much sought as confessed, for it is derived from a faithful response to the Word.

In its twentieth-century form kerygmatic transcendence can be described in terms of two priorities: the priority of *epistemology* in relation to *ontology*, and the priority of *existence* in relation to *essence*. Brunner has said that transcendence in the "theology of crisis" is epistemological rather than cosmological. Although Brunner did not elaborate this suggestion, we can guess the meaning. The problem that provided the setting for Barth and Brunner was not the ontological problem of the being of God, but the problem of the *knowledge* of God. And it was against an epistemological immanentism that they revolted, i.e., against any claim that God is a reality to be established by and within inherent capacities of human virtue and wisdom. God is the Transcendent because he is not continuous with man's *Erlebnis* or consciousness. Such transcendence is "kerygmatic," for it insists that salvation is *sola gratia* (by grace alone). Further, to say that Jesus Christ is himself the "good news" means that he is decisive in making our knowledge of God possible.

The nineteenth-century figure who marked out the problem of transcendence in its epistemological dimension was Sören Kierkegaard. In the *Philosophical Fragments*, Kierkegaard contrasted two types of relations between a seeker after truth and the truth he seeks. One relation is a continuous or immanent relation between the seeker and the truth. Truth thus is in some latent sense "in" the seeker. Nothing therefore outside the seeker can be decisive in giving him the truth. At best, outside forces can serve as occasions or Socratic midwives by which this immanent truth is liberated. In the second relation truth may be related to the seeker as something "transcendent" where the seeker does not have the truth in and of himself. If this is the case, he does not even recognize the truth when he sees it, for that would presuppose some truth-receiving capacity and thus a continuity between himself and the truth. But when truth is transcendent, the seeker gains truth (salvation, knowledge of God) only when it is given to him, and to receive it he must be transformed in the process. In this case the giver of truth is not merely a dispensable occasion or midwife (dispensable in that *any* midwife might do). The giver of truth is an indispensable, without which *this* truth would not be had at all. Here we have a classic statement of epistemological transcendence, where the transcendent is that which does not reside in man's epistemological capacities. This is not to say the transcendent is unknowable. Rather, knowing it depends on a transformation it brings to those capacities. Epistemological transcendence, then, is another way of saying salvation is of God alone.

The second priority that describes kerygmatic transcendence is the priority of *existence* in relation to *essence*. One might say this actually is an extension of the first priority. The first priority stressed the question, How do we *know* the transcendent? Its answer was, We do not *know* it except from itself, and in this is its transcendence. A further elaboration of this is, We know it only when it *gives* itself to us. We know the transcendent only in its (or his) revelation or givenness. That is, we know it only when our *existence* is grasped and transformed by it. We know *its* existence or actuality within such transformation. In this sense existence precedes essence, i.e., kerygmatic transcendence is "existential" not "essential" transcendence.

If essence preceded existence, we would then ask, What is the essence or idea of transcendence? And this inquiry would precede or at least bracket the transcendent in its revealing actuality. Then it would attempt to get behind the transcendent as it exists *pro nobis* (for us) to the transcendent as it is in itself, that is, in its essence. In contrast to this the kerygmatic point of view never tries to get behind the revelational processes that make it possible to speak about the transcendent in the first place. A more familiar way to describe this "actualism" or priority of God's givenness is to say that *revelation* precedes (though not necessarily annihilates) *reason*. It is transcendence conceived only from the Word. The framework in which we inquire about transcendence is thus the Christian kerygma, which means the event of Jesus Christ and the dialectic of sin and grace that this event extends to all existence.

6. The Problem of Transcendence: The Metaphysical Side

The "theological revolution" of recent decades has been a complex one. In addition to the confessional and neo-reformation theologies just described, theologies ultimately derived from the Schleiermacher side of nineteenth-century theology have continued. These "apologetic" or "correlation" types of theology have also been affected by twentieth-century realistic moods. However, to them the framework of the problem of transcendence is broader and more complex than the kerygma. Rather than stressing the problem of the knowledge of God (the epistemological priority), which comes through his self-givenness in existence (the existential priority), these theologies see also a metaphysical problem. This may be partly because they are "apologetic" theologies and feel therefore that they are responsible meaningfully to communicate or correlate the transcendent to the "situation." It is also because they see, over and above epistemological transcendence, an ontological problem of the relation of the being of God to the world.

It is the thesis of this study that contemporary theology has come to more or less of an impasse between kerygmatic and metaphysical types of theology.[37] Assuming that God is both the transcendent one who is given in the Word made flesh, and the metaphysical *Ens realissimum,* what is the relation between the two? How are we to relate, to use Pascal's words, the God of the philosophers and the God of Abraham, Isaac, and Jacob? At least three men in this study see the problem in this way: Heim, Tillich, and with qualifications, Niebuhr. The other two, Wieman and Hartshorne, although primarily working from philosophical commitments outside the kerygma, are helpful in providing metaphysical grist for the mill.

II

GOD AS TRANSCENDENT SELF AND SOURCE:
Reinhold Niebuhr

The background of Reinhold Niebuhr's thought is the disillusionment that captured sensitive liberals of the early 1930's when the cumulative effects of the war, the depression, and mass production were realized. The more "realistic" appraisal of "immoral society" drove Niebuhr along with others not only to question the gospel of theological liberalism but to re-evaluate traditional Christian doctrines. This, helped by his participation in the Theological Discussion Group and his encounter with new currents from Europe, pushed Niebuhr beyond his liberalism in politics to a "conservatism" in theology. But as a conservatism it was something new, being neither orthodox nor neo-orthodox in any simple sense. What this "something new" was now remains to be told.

1. God as Transcendent Self ("Biblical Faith")

There are two distinct and somewhat fluctuating strains in Niebuhr's writings on transcendence. The first strain concerns a more familiar aspect of Niebuhr's thought, namely, a prophetic exposé of the pretensions of individual and collective man, which sets such pretensions over against a righteous and holy God who is a personal and free Self. This is the dominant mood in Niebuhr. The second strain is more implicit, yet clearly present. God's transcendence is stressed as the solution to certain traditional metaphysical problems.

The first strain deals with transcendence primarily in the setting of " Biblical faith," which for Niebuhr often means the eighth-century prophets, their predecessors and successors. The road from Niebuhr's early works in Christian social ethics to this understanding of transcendence is a clear one. The sorry tale of man's self-sufficient finitude and his prideful pretensions, especially at the collective level, has been a familiar part of Niebuhr's writings since 1932. Even in 1927 Niebuhr's disillusionment drove him to assert a transhuman, transworldly reference in religion.[1] By the time of the appearance of *Beyond Tragedy* in 1937 it becomes clear that this transhuman reference is none other than the God of the Old Testament prophets.[2]

The stage is thus set for the controlling analogy that Niebuhr uses to describe God's transcendence. He has always been aware of the semimythologized and spatialized nature of the claims that God is " beyond " the world. However we choose to communicate transcendence, we will be " deceivers yet true." When Niebuhr attempts to communicate God's transcendence in the Biblical setting, his basic analogy is that of a human self in its freedom. This analogy is found in Niebuhr's works from the 1930's to the elaborated dialogic theology of *The Self and the Dramas of History*. But first, what does Niebuhr mean by the transcendence of a human self?

a. *Man as Transcendent Self.* Freedom is the key word in Niebuhr's doctrine of the transcendence of the human self.

For the transcendent self is always described in contrast to various types of structures. Niebuhr seems to see these structures as unbreakable necessities, both spatially and temporally. Therefore when he says that the self transcends nature, he is referring to the fact that human nature cannot be understood merely in terms of a cluster of impulses and drives acting on man as determining necessities. To say that the self transcends the structures of history means that the self is not merely a necessary product of such structures. And to say that the self transcends the self means that there is an ultimate freedom even over the necessities that flow from the character and structures within the self. Thus, negatively speaking, human transcendence means that human nature is free from all structures in that it is not simply determined by them. It follows from this that the self cannot be understood just in terms of determinate, identifiable structures.

One example Niebuhr gives for evidence is the self's transcendence in relation to the structures of reason. The evidence that the self cannot be understood just within such structures appears when we realize that the self can use reason to justify itself and the consequences of its freedom to itself.[3]

On the affirmative side, transcendence refers to the relation between the free self and structures whereby the self can survey such structures from a perspective above them. Temporally, man can survey a span of time, and because of this he can know history, he can " have " a history, and he can " make " history. Thus, man's consciousness or awareness of his " self " is the most specific witness to the transcendent aspect of human nature. Man transcends structures in that he is conscious of them, and he transcends his own self because he is conscious of that self. " Consciousness is a capacity for surveying the world and determining action from a governing center. Self-consciousness represents a further degree of transcendence in which the self makes itself its own object."[4] A corollary of this doctrine of transcendence is the fact that the self is both unique and mysterious. It not only evades scientific and conceptual grasping; it cannot find its completion in any structure of nature or reason. Yet this is not a sheer indeterminism, for the human self is always both an object in space and time as well as an entity transcending all objectification. All existence is a mixture of both freedom (spirit) and structure. Therefore it is in part predictable and in part not: amenable at certain levels to scientific method, and at others only to mythic and symbolic grasping.

b. *God as Transcendent Self.* Niebuhr's favorite designation of the *how* of God's transcendence follows the above analogy of a self which in its freedom cannot be reduced to structure. His starting point is the prophetic picture of the God whose transcendent will is over against the nation, thus not totally reducible to tribal or national loyalties. This seems to be the earliest conception of divine transcendence in the Biblical tradition, namely, God as a transcendent will. But what does it mean for God to "transcend" man and the world in this sense? What is the content of the spatial metaphors "above" and "beyond"? Niebuhr's answer follows closely his description of human transcendence. God is not transcendent in the sense of a simple separation from the temporal, as in the "side by side" theology Tillich despises so much. God transcends structures in that he is free in relation to them. This is the main reason Niebuhr feels that the analogy of God as personal cannot be given up. He is aware of the finitistic overtones in the analogy, but feels the real value is that only the analogy of personality " connotes precisely that freedom on the one hand and that relation to organic process on the other which prophetic and Christian faith assumes in understanding God's transcendence over, and his immanent relation to, the world."[5] Therefore in the context of this analogy, when we ask *how* God transcends the world, Niebuhr's answer is that he is free in relation to all its structures, even as a personal self is free in relation to the structures of nature. This freedom of God means that he is not identifiable with any created structure, nor is he a necessary product of such structure. This by implication would rule out the evolving deity of Samuel Alexander. If we follow out the analogy from Niebuhr's doctrine of human transcendence, we infer that God's freedom over structures refers also to his consciousness of them, the fact that he can survey all such structures from some point beyond them.

In using the analogy of personality, Niebuhr is willing to describe God as a Self. This gives rise to another facet of Niebuhr's description of transcendence. He now goes farther than saying God is free in relation to all structures. As a Self, God transcends not only the structures of nature-history; he also transcends other selves. Thus the contrast ceases to be merely one of person-structure, and becomes one of person-person or I-Thou. Niebuhr finds support for this in the Bible where he feels, following Buber, that the God-man relationship is that of dialogue. Therefore, he can describe revelation as *self*-disclosure, and revelational *knowledge* as akin to the knowledge of persons rather than things. One self transcending another self inevitably means the presence of mystery as well as revelation in the dialogue. Hence, one correlate of this notion of transcendence is the stress on *deus absconditus*. This is rooted in Niebuhr's view of reality as not completely open to rational schemata, but more directly traceable to his doctrine of dialogue. Why specifically is there mystery in God? Niebuhr's answer is partly historical, partly ethical, and partly anthropological. God rules history, but history is so morally ambiguous on the surface that his rule is not clearly apparent. God deals with history both in wrath and mercy, but the relation between the two is ultimately insoluble, hence the mystery behind and in the acts of God. God is essentially mysterious for the same reason that every self is mysterious. Because of transcendent freedom there are hidden depths in every self which can be only partially communicated. For these reasons we say mystery is a correlate of God's transcendence and one way of expressing it. There is mystery both *behind* his revelation (because of God as Self), and *in* his revelation (for he is revealed as both wrathful and merciful). This view of mystery is obviously nearer Heim than others in this study. It especially contradicts Tillich, who sees mystery in God not because he is a Self but because he is not, i.e., because of the divine abyss beyond all such polarities such as self-world.

c. *Divine and Human Transcendence: Differences.* The analogy between divine and human transcendence, is, of course, only an analogy. Where then does the analogy break down? What are the differences between the way man transcends nature-history, other human selves, and himself, and the way God transcends them?

Finite and Infinite Surveys Over Structure. In the context of freedom in relation to structure, the difference between finite and infinite being is clear. Man is free over against structure, but it is a finite freedom both in time and in space. Man can survey and be conscious of structure, but only from one point in the flux. God, on the other hand, is not related to structure by means of a spatial-temporal (finite) perspective.

Individuality and Freedom. In the context of the dialogic philosophy, the difference between *corrupt* finitude and *incorrupt* infinity emerges. Man is not only free, but he has used his freedom to rebel; thus history is not just a God-man dialogue but a God-man contest. One way Niebuhr states this difference is to say that only God unites perfect power and perfect goodness in freedom. This gives rise to two consequences of God's transcendence in relation to man: God as Judge and God as Redeemer.

A familiar aspect of Niebuhr's thought is his prophetic declaration of God's judgment. Thus he witnesses to the God of the prophets who, in contrast to a merely tribal deity, announced that he could be against his own people. Furthermore, God is able to judge, for only God is righteous and only God is powerful. Judgment, however, is not his last word, nor is it the most profound vindication of his freedom and transcendence.

The final proof and most profound expression of God's transcendent freedom is the fact and act of his mercy with its purpose of redemption. Niebuhr's point seems to be that the freedom of sheer power is a limited freedom, and the transcendence of a mere monarch a limited transcendence. These limitations are especially apparent within the framework of freedom, sin, and salvation. God shows his discontinuity with man in judgment, but this does not establish his sovereignty, because "judgment" is not his deepest or final purpose. Finding a way not only to judge but to redeem man is what is necessary if God is sovereign in the sense that he is free to accomplish his purposes. Therefore, God's mercy, which is the *how* of his redemption, is a sharper disclosure of transcendence than either his acts of creation or judgment. "His mercy is the final dimension of his majesty." The central symbol of this disclosure is the cross, for it points up the fact that God is free not only to judge but to forgive. Therefore, God involves himself in the guilt and suffering of free men who in their freedom have come into conflict with the structural character of reality and with God. This raises the question of the suffering God, which will not be elaborated now except to say that for Niebuhr, God's suffering is the final proof of his freedom in relation to all structures, and in relation to other selves. This is so because redemption is not accomplished apart from suffering. Hence, suffering is the profoundest symbol of God's transcendent freedom.

The Self-Body Analogy. So far two differences have been noted between divine and human transcendence: that of finite and infinite perspectives over structures, and that of corruption and righteousness involving the distinction between God as Judge and man as judged, God as Redeemer and man as redeemed. A third difference raises one of the most difficult problems for the interpreter of Niebuhr, namely, the relation of the self to the organism. In his account of the human self Niebuhr makes it clear that the self includes both a space-time object and a dimension (freedom and consciousness) irreducible to such.[6] There is one tripartite organism: body, soul, and spirit, and all three are facets of the self. In so far as the self experiences the unity of the body it is the "soul." In so far as it is free from all such divisions it is "spirit." But how far does this analysis hold in the analogy concerning God as Self in relation to the world? Is the world related to God as the human body to the human self? There are several passages that would indicate an affirmative answer. In one passage Niebuhr says that an adequate religion needs a "transcendent center of meaning," which though not exhausted in any concrete reality is incarnated there. " Like the human personality in the human body, it lives in and through the body, but transcends it."[7] In the Library of Living Theology symposium, he replies to Wieman's criticisms concerning a God above temporal processes. " God is certainly in the structures and temporal processes just as the human person is ' in ' its organism. But both the human and the divine person possess a freedom over and above the processes and structures."[8] The problem is how much to make of this. Niebuhr's doctrine of creation bears out this analogy, for he rejects any chronological interpretation of *creatio ex nihilo,* saying that its meaning is that temporal process is not self-explanatory. Also, the fact that he can cite both Whitehead and Hartshorne with approval lends weight to a serious stress on this organismic metaphor. Yet the picture is still vague. Is Niebuhr ready to say about God and the world what he says about the human self and the spatial-temporal object to which it is intrinsically related? Is Niebuhr ready to say with Hartshorne that God's self is intrinsically and dependently related to a body, namely, " the structures and temporal processes " ? If so, there is little to set him apart from Whitehead's doctrine of Primordial and Consequent Natures of God. But for Whitehead processes are eternal in that they are neverending. Yet there are passages in Niebuhr that seem to give a different picture, stressing the contingency, createdness, and derivedness of the world. In one place he even insists that " eternity outlasts time."[9] The unitary relationship of the human self and its organism means that the self is ontologically dependent on the organism, its structures and processes. Does this mean that this is the way God and the world are related? If so, Niebuhr is closer to some version of evolutionary theism than any of the other realistic theologians. By way of anticipation it should be said that there is another strand in Niebuhr's thinking that seems to undercut this organismic metaphor, namely, his antithetical way of relating time and eternity. Thus this self-world metaphor does not exhaust Niebuhr's description of the relation of God and the world.

In summary, then, God as a transcendent righteous will threatening and transforming the nations was one of Niebuhr's earliest theological affirmations. Because this God stands in dialogic relation with man, the chief analogy for God's transcendence is that of a self both related to and free over world processes and human selves. The primary way this freedom of God is manifested is in his judgment and redemption, the latter of which is the highest expression of God's free majesty. *What* God's transcendence is over against is history, civilization, and the nations. God is over against them, breaking them up, and calling them to repentance and redemption. Such is the "kerygmatic" strand of Niebuhr's doctrine of transcendence.

2. GOD AS TRANSCENDENT SOURCE ("ONTOLOGICAL ANALYSIS")

The second strand in Niebuhr that can be isolated concerns an unfamiliar side of Niebuhr in which he ceases to be the prophet speaking only out of the Biblical tradition and becomes the thinker addressing philosophical problems. Obviously, such a statement presupposes a distinction between what Niebuhr says about ontology and the ontology he develops.

a. *Niebuhr's Conception of the Ontological Enterprise.*[10] A passing glance will show that one of the issues between Niebuhr and his more philosophical critics concerns the nature of ontology. Niebuhr's attitude toward ontology, especially ontology's relation to the Christian faith, is one of elusive vacillation. The most familiar passages in Niebuhr are those which either historically or normatively treat the two as block entities to be related by antithesis. When this is put historically, Hebraism and Hellenism are the two poles of contrast, and Niebuhr has lately said that " The essence of the Christian faith is drawn from the Hebraic, particularly the prophetic, interpretation of life and history, and is erroneously interpreted as the consequence of a confluence of Hebraic and Hellenic streams of thought." [11] In this mood Niebuhr sees ontology as an enterprise that perennially distorts the Biblical drama, so that one must choose one side or the other. The antithesis is seen at every point of Christian doctrine. In the doctrine of God, impassible Being becomes the ontological distortion of God the Creator. Christologically, the doctrine of the two Natures is the ontological version of the dramatic fact that Christ was a historical figure who also disclosed the divine mystery of God's wrath and mercy. In the doctrine of sin and Fall ontological analyses reduced these dramatic symbols to necessities thus eliminating freedom. In the interpretation of history ontology obscures the drama of history (which is the mixture of freedom and structure) by seeing only structures and necessary patterns. And Niebuhr can see the above distortions in almost every period of Western history: the church fathers, the Councils, the medieval synthesis, the Renaissance, and contemporary liberalism. Therefore he can say that all ontologies lead to a " blunting " of the kerygma.

Such is Niebuhr's " No " to ontology. But in other moods he displays a different and perplexing attitude. For Niebuhr not only fears ontological " blunting " of the kerygma, he also fears the unontological obscurantism that arises when the kerygma is kept in isolation. Thus in spite of Christianity's Hebraic essence, Niebuhr writes that revelation must "be brought into conformity with the truth which may be known by analyzing the structures and essences of reality at all levels."[12] In this mood Niebuhr admits that the Biblical drama had implied ontological presuppositions. He wants no falsification of the drama, but he does want theology to "show how what is implied about the nature of God, man, and history is related to what may be known about man, history, and reality through all the disciplines of culture."[13] The most positive statement of all is in his "Reply" to Tillich in 1952 when he denies that he sets Hebraism against Hellenism: "My thesis is simply that both modes of thought are necessary."[14] His point is that reality is dual, involving both structure and freedom. Ontology grasps structure, but dramatic and historical modes of apprehension are necessary to grasp freedom. Ontology without Biblical faith misses the vital dimensions of life. Biblical faith without ontology tends to be obscurantist. Neither side can be dismissed, nor synthesized. Unfortunately, Niebuhr never elaborates exactly how they are to be held together and what it means to "relate" the kerygma to the truth of ontological and cultural analyses.[15] In the end he can only say that we must "hold fast to the mystery and meaning beyond these coherences," plus having "a decent respect for the order and meaning of the natural world."[16]

What is this ontology which by definition can not grasp the dimension of freedom? Niebuhr seems to see the matter in terms of levels. At the level of life or existence we find a complex mixture of structure and freedom, which when expressed religiously (as in the Bible), is essentially mythic. Theology is one step removed, for though it retains the myths, it attempts to synthesize them, and tries to relate them to culture at large. Ontology is a further step away because while it is covertly theological and semimythical, it dismisses the myth in its attempt to gain coherence. The significance of theology's retaining of myth is that it retains a means of apprehending the freedom side of existence, while ontology in dismissing it, gives itself over to the attempt to reduce everything to a system of necessities. The meaning of the levels now becomes clear. Niebuhr's thesis is, the higher the level of abstraction and conceptualization, the more patterned and deterministic an enterprise of apprehension and expression becomes. Ontology thus for Niebuhr must always by definition search for "necessary patterns." Therefore, the ontological analysis of history, for instance, reduces history to such patterns of necessity that are either cyclic or progressive, inevitably assuming some "necessary development." Ontology thus imposes a deterministic or at least ratiocinative scheme on the reality with which it deals, and this view of ontology, which finds its chief illustrations in the ontology of Hellenism, is the clue to Niebuhr's vacillating treatment of it, as well as the overt unphilosophical tone of his writings.

Such vacillation about ontology is reflected in Niebuhr's total thought. Thus while Niebuhr's thought is basically kerygmatic in tone, it has an ontological dimension, not in the narrow sense of Niebuhr's characterizations of ontology as finding "necessary patterns," but in the broader sense of reflection on "the universal conditions of any real existence."[17] Thus Niebuhr like all ontologists characterizes nature, history, meaning, individuality, and form. Nor are his characterizations merely derived from the kerygma. They have an independent basis, namely, the immediate world of experience and common sense.

b. *Ontological Problems and God's Transcendence.* We shall attempt to delineate Niebuhr's ontology by isolating four major " fields of being," or areas of ontological analysis in Niebuhr's writings: individuality, meaning, history, and nature. These will be drawn together by a consideration of his total picture of reality.

Individuality and Freedom. What is the problem of individuality for Niebuhr? By " individual " he does not mean the complex entity of Whitehead's analysis, but man as a unique self-transcending self. He sees existence in terms of many levels, but individuality comes only at the level of human life, for it is based on the capacity of man to distinguish himself as an object. At the level of nature unique events can occur, but individuality for Niebuhr is always this consciousness of the self and hence freedom over all structures. Niebuhr describes the " problem " of individuality historically. Once this free " individual " emerged in and from nature, he began to vacillate between the peril of total autonomy, a phenomenon especially seen in Renaissance and modern bourgeois civilizations, and the perils of being reduced to some system that annihilates him as an individual, such as absolute idealism or communist collectivism.

This historical analysis illustrates the " realistic " (or as might be said now, existentialist), nature of his ontology. Thus Niebuhr does not see individuality as just a theoretical problem to be solved on paper, but a perennial problem man faces in his existence. Yet it is an ontological problem because individuality is the distinguishing mark of the human (way of) being. The ontological aspect of this is revealed in Niebuhr's attempt to contrast Christianity's way of " solving " the problem with that of naturalism, idealism, and romanticism. Niebuhr seems to mean by this both historical and intellectual solutions, and the content in Christian faith that enables such a solution is the doctrine of a transcendent God.

How can this be? One peril man faces as a free individual is that of chaos and arbitrariness, and this is the fear that the fascist wing of romanticism exploits. How does the affirmation of God transcendent " solve " this problem? " In Christianity the unique individual finds the contingent and arbitrary aspect of his existence tolerable because it is related to, judged, and redeemed by the eternal God, who transcends both the rational structure and the arbitrary facts of the universe."[18] The other side of the peril of individuality can be seen in those systems which translate the individual to some lower (or higher) level of necessities such as natural or historical determinants, or the Absolute of idealism. Niebuhr says only God transcendent can save the individual here, because man realizes his own individuality only over against God. " In this divine transcendence the spirit of man finds a home in which it can understand its stature of freedom. But there it also finds the limits of its freedom, the judgment which is spoken against it, and, ultimately, the mercy which makes such a judgment sufferable."[19] Niebuhr finds this historically verified by the fact that " both the idea and the fact of individuality achieve their highest development in the Christian religion."[20]

The point then is that the characterization of man as a free individual is an ontological problem. Niebuhr struggles with the problem, recognizes certain basic alternatives, and attempts to " solve " it by means of the content of Christian doctrine, especially the doctrine of God as transcendent self. God transcendent in this case becomes a means of dealing with an ontological problem, and not just the result of propounding Biblical tradition.

Meaning and the Source of Meaning.[21] Niebuhr's concept

of individuality and freedom is the starting point for his understanding of meaning. Apart from a being who could transcend the process and survey it in memory and anticipation, the problem of meaning would never arise. Man can review large blocks of the world process and therefore can ask, What is it all about? But he never would ask this question unless the process were in some sense a threat to him. Nature and history are full of contingencies and unpredictabilities. Animals encounter them and go down before them without the threat of meaninglessness. But when man as a transcending individual confronts a process that offers a mixture of stability and instability, he asks, what does it mean? He sees that he himself is involved in the instabilities, and that the insecurity is partly within his own self, and there is no easy or immediate answer to the question, why?

Before going any farther, we must note again the existential setting of Niebuhr's discussion of meaning. To have meaning for Niebuhr is not the same as rational certitude, and therefore, man's search for meaning is not something that goes on primarily in academic disciplines. The opposite of meaning is not intellectual uncertainty, but personal insecurity. Therefore, the test of meaning is not objective certitude, but personal orientation, which means that mystery is not the antithesis of meaning. In fact, Niebuhr goes on to say mystery is an inevitable concomitant of meaning, for if we make things too neat and pat, we will eliminate the necessary depth that provides meaning.

So man quests for meaning in the sense of an environmental security, and he seeks first of all for sources of meaning in those environments nearest to him such as human ideals or nature and its laws. However, for Niebuhr no finite principle or temporal process can adequately serve as the source of meaning. Not that finitude or temporality is meaningless. We do find meaning there, but it is not clearly apparent that such is the ground of meaning. Every temporal process is a mixture of structure and contingency. Thus, Niebuhr can speak of " the caprices and contingencies of the physical order." Because of these dysteleological aspects the finite order is a source of partial, not final, security. Partial meaning seems to be manifested in the presence of a threat that all will come to nothing in the end. Niebuhr exemplifies the attempt to operate solely within the framework of finite meaning by citing science, which by narrowly limiting its field can do consistent and successful work. But such success is possible, he says, because no ultimate questions are asked. Thus science gives no " adequate account of the whole complex interwovenness of moving reality." [22] The best we can do in the finite order is to isolate a plurality of meanings. There is no one immanent principle that is a clear and certain key to the " universes of meaning " in the temporal order.

But what is this " meaning " which man searches for, and which is necessary to render a process " meaningful " ? We have already stressed that in the context of man's encounter with the instabilities and insecurities of nature and history, the problem of meaning is the need for a sort of environmental or " existential " security. But what will provide such a security? At this point a more explicit doctrine of meaning arises. The problem of meaninglessness occurs at the point of man's encounter with the sequences of events in nature-history. And two conditions are required for a " sequence of events " to be meaningful.

In the first place the mere fact of a sequence carries with it no intrinsic meaning. Such a sequence takes on meaning only when simultaneously comprehended by a consciousness. " The divine consciousness gives meaning to the mere succession of natural events by comprehending them simultaneously, even as human consciousness gives meaning to segments of natural sequences by comprehending them simultaneously in memory and foresight."[23] Yet merely remembering or beholding a sequence of events is not enough to make such a sequence a source of meaning. In addition some structure of meaning is needed, and this structure is established by some significant clue that enlightens the whole sequence. George Washington, the Father of his Country, thus provides a clue for the sequence or "story" of American history. But the *locus classicus* of such a decisive clue is the Hebrews' apprehension of their own story via the covenant events. A sequence of events, thus, is a source of meaning if it is, as a total sequence, comprehended by a consciousness, and if this comprehension is provided with a clue to how the sequence is structured. The problem of meaning, then, is not for Niebuhr a matter of words and their referents, but a problem of the relation between man and his environment. And "meaning" arises when the above two conditions are fulfilled.

This sets the stage for Niebuhr to "solve" the problem of meaning by reference to a transcendent source. He has already done his work negatively by asserting the impossibility of a source of meaning immanent in the finite order. With reference to the first meaning of meaning, Niebuhr says that only a transcendent God can provide the context or environment that is source of final security, for a God "in" the finite order would himself embody the threats of chaos and contingency and offer no guarantee to overcome them. With reference to the second meaning of meaning, Niebuhr raises this question. Granting that human consciousness lends meaning to a sequence of events by remembering it as a "story," what can fill this condition concerning the *total* order? Although particular events can provide clues as to the structure of a particular sequence, what can do this for the whole of nature-history? Therefore, to provide this kind of meaning, the transcendent is necessary, for only the transcendent can provide an event decisive enough to serve as a clue to the meaning of the whole.

How does God provide this "frame of meaning" and clue to the whole? Not in the otherworldly way of ascribing meaning to a divine world but meaninglessness to our world. God is the "ultimate center of meaning"; yet the world is meaningful, for God both creates it and is incarnate in it. The basic clue to the story is found not just in the fact of God's transcendence but in the acts of his self-disclosure culminating in the Christ.

History.[24] History also can be the object of ontological analysis because it a *way* of being, or a way beings can "be." Even if history is a realm that includes freedom, freedom itself is a way of being even as structure and necessity. Niebuhr approaches history not at the level of historiography but in terms of certain problems history raises for existence. Hence, we have here another way Niebuhr characterizes reality. What is "history" for Niebuhr? Although Niebuhr never explicitly defines history, he seems to mean that process or sequence of events which arises when the structures of nature (including human nature) and the creativity and freedom of man are combined. That sequence of events which results from this combination is "history."[25] History is what happens when man in his freedom operates within and on the physical order. Thus history is rooted in nature, yet because its sequences are partially consequences of man's individuality and freedom, it is not reducible to nature. "Human history is rooted in the natural process but is something more than either the determined sequences of natural causation or the capricious variations and occurrences of the natural world. It is compounded of natural necessity and human freedom." [26] Niebuhr's favorite term for characterizing history is "drama," which means a realm of freedom, conflict, and partial resolution. The stress here is on the novelty and even the "cunning" of history, which makes it impossible to grasp it in "necessary patterns" or in any detailed conceptual system. History is a machine driven neither from below (nature) nor from above (divinity).

Almost everything Niebuhr says about history follows from his belief that history is the "fruit . . . of man's freedom." He wants above all, to show that history is a complex combination of law and chaos, meaning and meaninglessness, and good and evil. He insists against both classicism and naturalism that history is both good and meaningful. Naturalism reduces history to a system of necessities, such as the cyclic patterns of nature, thus undercutting its meaning. Classicism contrasts "bad" history to a "good" eternity thus undercutting the goodness of history. This is the "problem" of history for Niebuhr: it must be conceived in such a way as to do justice both to its structures and patterns and to the element of freedom contained within it. The problem, then, is, On what basis can we assert the meaning and ground of history and yet preserve the distinctiveness of the historical way of being?

In addition to having a minimal unity and coherence, and a minimal goodness and meaning, history is also a precarious and insecure realm. It is morally ambiguous because it does not providentially separate the innocent from the guilty in its catastrophes. And it provides no guarantee that this will be remedied in the historical future, since history follows no pattern of inevitable progress. Good and evil increase dialectically to the very end. Therefore, incompleteness, insecurity, and sin always characterize man in his historical way of being. This is another " problem " of history, namely, its perennial corruption and the consequent impossibility that the salvation of the historical will arise from history.

Such is Niebuhr's characterization of historical being. How does he attempt to deal with these " problems " of history? Negatively, he reviews the way history is handled by other ontologies such as naturalism and classicism and finds that they do not do justice to the complexities of freedom and structure or good and evil in history. He thus feels that only a transcendent reference will do. Historical beings are partial and incomplete, but they tend to claim the opposite for themselves. Further, if such claims are challengeable, the source of criticism can not be some other incomplete being, but rather some ultimate being, and this pushes us " beyond history." Because of both ignorance and corruption, historical beings are caught without a norm, and the kind of norm needed must be transcendent, yet in such a way as to be a norm *for history*. Niebuhr finds such a norm in the transcendent God who not only has established a norm in history in the *justitia originalis,* but who in the Christian revelation has revealed the content of the norm as sacrificial love. At first glance history is a plurality of sequences and meanings not easily brought into unity and coherence. This too is accomplished in the transcendent, for all historical destinies can then be seen as under a single divine sovereignty. The way past and present systems have interpreted history shows how difficult it is to embrace both freedom and structure in history. Again, the transcendent reference is relevant. The structures can be affirmed as good and meaningful because they are derived from the transcendent, and freedom can be affirmed because of the dialogic relation between the transcendent and man.

So far Niebuhr has "solved" the problem of history by reference to a transcendent dimension "above" history. Another dimension is needed, however, for if history is to be meaningful, there must be some basis for anticipating and affirming a meaningful outcome, in which present partialities and corruptions are fulfilled. The basis for such a hope must be a transcendent God who not only is the source of history and its present sovereign, but who in some sense is its goal and the guarantor of the victorious outcome.

Nature.[27] At first glance Niebuhr's treatment of nature seems to be closer to the eighteenth century than to the twentieth. The contrast he makes throughout his writings is between nature and its "necessities" and history and its freedom.[28] For this reason man and his history transcend nature. The picture conjured up is that of a system of mechanisms within which dwells a being who has partial freedom over the system. A second glance, however, reveals that not mechanism but organism provides Niebuhr's controlling metaphor. On the one hand he can speak about nature as a realm of necessities, forms, laws, and structures, yet on the other hand he can speak of vitalities, novelties, contingencies, and accidents in nature. In spite of the latter there is no "freedom" in nature in the Niebuhrian sense. Nature is a process, a flux of events at various levels, and not the operation of a mechanism, yet efficient cause controls the flux. Thus the contingencies and accidents of nature appear as necessities when compared to individuality and history. However, by "necessity" Niebuhr does not mean mechanistic causality, but rather certain inevitabilities that nature presents to man such as death.

Nature does have several fundamental levels such as the organic and inorganic, but on no level of nature is "individuality" to be found. When individuality emerges, nature is transcended. The highest level of nature for Niebuhr is that of a unified organism with a central nervous system, which nevertheless is governed by instincts or impulses traceable to the characteristics of a species. We do find uniqueness in nature, but it is a uniqueness of events such as earthquakes, and not the uniqueness of personal centers that we have in individuality. What Niebuhr seems to be saying is that the physicochemical order, whether at the inorganic or organic level, does not contain the consciousness or awareness that is necessary for individuality. Thus even nature's processes and novelties operate within the framework of efficient cause and hence are " necessities." That realm called nature is a realm of pushes and pulls, not free creativity. Putting the picture together, we might say that for Niebuhr, nature is that realm of spatial-temporal structures and recurrent processes which operates in the framework of efficient causes, and which with varying success can be predicted.[29]

In relation to man, nature is both a source of meaning and threat. Niebuhr always insists that in the Biblical tradition nature is " good," and therefore not something to be escaped from in the present or annihilated in the end. However, the meaning of nature is not easily discernible, and this is one of the " problems " that nature presents to us. One reason for the obscurity of the meaning of nature is the fact that the relation of nature to man and his purposes is one of indifference and even capriciousness. Nature is not " reasonable " if " reasonable " means supporting the patterns and plans of human history. Nature often threatens such plans either by recalcitrantly resisting them, or by capriciously wiping them out, the final example being death. The second reason nature is a problem is that the clue to its meaning is not found in nature itself. There is a mystery about nature that is not solved by reference to the spatial-temporal structures and processes themselves.

Such is Niebuhr's description of "natural being" and the problems that arise with its characterization. As before, he resorts to a transcendent reference for a solution. God as transcendent Source is the only way to solve the mystery of nature's derivedness, as well as the meaning and goodness of nature, for God is the "ground of the natural." Also, the God who transcends nature as both ground and goal solves the existential problem of nature's threat to man by providing a hope that such threats (especially death), are not the last word.

c. *Niebuhr's World Picture: God the Transcendent Creator.* Niebuhr's "ontology" goes beyond merely characterizing various dimensions within being such as history or nature. At times he is willing to discuss the "all-encompassing system," which includes individuality, history, and nature. And he discusses it under such all-inclusive terms as the temporal order, existence, world, finiteness, creation, the universe, and nature-history. Niebuhr therefore not only addresses the specific types or ways of being outlined above. He does have a world picture of sorts, which can be expounded by putting together various facets of his particular characterizations.

The final result is not unlike that of many contemporary naturalists. Like the naturalists Niebuhr's world picture is broad enough to include such dimensions as history, freedom, value, and a minimal coherence running throughout. Also with the naturalists, Niebuhr recognizes distinct levels in the total system which can not be reduced to one another such as mechanism or panpsychism would tend to do. The lowest level is that of nature which as we have seen ranges from inorganic spatial-temporal structures to organisms with a central nervous system. Rooted in but transcending this level is history, which is a fusion of nature and human will. Standing in both nature and history, but also transcending both, is man, who is a unique, self-transcending individual, free even in relation to the structures of his own self. Again, with the naturalists, Niebuhr says that these levels are not distinct realms separable from one another, but rather overlap, each one serving as the ground of the next. Yet we must not give the impression that this world picture is a neat system that can be confidently marked off. Niebuhr, also with many naturalists, insists that it is not easily apparent that the world is one single order, for there is no one principle immanent in the world that can serve to tie it all together. At face value what confronts us is not a single, unified order, but a pluralism of meanings and orders. Even though man may instinctively assume a unified cosmos, there are in the one cosmos many worlds and realms of meaning "not easily brought into one system." Niebuhr's metaphysical pluralism is never more explicit than in this statement: "The forms of life are too multifarious to be ascribed easily to a single source or related to a single realm of meaning if the source does not transcend all the observable facts and forces, and the realm does not include more than the history of the concrete world."[30] Why is Niebuhr agnostic about such attempts? Two reasons stand out. One is that no one principle such as natural causation can explain the "specific givenness" of things. It can only relate things in one particular chain to one another. Second, man as he attempts to construct some total coherence must do so from some particular or finite perspective, but to find the key to the total process, a less limited perspective would be necessary. This problem of limitation is increased when we take into account man's willingness to absolutize the particular perspective he adopts, or in short, when we take into account man's sin.

Another similarity to the naturalists, which also helps to explain both the breadth of his world picture as well as Niebuhr's pluralistic bent, is what might be called "common-sense empiricism." Niebuhr tackles many of these problems from a common-sense perspective. Thus he gives a common-sense definition of "facts" as realities assumed and encountered in everyday life. Such "facts" are human freedom, its mixture with egoism, and the "dramatic essence of history."[81] Hence the data for empirical reference is not merely sense data but the realities of life known by "every man."

Such is Niebuhr's world picture, with each level a series of unexplained dead ends. But now we come to the place where Niebuhr begins to depart from naturalism. Not content to rest with the pluralistic picture, Niebuhr like many ontologists before him, searches for a Source. For although nature is the base of a series of transcendent levels, it nevertheless points beyond itself and provides no immanent self-explanation. While many naturalists look to the future work of science to provide the clue to the single order, Niebuhr affirms an ultimate Source and Ground.

The ontological tone in this strain of Niebuhr's thought is clear in both the nature of the problem and the terms he uses to solve it. Hence he can speak about the need for a "foundation," a "Ground of nature and existence," an "ultimate Source," and even an Absolute. However, this does not mean that the kerygmatic or dialogical strain is now overthrown, for the content of these terms is always the creator God of the Biblical tradition. Niebuhr will have nothing to do with any ontology that solves the problem of the givenness of existence by referral to a "distinctionless ground," or an "ultimate abyss of the natural where all distinctions vanish and all dynamic processes cease."³² He admits that such contentlessness is what the Ground of existence seems to be from the human perspective. But for Niebuhr the Ground is the personal God of the Biblical tradition, and though this lacks the sophistication of the negative theology, its superiority is that it gives a specific meaning to the divine.

Niebuhr's version of transcendence in this "ontological" strain in his thought is that of God as the transcendent Source and Ground of all structures, processes, and finite selves, rather than God who is over against such structures as a free Self in the present.³³ But when Niebuhr insists that God as personal creator is the content of the Ground, we have the bridge between the two.³⁴

How is God the transcendent Source? Niebuhr says from the beginning that creation is a mythical rather than a scientific concept. It is not, therefore, the doctrine of efficient cause applied to the "beginning" of everything. What then does the myth denote? Negatively, it denies both the doctrine of absolute temporal beginning and the eternal and underived self-sufficiency of the world. Unwilling to say that creation is necessary to God's perfection, yet also unwilling to say there was a time when God did not create, Niebuhr joins Augustine's company and leaves it a paradox. In one of the most explicit passages illustrating the positive meaning of creation, Niebuhr uses the Biblical analogy of the potter and his clay, the point being that the potter is " in a different category of existence " from the clay. In his Gifford Lectures creation denotes an absolute contrast between God and the world. " In the Biblical view the contrast between the created world and the Creator, between its dependent and insufficient existence and his freedom and self-sufficiency, is absolute." ³⁵

d. *Time and Eternity.* The above passages however are still vague, and to be any more specific we must raise the question concerning the relation between God as Source and the world, which means we must look at Niebuhr's doctrine of time and eternity. Three facets of this problem are isolated here for analysis: the " Platonic strain," the dialectic, and the *Passibilitas Dei.*

The " Platonic Strain." Hammar has said that the " dialectical interpretation of the relation between time and eternity " is Niebuhr's central idea.[36] That it may be. It is certainly the most elusive part of his thought. One reason for this is the tension between time and eternity in Niebuhr's thought. At first glance he seems to subscribe to the traditional Hellenistic [37] framework of early Christian orthodoxy in which eternity is an atemporal and changeless realm related to time only by contrast. A case can be made for this side of Niebuhr's thought by drawing out the implications of his treatment of finitude. Like the orthodox tradition he says that finitude (creation, temporality, etc.) is good. However, it is also " incomplete," " partial," " peripheral," " relative," " conditioned," and the realm of flux and change, the *stage* of which is time. The implication of such language about the eternal is that it therefore is complete, total, immutable, and unconditioned, which transports us (with qualification) to the world of Parmenides and Plotinus. It must be said that this distinction is best established not in clear passages, but as the underlying presupposition that lends power to Niebuhr's prophetic denunciations of arrogant finitude. Finite entities are not infinite; temporal entities are not eternal; conditioned entities are not unconditioned. Hence he can attack their pretense to be central, final, and absolute by contrasting them with a realm that is final and absolute. As we have seen, Niebuhr at times was willing to designate God as Absolute and the ground of existence, the connotations of which seem to undercut the Biblical and personal side of his thought. In one passage he even goes so far as to say God's self-sufficiency is absolute.[38] Another passage implies that God has an unrelated as well as a related side. Biblical religion, he says, equally stresses " the transcendence of God over, and his *intimate relation to the world.*"[39] The implication is that transcendence means God's *un*-relation to the world.

Possibly the passages that best reveal Niebuhr's " Platonic side " are those which insist that the Christian doctrine of an eternity embracing time is absurd. " Christian eschatology looks forward to an ' end ' of history in which the conditions of nature-history are transfigured but not annulled. This picture of the fulfillment of life involves the rational absurdity of an eternity which incorporates the conditions of time: individuality and particularity."[40] In a similar vein, Niebuhr attacks the Christology of the Councils as " logical nonsense " for ascribing " both finite and historically conditioned and eternal and unconditioned qualities " to Christ's nature.[41] But what is the nature of eternity that makes its " incorporation of the conditions of time " absurd? Apparently, it is because eternity is antithetically related to time, as a changeless and foreign realm.

Qualification by the Dialectic. There are other dimensions in Niebuhr which radically qualify the " Platonic strain." The first qualification is that ultimately the relation between time and eternity is not one of antithesis but dialectic. The meaning of Niebuhr's use of this term might be negatively stated by saying that if time and eternity are identified or if they are absolutely contrasted, there is no dialectical relation between them. Thus he uses dialectic to establish relation and maintain tension. Platonism and orthodox supernaturalism imperil the dialectic by losing all relation between the two. In liberalism it is imperiled for the opposite reason that the tension is lost. What then is the Niebuhrian dialectic? Carnell stresses Niebuhr's dialectic as dialogue, a discourse of give-and-take between God and the world, not in the sense of miraculous acts, but in the sense that every moment of time maintains both relation and tension with the eternal.[42] Dialectic thus refers to Niebuhr saying both "Yes" and "No" to the question, are time and eternity continuous? This provides the basis for his dialectical treatment of time in which he affirms it as good and negates it as perennially corrupt. And the "Platonic strain" is qualified by this dialectic because it shows that in spite of his prophetic contrasts, he yet says eternity in some sense is relevant to and continuous with time.

The Qualification by the Passibilitas Dei. *"In some sense continuous with time"*; this is the puzzle. In spite of his "Platonic strain" Niebuhr always attacks any neat dualism or otherworldliness, and insists that eternity is related to and relevant for time. What does this "relation" involve? At this point we must consider Niebuhr's doctrine of immanence, which he expresses in a variety of ways. The Eternal is the source, ground, and end of the temporal. The temporal "reveals" the Eternal. The Eternal "bears," "embraces," "incorporates," and is "engaged in" the temporal. The second and sharpest qualification of the Platonic strain comes when the question is asked, What is the content of "eternity"? What is it that bears, embraces, and is engaged in the temporal? At this point Niebuhr rejects any "undifferentiated eternity," and says the content is that of suffering love. Thus a "permanent structure" is not the eternal in contrast to the "cycle of change," but rather *Agape*. Therefore to glimpse the Eternal is not to envision the immutable, but to catch sight of the " eternal love which bears the whole project of history." As *Agape,* God " suffers " and " takes the effects of evil upon and into himself." [43]

With this the hardest question of all is raised. In what sense does God " suffer " in time? Is Hammar right in denying any " substantial immanence " of God in the world to Niebuhr's thought? [44] How then does God suffer if not substantially? Does he actually undergo painful experiences, taking the new into himself, thus involving real growth as Hartshorne describes it? This is the point where ambiguity hides Niebuhr's position from his interpreters. If the " Platonic strain " wins out, whatever else God's suffering means, God does not undergo the processes and changes of the world. He does not suffer *in* history as either a part or whole of it, but suffers as a personal self who is the source and ground of history and concerned about his creation. But if the organismic side of Niebuhr wins out and God is " in " temporal processes " as the human person is ' in ' its organism," [45] then it seems we have a substantial immanence and a substantial suffering.

To summarize Niebuhr's ontology then, we should again make it clear that Niebuhr is fundamentally an ethicist-theologian and not a philosopher. The most apparent reason for this is his method and epistemology. He rarely gives sharp, technical definitions. He rarely explicates and elaborates his basic concepts, and he rarely systematizes. Even more important, his basic data originates in a correlation between Biblical insight and common-sense empiricism. However, Niebuhr does have a certain world picture, with many features in common with other philosophers. He does deal with various problems of being, and he does attempt solutions to these problems.

3. The Apprehension and Expression of the Transcendent

If we raise the question for Niebuhr about the spatial overtones of the language of transcendence, the answer would involve us in Niebuhr's doctrine of myth and symbol. Niebuhr is aware of the spatial-overtones problem involved in such terms as " transcend," but his way of dealing with it, unlike Heim, is not that of a reconstruction of the ancient or modern world picture. Any rational or coherent world picture will inevitably be embarrassed by transcendental symbols. Nor is this limited to *divine* transcendence. Selfhood, either human or divine, is the basic meaning of transcendence in Western thought, and any attempt to grasp such in a *Weltanschauung* will result in immanence only. Hence transcendence must always be mythically apprehended and expressed. Such mythic and symbolic expression will be more crude and inexact, yet it does more justice to the facts of experience than a rational immanentism. Originally, transcendence was a Hebrew myth and any attempt to translate it into a more rational context falsifies it because neat concepts can never wholly exhaust or embrace a transcending free self. Causal analysis can deal with the surface of a sequence of events but never with " the dimension of depth," and this is the function of myth.

Niebuhr's most striking illustration of this sounds much like Karl Heim. Painters, he says, can use symbols in such a way as to communicate the sense of three dimensions in a two-dimensional painting. This process invokes a deception (for it really is only two dimensions), yet it is a symbolic revelation of a dimension incomprehensible in other forms of communication. Myth and symbol perform a similar function of denoting the deeper dimension of religious realities. Niebuhr's favorite term for this kind of apprehension and expression is " drama," which for him is the only form that can do justice to the dialogue within and between selves and the patterns of freedom and necessity, which consequently emerge. Therefore, we find Niebuhr agreeing with Tillich concerning the inevitability of symbolic expression of the " eternal ground," but with one difference. Tillich sees symbols as necessary because the ground is also an abyss underlying every human category, including that of freedom and personality. But Niebuhr feels that it is because of freedom and personality in the divine ground that symbols are needed to grasp it.

III
GOD AS TRANSCENDENT GROUND:
Paul Tillich

1. The Religious Socialist Years: Transcendence in the Early Tillich

Until 1933, Paul Tillich's theological work was carried on in the confines of Germany. In these early years [1] Tillich was known chiefly as one who helped organize religious socialism in Germany, called at times the "*Kairos* Circle." These were the years of the rise of National Socialism under Hitler and its accompanying "German Faith." Furthermore, transcendental symbols played an important part in religious socialism's polemic against "immanentist" movements. Tillich thus saw the loss of transcendence in terms of a fluctuation between two powers, the demonic and the profane.

a. *The Demonic and the Profane.* One side of the fluctuation is the demonic. Many throughout the nineteenth century were aware of the creative depths of nature and life. Romanticism, especially as it was expressed in the *Lebensphilosophie,* sought to give vent to the irrational vitalities surging through nature and human nature. When this stress on creative force became coupled with modern political and economic blocks of power, the demonic emerged. Actually it is found in all history as a creative, form-destroying force, but rather than be a mere chaos, it forms its own *Gestalt* of evil. Thus both the Grand Inquisitor and Hitler mirror the demonic, for they tried to crush the rational forms of culture, and they made an absolute claim in behalf of the structure that subsequently emerged.

In what sense is the demonic a type of immanentism? In so far as it recognizes and utilizes certain creative depths not reducible to the surface of things, it itself retains a transcendent element. Yet it always ends up making absolute claims for the *Gestalt* which it produces, hence the horrors of fascism and nazism. The demonic therefore is always a piece of creative finitude making unqualified claims for that finitude, and in the process the true Transcendent is lost.

History has seen many ways of overcoming the demonic, but the way of the post-Enlightenment West has been that of profanization or " the capitalistic spirit." This is the way of complete rationalization, overcoming the depths by denying they are there. Clear, rational form replaces irrational transcendent vitality, therefore even the divine is reduced to a transparent clarity. " Rather they sought to see and make visible divine clarity in the perfection, completion, and rationality of form. But in the emphasis on divine clarity, the divine depth was lost: that which is inexhaustible, self-manifesting, unconditional, and transcendent." [2] In 1926, the same year of the publication of *Das Dämonische,* Tillich published his most elaborate analysis of profanization, *The Religious Situation,* in which profanization is called the " capitalistic spirit of self-sufficient finitude." Profanization here is not mere rationalism but complete self-sufficiency. The over-all world vision of this spirit is that of a world of surfaces without height or depth. Things are what they appear to be and therefore can be easily controlled. Epistemology reflects this spirit when it sees knowledge as a detached encounter with the surface world resulting in the possibility of control. The result of this is " technological reason " or the employment of reasoning processes in the service of technical utility. Self-sufficient finitude also worked itself out in a philosophy (Kantian) that split science and religion into autonomous spheres, a metaphysics that denied metaphysics, an art that imitatively reproduced the world of surfaces, and an education that gave objective information. God then becomes "the consecrating word for the closed world system, for the completed immanence and its rational structure."[8]

Although Tillich does not say so in so many words, one manifestation of self-sufficient finitude is supernaturalism. Strange as it may sound, supernaturalism represents a loss of transcendence. Tillich has several definitions of this elusive notion of the supernatural, but basically he means the attempt to understand and express God's relation to the world by a literalization of this-worldly categories. Thus God is described as an entity within the subject-object structures of the spatial-temporal world. The chief point here is that language with its inevitable spatial-temporal connotations is applied directly or nonsymbolically to God. The result is a God who *exists* as *a* being, *above* the world. For Tillich this is a loss of transcendence because the Unconditioned transcends this God who is *a* being and who exists *above* our world in another "world."

Thus we have two manifestations of immanentism in these early, fiery polemics of Tillich: the Demonic, which absolutizes a depth which is not the Depth; and the Profane, which recognizes no depth at all. Furthermore, the two are dialectically related in that they continually produce each other.

b. *The Unconditioned,* Kairos, *and Theonomy.* Granting this analysis of Western culture, caught between these fluctuating immanentisms, the problem was how to overcome self-sufficient finitude with its sterile rational world of the surface without submitting to the irrationalities of a demonic institution such as Germany's "blood and soil" religion. The self-sufficient side is that of autonomy where the only *nomos* (law) is that arising out of the *autos* (self). When this is overturned by an authoritarian power bloc, the source of the *nomos* becomes an alien *heteros* (other) which subjects man to itself in an authoritarian way; therefore we have no real improvement on demonic transcendence. What is needed is a transcendence that both judges and supports autonomy (self-transcending autonomy). Tillich's answer to this in *The Religious Situation* and other writings of the period was the *Unconditioned*, which challenges self-sufficient finitude via the *kairos*, producing the result, *theonomy*. In this sense all three are important transcendental notions in Tillich's early writings raised against the immanentism of both the profane and the demonic, both autonomy and heteronomy.

Das Unbedingte.⁴ The notion of the Unconditioned becomes clearer when we see Tillich against the background of a number of "revolts" against the capitalistic spirit with which he associates himself. These revolts, according to Tillich, discovered the subterranean ground of the easily manipulated bourgeois world of the surface. Metaphysicians like Bergson spoke of an *élan vital* or its equivalent. Expressionist painters overturned the ordered world of the nineteenth-century painters, and scientists began to suspect an ultimate arbitrariness behind the certainties of the laws of nature. All in all, the awareness arose of "something more." This "something more" is not reducible merely to the irrationalities of existence, but these revolts helped bring such to consciousness.

Tillich himself uses the language of the nineteenth-century German idealists, especially Schelling, to express his own understanding of the "something more." What is necessarily presupposed, he asks, in any normative endeavor? Inevitably permeating human endeavors are such notions as truth and goodness. Every attempt to have the truth or speak the truth (even the attempt to deny truth) proceeds on the basis of a norm. But is this norm something we "have"? No, as a norm it is something we do not have, but in the light of which all statements are made. Can we find it in existence, clearly identified with any person, object, or movement? No, even the attempt to make the identification is on the basis of a preceding truth, for it claims the identification is a "true" one. This universal, all-pervading prius of all thought is the *Unbedingte,* or Unconditioned. Human beings inevitably have a concern for the Unconditioned, for their endeavors are carried on in the name of some normative background. This background is Unconditioned, for there is nothing to qualify it; rather, all qualifications are made in the light of it. In this sense it is inescapable even when denied.

The Unconditioned serves both negative and positive functions. Negatively, it cannot be manipulated, or molded to human purposes and ideals. No finite enterprise ever attains an absolute standpoint or unconditional status, thus such enterprises have the "No" spoken against them. One aspect of the Eternal, therefore, is the "No" spoken against time. Positively, because the Unconditioned is the contrast to the relativity of finitude, because there *is* such a contrast, relativity does not swallow man, but there is a real ground of both meaning and responsibility. The Unconditioned as Unconditioned transcends every temporal form, but because it is the background of normative endeavors, it is both their basis and their judge.

Kairos. History does not move in neat cycles but rather is marked by decisive happenings in which Demonic structures meet their downfall and confident, well-structured movements and epochs come to an end. The self-sufficient surface world is perennially challenged and so are the self-absolutizing challengers. What is responsible for these challenges? The answer cannot be any finite entity or process, since they all fall under the possibility of breakup and transformation. What is it that breaks up and transforms and does not itself live under such a possibility? The answer again is the Unconditioned, which is another way of saying that the Eternal is not a static substratum of reality but rather " that which invades." This means that the Unconditioned manifests itself historically, in decisive " times," and the word for such a " time " is *kairos.*

We can see now that *kairos* in Tillich's early writings is one of the notions that carries a transcendent connotation, for it means " the critical transcendence of the divine over all conservatism and utopianism." [5] Immanentism sees only *chronos* (endless time) or *logos* (rational structure), but *kairos* is related in a transcendent way to both, for it is the possibility of the end and of a new beginning, overthrowing existing powers and structures.

Theonomy. The name for that which is created by the *kairos,* when the Unconditioned is manifested, is theonomy. In this concept Tillich tries to solve his former dilemma. The problem was, How can self-sufficient finitude be challenged without being subjected to a heteronomous transcendence that destroys man's nature by forcing it into a strange world? Tillich's answer again is the Unconditioned, for it is not only the " No " to finitude but its underlying ground: that by which it is. Therefore, the *nomos,* which the Unconditioned brings, is not something foreign to the essential *nomos* of the self; hence, "self-transcending autonomy" is possible. Theonomy denotes a situation in culture in which there is openness to the Unconditioned, which through various *kairoi* creates new beginnings.

All of this is relevant for the cultural problem because it provides a principle of protest. Individuals and groups can use such transcendent notions to show that particular absolutisms are not absolute. Clarification of what the Unconditioned is provides a basis for attacking the *Gestalt* of evil which arises with various demonries. The phrase that summarizes this criticism and the concepts involved is "the Protestant Principle," which is "the guardian against the attempts of the finite and conditioned to usurp the place of the Unconditional in thinking and acting."[6]

It is important to remember that the transcendent element in Tillich's early writings is not explicitly in the context of the metaphysical problem of the relation between God and the world. Immanence does not mean a doctrine of God-in-the-world, nor does transcendence refer to God-out-of-the-world. So far Tillich's interest is not merely theoretical or traditional. He rather addresses a situation at the level of culture, and brings to it certain rediscoveries about the depths of life that can relevantly challenge that situation. Although this "cultural" context is basic for Tillich's thought in his Religious Socialist years, the doctrine of the Unconditioned also overcomes the immanentism of supernaturalism. As the *Unvordenkliche* (Schelling), it precedes and grounds every temporal category and polarity, and cannot be drawn into any one of them. And it is this strand which predominates in the system that afterward arose.

2. The Doctrine of God: Transcendence in the Developed System

Tillich in his early years, as we have seen, elevated three transcendental symbols: the Unconditioned, *kairos,* and theonomy, against culture in its demonic and profane dimensions. Yet as a thinker on the boundary line between cultural movements and professional philosophical theology, Tillich while still in Germany had worked his cultural and philosophical analyses into a "dogmatics." This system proved to be not only the arranging of key theological concepts into a consistent relation with one another, but a thoroughgoing world vision that included a full ontological statement and a radical reconstruction of Christian doctrine. The purpose of this section is to describe Tillich's elaboration of his key symbol for transcendence (the Unconditioned) in the developed system of his later writings, an elaboration that shall be characterized as hypertheism.[7]

a. *Nonsymbolic Transcendence* (*The God Above "God"*). Because Tillich's hypertheism comes primarily out of his ontology, we must begin there. In good Heideggerian fashion he says that ontology begins with man. Man is the being who asks the question of being, for it is he who receives the shock of nonbeing. As man, he continually asks the child's question, How came the world? As man, he goes from thing to thing, discontent with all things, and searching for something more. Ontology thus is the systematic elaboration of natural curiosity and existential involvement. Such is its basis in human nature. When Tillich begins to describe the ontological enterprise, we find, of course, his own ontology governing the description. Yet we find an elusive feature here, for there seem to be at least two conceptions of ontology in Tillich's own system.

Ontology: What It Means to Be.[8] A frequent characterization of ontology in Tillich is that it is the discipline that asks, What does it mean to be? At first sight this seems to assume from the beginning that the world is one unified harmonious system. Although Tillich would hold to this, his claim at this stage is more minimal. The only unity he insists on is whatever unity is implied in the assertion: Something *is*. The phrases Tillich uses to denote this is-ness about us are "reality as such," or "the structure which makes reality a whole." Ontology is the inquiry that makes "reality as such" its object; thus it analyzes the structures common to everything that is: the "constitutive principles of being," "the most general questions about the nature of reality." In this view of ontology Tillich comes close to Aristotle, for he does say ontology asks a *what* question, and it is basically an analytical endeavor. The structures it describes are those found in and presupposed by experience. It is no accident, therefore, that Tillich finds himself in the line of Aristotle's "first philosophy." The basic question ontology asks when conceived in this way is, What does it mean to be?

How does Tillich deal with this question? To answer this we must concern ourselves with the basic categories of his ontological analysis. We mentioned previously that man was the key to the nature of being. Negatively, this means there is no ontology that successfully describes purely objective structures external to man, nor is there an ontology that successfully reduces such structures to self or mind. The starting point must be the interaction of the self and world, which is a polarity mirrored throughout all existence as its basic structure, namely, that of subject-object.[9] From this basic characterization comes the rest of Tillich's description of what it means to be. Everything that exists falls within this polar structure, and this has ramifications throughout Tillich's system. All language is conditioned by its participation in the subject-object structure; thus language can never apply directly to anything beyond it. Symbols attempt such a mediation, but because they are symbols they cannot directly denote anything beyond the polar structure. Tillich's treatment of supernaturalism also rests on this ontology, for supernaturalism attempts to describe spiritual realities as if they comprised another subject-object world. Also of crucial importance, Tillich's hypertheism is erected out of this polar vision. God does not " exist," for " existence " refers to actual entities or processes in the polarities. Nor is God a person or even personal in the literal sense, for personality is always rooted in individuality, which is a pole of one of the polarities. Therefore, Tillich's first answer to the question, What does it mean to be? is as follows. " To be " means to be structured within certain basic polarities.

His second key notion is that of finitude. Even though the finite-infinite is one of the polarities, finitude is more central than this would denote. For finitude is present throughout all the ranges of being and knowledge. It permeates the four categories, and all existence is characterized by it. Finitude's basic characteristic is temporality in the sense that existence comes into being and ceases to be. Before it comes to be it is " nothing," and after it ceases to be it is " nothing "; thus finitude means the presence of nonbeing in the past and future of a being. This is the meaning of the phrase, nonbeing limits and threatens being.

At this point we have the bridge to the second ontological question Tillich asks. The question of finitude is not just a category spun out of the philosopher's curiosity and leisure. Because it characterizes all being, it also includes man's being; for man is the only being who can be conscious of the threat and limitation of nonbeing. As a being who faces having-to-die, he faces the *nothing* of the future, which is the source of "ontological anxiety." Such anxiety is also rooted in man's realization that he has no definite space. And causal finitude produces ontological anxiety when man realizes he is not the source of his own being, nor does the alternative of an infinite regress provide an answer to his question of source. The finitude of substance arises, producing anxiety when man experiences change and the possibility that his substance may be lost. Because of this existential experience of finitude and its accompanying anxieties, man is not content to inquire into the *what* of being, merely describing its polarities and categories. His anxiety ("the shock of nonbeing") pushes him to ask a basic question about the whole network of polarities: Why anything at all?

Ontology: Why Not Nothing? This question leads us to the second and less Aristotelian way Tillich conceives the nature of ontology. Here Tillich is not so much concerned to characterize the *structures* of being as to ask the more inclusive question, Why is there anything at all? In 1951, Tillich had a technical objection to stating the question as Schelling had, Why is there something, why not nothing? For this seemed to lead to an infinite regress.[10] However, in *Biblical Religion and the Search for Ultimate Reality* he seems to forget his own warning: "He who seriously asks the question: 'Why is there something, why not nothing?' has experienced the shock of nonbeing and has in thought transcended everything given in nature and mankind."[11] In spite of the problems connected with the actual phrase, one strand of Tillich's ontology has to do with this more unifying search; hence, ontology is not just an analytical but an analogical inquiry. Furthermore, its object is not just the texture of reality as such, the structures presupposed by the world of experience, but that which precedes such structures. "It is the function of an ontological concept to use some realm of experience to point to characteristics of being-itself which lie above the split between subjectivity and objectivity and which therefore cannot be expressed literally in terms taken from the subjective or the objective side. Ontology speaks analogously."[12] The basic question here is not a *what* but a *why* question. "*Why* is there something, why not nothing?"[13] When this question is asked, the stage of ontology arises that parallels the traditional quest of religion, since for both, the goal is nothing less than the Ultimate. The two types of ontology in Tillich involving the *what* and the *why* are not merely separated, but as we have seen are bridged by the fact that due to the shock of nonbeing and due to the analysis of the structures of being, man is pushed to ask, Why not nothing? Whence and why the whole world of polarities? Its existence is not illusion, yet it is not completely self-evident or self-authenticating. Here we have Tillich extending ontological analysis to the question of the world's coming-to-be. And as we have said, when this is done, analogy must be the method, for here we are moving past the world that can be spoken about in direct or literal terms.

It is at this point in his ontology that the notion, *das Unbedingte*, of the days of his early writings, appears; however, this time in the term "being-itself." The answer to "Why not nothing?" is a fountain of being that is the ground of the polarities and the source of finitude.

Tillich begins by recalling the ordinary experience of disillusionment. We suppose an entity to be one thing and closer investigation reveals it to be another. One of the results of a scientific inquiry is that we are shown that things are not what they seem to be, or at least *all* they seem to be.

The world of superficial encounter with the surface of things gives way to a world below the surface. For example, in the area of truth we discover truths about things but hesitate to identify any particular thing with absolute truth. Even if truth means workability or a correlation between a statement and certain facts in reality, we hesitate to claim that such are realized absolutely. Absolute truth is something else, yet not "something" at all, since we find it in all things or find all things in it. The same holds for being. All things "are" but not absolutely, for as finite entities they are all threatened by nonbeing and go down before it. Being adheres in them but in the absolute or complete sense is not identifiable with any of them. This being which "is" yet is identifiable with no "thing" is being-itself. There is something in common with all beings by which they "are" and this something is being-itself.

How is this related to God and transcendence? In *Biblical Religion,* Tillich pictures both the traditional ontological quest for ultimate reality and the religious response to a God who is ultimate. But there cannot be two ultimates, says Tillich; rather, only one, and this is being-itself. And this is the only nonsymbolic, completely literal way of denoting "God."[14]

However, it must be made clear that Tillich is not applying being-itself to God as one would apply a name to an object or an adjective to a noun as when we say that water is (literally) wet. This would be subject-object language, and neither subject-object categories nor the way of applying them is possible at this level. Being-itself is Tillich's concept which denotes whatever-it-is which is not subject to the world of polarities and finitude. This is why for Tillich at least it is not a symbol or myth. For symbol and myth are always concrete pictures drawn from the subject-object world. Being-itself is a phrase that designates the unmythologized, and literal whatever-it-is that grounds the world of polarities.

One clue to the nature of the transcendence of God as being-itself is found in the term " ground." Schelling in his later period used the concept " ground " as a substitute for the purely logical process in Hegel's *notions,* and in so doing wanted to account for real process at the level of existence. Tillich uses the word in a similar way, and also to mark off his position from certain alternatives. God as the ground of being is not a universal essence, nor is " God " a word denoting the unity and totality of finite things. This would empty God of all true transcendence. Nor does being-itself connote the being or substance of beings. Like Schelling, Tillich wants to know why the totality, why the unity, why the substance, and why the process at all? Thus to understand this metaphor, ground, the problem of becoming must be seen as central. In this sense it is not entirely unlike the Plotinian imagery concerning a fountain of being. It is certainly nearer to *fons* than to the basic source of a premise in the context of logic, which Dorothy Emmett once suggested as an interpretation. This implies that epistemology rather than ontology is the decisive background. In this metaphor, ground, Tillich wants to avoid all merely static connotations that often cling to philosophical categories, such as the Absolute. He also wants to avoid any notion of God which like the God of deistic supernaturalism or even the Absolute of some versions of idealism excludes the finite from itself. It is the ground because the finite is grounded in it, thus the spatialism of the vocabulary of supernaturalism is replaced by qualitative meanings.

So far, being-itself as the ground of being seems to be transcendent in the tradition of the *via negativa.* As the ground of being it cannot be reduced to any being, any category describing being, or even the totality of being. The world of polarities and finitude is neither a self-explaining nor self-sufficient world; therefore, that which does explain and ground it cannot be simply identified with any describable, namable thing.

Of course, Tillich means more by being-itself than a series of negations. When we attempt to say more positively how being-itself is transcendent, the phrase " the *power* of being " must be considered, and this is what prevents Tillich's being-itself from being a category in an unqualified substance ontology. Being-itself is not a static substratum of being but the creative fountain of being, that by which being comes to be. Tillich follows Schelling here in seeing the difficulty of explaining becoming from a completely self-enclosed and self-sufficient absolute. In order to account for being, being-itself must itself be eternally dynamic. Hegel's introduction of movement into logic (an attempt that Kierkegaard thought to be a contradiction in terms) is an endeavor to conceive the eternal dynamically. However, there is always the suspicion that Hegel identifies logical with historical processes in his description of the life of the *Weltgeist*. At this point Tillich follows Schelling's revolt against Hegel and against his own earlier principle of absolute identity. It became clear to Schelling that mere self-contained identity left unsolved how things came to be, the problem of differentiation. " If there were only unity, and if everything were at peace, then truly nothing would want to stir, and everything would sink into listlessness." [15] " If primal nature were in harmony with itself, it would remain; there would be an abiding one and never a two, an eternal immobility without progress." [16] Schelling solved his problem by combining his former Absolute Identity with Boehme's

Ungrund, seeing thus an eternal contrariety in God. For Tillich also, God faces " eternal contrariety " within himself. God is the ground of the polarities and therefore the polarities are in God. However, they are " in " him without the threat of overcoming him. Another way of putting it is that nonbeing is in God, but not in the same way that it is in finitude. Nonbeing participates in finitude as a threat to its existence, thus causing the ontological instability that is the essence of finitude. Finite being goes down before nonbeing, for it arises out of it and passes back into it, but God as the *ground* of being eternally overcomes it. And this overcoming of nonbeing is the dynamic element in God by virtue of which he is the *power* of being. The ground of being therefore is dynamic in the sense that it is a primordial dialectic going on in the heart of reality. If this were not so, differentiation and creation (becoming) would not be possible. To summarize, God as the ground of being does not *exclude* being, for being participates in God. This means that the polarities of being, including being and nonbeing, are in God, and he is that power of being which eternally overcomes the nonbeing that is such a threat to particular beings. The whatever-it-is that gives beings the power to be is itself not subject to dissolution. Therefore, in addition to the negative transcendence implied in the categoryless being-itself, there is a positive transcendence of the ground of being in that it is the dynamic and creative source of all being, the perpetual power in being.

We previously termed this section " nonsymbolic transcendence," in order to isolate the type of transcendence implied in Tillich's hypertheism. Although symbolic language is inevitably used in connection with this hypertheism, the approach is that of ontological analysis, and the transcendence is that of an unconditional ground rather than the "God" pictured in the terms and categories of ordinary theism. It is therefore "hypertheistic" transcendence, and it is nonsymbolic in the sense that that-which-transcends (being-itself) is both "ecstatically and rationally" denoted as whatever-it-is that precedes and grounds all qualifications and descriptions of it. This nonsymbolic and hypertheistic side of God is clearly portrayed by Tillich in the following passage: "But we cannot simply say that God is a symbol. We must always say two things about him: we must say there is a *nonsymbolic element* in our image of God — namely, that he is ultimate reality, being itself, ground of being, power of being; and the other, that he is the highest being in which everything that we have does exist in the most perfect way." (Italics mine.) [17]

b. *Symbolic Transcendence: "God"*
"*God.*" Tillich has made it clear from the beginning that he stands in both philosophy and theology. Therefore he does not posit an either-or between the Unconditioned of ontological analysis and the "God" of historical (Christian) religion. But how does he get from one to the other? Dorothy Emmett has raised the question, "Why should not the 'ground of being' be something valuationally indifferent, or even, from a human point of view, sinister?" [18] Tillich does have an answer to this question, and it is found in the nature of being-itself. As a dynamic concept (the power of being) being-itself is creative and self-manifesting as well as abysmal. Even though finite beings under the conditions of existence are estranged from their ground, yet because it is their ground, each can be the bearer of its self-manifestation. When this occurs we have revelation. In this revelational encounter with the self-manifesting ground of being, which is always at a deeper level (ecstatic reason) than that

of technical reason, symbols grasping and expressing the encounter are spontaneously generated and carried by historical communities. The presence of symbols means that man never receives revelation directly. He receives it in the way he receives anything, through the language conditioned by his subject-object experience and polar world. The cluster of symbols which arises as the result of this revelational encounter and which participates in being-itself is "God." "God" is the religious word for the ground of being, the symbol for that which is not symbolic.

Therefore, Tillich's answer to Dorothy Emmett would follow this line. If "God" were not also being-itself, the ground of being, he would not be God in any traditional sense, for it is ultimacy that makes God divine. However, being-itself as dynamic, self-manifesting, and related to the world, has besides the aspect of unconditionality, a face turned toward the world, which is grasped and symbolized in "God." This "God" of theism is inevitable if the hypertheistic ground of being is something we can be related to, and if we try to express this relationship.

"God" as Personal. We have tried to see how Tillich's hypertheism and the notion of being-itself is a way of reconstructing transcendence. There is also a transcendence in his theism in connection with the "God" that arises by way of revelation. Because personality is the central symbol used to denote the theistic God in the *via revelatus,* we must analyze Tillich's doctrine of the personal God.[19] The result is a clue to the way in which "God" is transcendent. Of central importance is Tillich's definition of person and personal. In 1929, before the systematic elaboration of his ontology, he described personality as essentially rooted within the categories of finitude. As " self-determining freedom " in and above one's nature, personality presupposed *individual-*

ity. It was not merely identified with individuality, but rather was the nexus of individuality and the universal structure of being, which means the freedom in the depth of reality becoming manifest and actual. Personality is what happens to individuality at the level of human beings who can be both self-related and world-related. In his developed ontology this basic analysis is retained, for in his *Systematic Theology* person and personality become correlates of one of the polarities, namely, individualization. Personality is thus seen as the most perfect form of individualization, but it occurs only over against the opposite pole, participation. It is in other words " life within the subject-object structure conditioned by time." In the light of such an understanding of personality, it is not surprising to find in Tillich a constant polemic against God as " *a* person." For such a doctrine identifies God with one side of a polarity that he transcends as its ground. Tillich recognizes that in the process of historical religion God continually becomes *a person,* but he insists that this must be seen for what it is, a symbol.

This does not mean, however, that God is impersonal. In so far as God is related to man he is not only being-itself but being-for-us. Being-itself is not a full description of God, for God has a concrete aspect that is manifest in revelation. In this concrete aspect God plays the role of " God " : he " forgives," " loves," " judges," answers prayers, or in other words meets man in his personal center. Hence, because God is reciprocally related to man, he is at least personal.

God therefore is neither *a* person nor subpersonal but is *symbolically personal*. This does not mean, however, that God is not personal at all, which position Nels Ferré has accused Tillich of holding. Tillich's use of symbols is not devaluative, thus he opposes those who want to say, " Only a symbol." How is God symbolically personal? The key issue here is how the polarities (especially individualization-participation) are related to the ground of being. Tillich sees the concept, person, arising from the subject side of the polarities (individualization), which includes " finite separation." Because God as ground transcends the polarities, he is not graspable by categories within them, yet because he is *ground* of the polarities, his relation to them is not that of exclusion. If God were completely excluded from the polarities, he would inevitably be impersonal, but as ground he includes personality and is at least personal. As the ground of the polarities God is never less than or inferior to the reality that emerges as their content. He is the preceding ground of the personal (individualization) and communion of persons (participation). In this sense God is the Personal-itself.[20]

" God " Transcendent. Because Tillich can so reconstruct the doctrine of a personal God, there is at least a place for the " kerygmatic " type of transcendence expressed in the various corollaries of personality: love, judgment, mercy, will, etc. Therefore he can even say that in revelation there is an I-Thou relation between God and man. In this relation the God who is the unconditional ground of being plays the role of " God."

How does he do this? The world is a split world; estranged from its own ground, with particular processes autonomously and independently becoming actualized and separated from the ground. But there is a power working in these processes constantly, judging them as demand and norm. This is the God who is *justice*. But God also works in the world as a power that reunites being, allaying its tension and estrangement. As such he is *love*. These are symbols, but as participating symbols it means that being-itself is transcendent love and transcendent justice over against the structures of existence.

But the main way "God" is transcendent is that he is free. Tillich's clearest passages on the transcendence of God are in this vein. Thus he says that the spatialism in expressions like "God above the world" can be reconstructed only in terms of God as creative freedom. "If we then answer that the relation of God and the world is not spatial but must be expressed in terms of creative freedom, an ontological answer is given, but an answer in terms of freedom. The freedom of the creature to act against its essential unity with God makes God transcendent to the world."[21] Although transcendence is limited here to the freedom of the creatures, Tillich extends the concept to the divine as well as to the human side in *Systematic Theology*. There he reconstructs the spatiality problem of transcendence in terms of a qualitative relation of freedom. "Transcendence demanded by religious experience is the freedom-to-freedom relationship which is actual in every personal encounter. Certainly the holy is the 'quite other.' But the otherness is not really conceived as otherness if it remains in the aesthetic-cognitive realm and is not experienced as the otherness of the divine 'thou,' whose freedom may conflict with my freedom."[22] The setting of this passage is clearly that of "God," which is a symbol involving a cluster of symbols all rotating around personality and its correlates. The picture here is the traditional one of a free self who is analogously "other" in much the same sense that persons transcend one another as "other." At this level his reconstruction of transcendence does not sound unique. But when we see it in the full setting of his doctrine of God, it begins to take on a distinctive hue. The obvious criticism of transcendence as freedom is that nothing has yet been said. *What* is it that is free? How do we know there *is* anything? At this point Tillich's full analysis of being and the ground of being comes to the fore, undercutting every literal attempt to pin down that which transcends. God as being-itself is transcendent as the ultimate and metaphysically transcendent *Prius,* from which all reality comes and over against which all structures have their being. However, God is more than this unconditional aspect even though this is what makes God God. God is also a dynamic, self-manifesting power which when grasped in revelation is received as a creative freedom which is at least personal. Therefore, God is not only a transcendent depth of things (being-itself), but as " God," a transcendent " beyond " in the sense of the otherness of a freedom-to-freedom relation (being-for-us).

To summarize, Tillich, like Heim and Niebuhr, sees both metaphysical and kerygmatic aspects of transcendence, or to use his terms, God is being-itself and also " God." To say that " God " is the theological " answer " to the question of being is only the formal way they are related. Actually, Tillich relates the two by having " God " *participate* in being-itself, or to reverse it, being-itself *transcends* the symbolic " God " of theism. This is not a transcendence of exclusion, however, but of inclusion. Being-itself, remember, is dynamic, not static, and in a dynamic act it has revealed itself, a revelation that is received and expressed in terms of the symbols that make up " God." We dare not identify the symbols (" God ") with God *an sich.* Yet we dare not ignore them, for as " participating " symbols, they really do speak of God.

3. The Principle of Correlation: Transcendence and Theological Method

So far our problem has been to set out the senses in which Tillich sees God as transcendent. Now the question is, How does this affect the rest of his theology? How might it serve as a clue to clear up some of the more elusive features of his theology? There is no mystery in the fact that the way Tillich relates God and the world, eternity and time, is reflected in the way he conceives theology and thus relates it to philosophy. Tillich's own term for this relation is " correlation." Thus he " correlates " the questions of philosophical (existential) analyses with theological (revelational) answers. He correlates revelation to reason, the Kingdom of God to history, etc. In fact, five of these basic correlations comprise the structure of Tillich's system. One would not go too far to say that the essential feature of Tillich's theology is this principle of correlation. And it has been precisely at this point that the most serious criticisms of Tillich have arisen. What most bothers critics is the suspicion that correlation is basically a synonym for adaptation, amalgamation, and compromise. Many feel that what Tillich really wants to do when he " correlates " theology and philosophy is to " synthesize " the two into an eclectic mixture.[23]

a. *The Principle of Identity: Schelling and Hegel.* Those interpretations which stress correlation as synthesis are apparently reading Tillich via the " identity " principle as it is found in Hegel and the early Schelling. Undoubtedly, the most important influence on Tillich in his formative years was Friedrich Schelling, on whom Tillich wrote two theses for graduate degrees.[24] However, Tillich does not follow the early Schelling of the system of identity and the system of transcendental idealism,[25] but the later Schelling, who (influenced by Boehme) elaborated an "existential" and anti-Hegelian philosophy in his Berlin lectures of 1841–1842. It is the thesis here that the core of Tillich's thought derives not from Hegel directly but from German philosophy at the moment of its break from Hegel.

The *Identität-system* in the narrowest sense refers to a principle Schelling worked out to solve the epistemological problem. In his early works he saw philosophy primarily as the science of knowledge. But the problem of knowledge was two-sided. It included not only the problem of how the *subject* can know (Fichte's problem), but how *nature* can be known. He concluded that both a "philosophy of nature" and a "transcendental philosophy" were necessary, thus both nature and the Self, both reality and ideality, had equally valid claim on truth. And the way Schelling dealt with this dualism that was beginning to emerge was to recognize a common identity, a truth, or "reason," running throughout everything. Everything that "is," and that can be the object of knowledge, must have something in common, be it the world of the ego or the natural world. This something in common is the Absolute Identity.

In the broader sense the principle of identity is also found in Hegel's philosophy. Hegel saw "identity" as the very definition of the Absolute, for the Absolute was that which was identical with itself.[26] Hegel, however, felt that Schelling's identity (absolute) was merely an abstract, contentless principle [27] and instead of that he wanted a "true identity." By this he meant an all-inclusive identity that embraces, explains, and thus overcomes all difference and contradiction.[28] Therefore, if there is estrangement, it is estrangement within a more inclusive identity, the Absolute. On this basis philosophy and theology, reason and revelation, really can be "synthesized." That is, they always have a necessary, dialectical relation to one another, and thus can be derived from one another.[29] Knowledge of God thus always exists in and through estrangement. It is never undercut by estrangement. Accordingly, Hegel can say that the content of religion and of philosophy are really the same, differing only in form, in that religion deals in figures (*Vorstellung*) while philosophy turns such into the more specific knowledge of the concept (*Begriff*). Such is the method of synthesis par excellence.

Against this principle of identity Schelling revolted, and Tillich followed after. Schelling's thought cut across this principle in at least two developments. The first arose out of a metaphysical problem Schelling had difficulty solving. If there is an undifferentiated identity embracing spirit (self) and nature, being and thought, how is it that finitude and especially evil ever develop at all? How "does God transmute himself into the world"? Schelling in his later years went through several stages trying to answer this problem, first suggesting a "falling away," which is not a necessary, deducible act but something that occurs out of sheer freedom. Later in the *Weltalter* he followed Boehme in asserting that this falling away or negation occurred eternally in the divine itself. Whatever the explanation, Schelling came to see existence, finitude, or actuality as somehow estranged from the divine unity, and furthermore this estrangement cannot be rationally explained. In brief, a principle of identity (or in Hegel's terms a dialectic) will not rationally embrace both the divine and the finite. Real freedom is involved. Thus the estrangement can never be totally explained, nor *necessarily* overcome.[30]

Secondly, Schelling in his later years elaborated a distinction taken from Scholastic philosophy, the distinction between a philosophy of the *what* (*quid sit*) and a philosophy of the *that* (*quod sit*). When philosophy dealt with the *what* of things, it dealt with ideas or essences, and this is essentialist or negative philosophy, as Schelling termed it. " Negative philosophy " could relate and explain ideas, but it could never account for a single actuality or existence. Thus it could never deduce the why of actual estrangement or an actual overcoming of estrangement. For that we need a " positive " or existential philosophy, that is, a " philosophy of mythology and revelation." Here the answers are not deduced but experienced as God reveals himself in the religious life of mankind.

What all this amounts to is a split between God and the world, which a philosophy of identity cannot account for or overcome. God always remains the prius (*Unvordenkliche*) or ground of the world, but the estrangement of existence renders impossible any automatic or immanent revelation that coheres with the structure of human reason. In all this Tillich follows Schelling. God is the prius of an *estranged* existence. For this reason estranged existence and ultimate ground can never be merely lumped together, adapted, compromised, or synthesized. To do that would be to return to the principle of identity, which means estrangement is interpreted and explained by an all-inclusive rational principle.

b. *Participation and Estrangement.* How does this illuminate Tillich's doctrine of correlation? Our thesis has been that correlation is not synthesis or compromise. What is it? The clue to correlation is a relationship where the finite both *participates* in and is *estranged* from its ground.

In so far as man is estranged from God, every point of his existence is so radically affected that he is incapable of deriving a revelation or salvation out of anything in and of himself. Estrangement robs man of any "identity" with God on which basis he might naturally work out his own salvation. For this reason revelation comes independently of anything man does to bring it about. "Existential questions and theological answers are independent of each other." [31]

On the other hand estrangement (and independence) does not mean being totally cut off from God. If this were the case, salvation would be something absolutely foreign to man. But Tillich denies this, not because he wants to make salvation a co-operative affair, but because he insists that man even in his estranged state remains God's own creature. Estrangement means that man's "essential being" does not remain intact in existence, but in so far as man is man who has his being ultimately from God and is made for God, he is "essentially" better than he is "existentially." Man's essential unity with God still remains that for which man was made, even if man is estranged from it. This is what Tillich means by *participation*. And although this is a philosophical term ($\mu\epsilon\tau\alpha\lambda\alpha\mu\beta\acute{\alpha}\nu\epsilon\iota\nu$, Plato), Tillich employs it theologically to show that man continues in and for God in spite of his estrangement. Or to put it another way, God remains man's God in spite of the disruptions of existence.

Man is related to God both by participation and estrangement. However, even Hegel could say this. Wherein, then, would Tillich differ? The crucial issue concerns the way estrangement is held along with participation. For Hegel, man's essential unity with God always pervaded and overcame estrangement; thus man in and of himself, in and through estrangement, can know God and thus theologize. For Hegel, participation is a *saving* participation. For Tillich, estrangement destroys any saving efficacy participation might have. Thus man really is dependent on a salvation that must come to him and that he can only receive.

But because even in estrangement man participates in his ground, the salvation that comes to him is not something strange to his being. It really is addressed *toward* man, which means toward his questions. Such " questions " are not merely verbal formulations but questions that cohere in man's existence, since man's " very being is the question of his existence." For this reason revelation does not wait for man to ask; it does not depend on man's asking a question, for man himself inevitably *is* a question. Revelation thus is not produced by man's questions but comes independently. But " independently " does not mean that it comes as something totally strange to man. Rather it comes *to* man's existence, and in so far as that is true, the reception and expression of revelation are influenced by man, but not the fact of its coming.[32]

Now this double situation of real estrangement (requiring a revelation not immanent in man or his situation) and a real participation (requiring revelation to be addressed to the man who is God's own creature) is the principle behind correlation. The correlation principle is an attempt to take both equally seriously, and, for this reason, is meant to replace the Identity principle. To put it another way, Tillich seems to be trying to combine two decisive streams of the nineteenth century, Hegel and Kierkegaard. Kierkegaard denied any immanent possibility of the knowledge of God, while Hegel assumed that saving knowledge was continuous with man's being in that man's being was a being within the Absolute. The distinctiveness of Tillich's principle, and also its strangeness, the reason he can at times be called both " neo-orthodox " and " neo-liberal," is his attempt to do justice both to estrangement and participation, and this is the meaning of correlation.[33]

IV
TRANSCENDENCE IN A DIMENSIONAL METAPHOR:
Karl Heim

Although Karl Heim has been relatively in the background in the theological currents of the last two decades, Edwyn Bevan once ranked Heim with Barth as one of the two most influential theologians in Europe prior to the Nazi revolution. This early period of popularity extended to the English-speaking world especially in the person of E. P. Dickie, possibly Heim's most enthusiastic disciple and the major translator of Heim's works. Now that the first five books of Heim's famous *Glaube und Denken* are translated into English, Heim's theology may yet come into its own.

Born in 1884, Heim, like Tillich, lived through the various crises that rocked Germany in the course of the first half of the twentieth century: nihilism, the First World War, the Communist challenge, and the Nazi revolution. Also like Tillich, Heim has stood on the boundary of many things: theology and philosophy, the evangelical tradition and contemporary world views, and the church and academic life. Heim came from the pietistic setting of Württemberg, where he was born (at Frauenzimmer) and where he served as a pastor (at Giengen). After a few years in the pastorate, and three years as Secretary of the German Student Christian Movement, he taught first at Halle, then Münster, and finally Tübingen, where he has been since 1920.

Heim's magnum opus is *Glaube und Denken*, which he began to publish in 1931. The central problem of the opening volume of this work is the problem of transcendence. This problem as Heim saw it is a combination of a cultural and a metaphysical crisis. The earliest cultural background of Heim's reconstruction was the relativism and nihilism that he felt accompained the Communist world view. With this as the background, Heim wrote the first edition of *God Transcendent* (1931). However, Heim follows a type of apologetic method that attempts a continual dialogue with whatever crisis is current at the time. Thus in 1933 when Hitler came to power, Heim saw another more fearful cultural crisis and accordingly rewrote *God Transcendent*. With Hitler and the cult of *Blut und Boden*, no longer is the problem that of providing a Transcendence in place of a vacuum. Now the divine is quite crudely identified with "faith in the power of the German people."[1] Such is the cultural crisis immediately behind Heim's work. However, in addition to this, and accumulating over centuries of radically changing world pictures, was a profound metaphysical problem, and it is this we must now consider.

1. The Metaphysical Problem

Heim had felt that in both Spenglerian nihilism and in German Faith, the case was one of a simple monism where there was no God in the sense of an "Archimedean point beyond the whole world." This meant that transcendence was not only lost in a cultural immanence; the very notion was metaphysically meaningless. At this point Heim's apologetic theology came into conflict with Barth. Barth, he felt, was valuable in denouncing the cultural idolatries of the time. Yet he felt that Barth's language of transcendence was powerless and meaningless because of what had taken place in the realm of modern secular world views. We cannot simply address the immediate cultural crisis with a direct statement about transcendence without going behind that crisis to the *Weltanschauung* it represents. Heim is not willing to operate in terms of a dualism between Christian proclamation and secular *Weltanschauung* but feels responsible as an apologist to analyze critically that world view, and to use new materials in reconstructing a meaningful distinction between the Transcendent and everything else.

a. *The Collapse of the Ancient World Picture.* But what is the " problem of transcendence," and why has it arisen? Heim sees the matter as a conflict between two entirely opposing world views. This is not, however, the clash between the " scientific " and the " religious " ways of looking at the world, but rather theism's clash with secularism in the purest form that history has yet seen. This secularism is not unrelated to the rise of modern science, since it is rooted in the breakup of the ancient world view. Heim attributes this breakup not so much to Copernicus, to whom it is often assigned, but to Bruno. For while Copernicus kept a sun-centered universe in a definite space, Bruno " struck the roof off " and centerless infinity was the result. Gone were the outer spheres, the territory of the divine, and thus gone was the referent of the vocabulary of transcendence.

All of this has had more far-reaching results in Western culture than merely as cosmological theory. Not only the world picture (*Weltbild*) is changed but a whole new picture of reality (*Weltanschauung*) has arisen, namely, a pure and contented secularism where the very word " God " is a meaningless sound. Such atheism differs from older atheism in that traditional atheism had no trouble conceiving the

God it rejected. In place of the traditional theistic world view where debates about God could at least be meaningfully held has come a view based on *Bios* (life) where the only meaningful referents have to do with the struggles of organisms for life.

Therefore, in summary, the real " problem of transcendence " is broader than the attempt to counteract the great fanaticisms that German Faith represented. These are only reflections of the secularism that pervades all of culture. This secularism is not just an idolatry, the absolutizing of one god over another. It is nearer a vacuum, a maze, or a jungle, and out of the subsequent disillusionment and nihilism come the fanaticisms and claims of absolute loyalties. Therefore, cultural immanentism may be the immediate threat, but nihilism and pure secularism comprise the general background, and the challenge of the former involves a reconstruction that must attain the level of a total world view. Thus to *God Transcendent,* Heim gives the subtitle " Formulation for a Christian Metaphysic."

b. *The Newtonian World.* So far we have seen Heim reacting against the cultural immanentism embodied in the absolutist claims of German National Faith, and insisting that if the truly transcendent God can be asserted against such, the breakdown of the world view that gave the *trans* its meaning must be reckoned with. This does not mean, however, that he is merely dropping the ancient world view and accepting that which took its place. He makes clear that the apologetics for which he stands must not merely adopt the science of a particular age and then somehow fit religion into it. He rather insists on a philosophical examination of the world view of each scientific epoch. Armed with some metaphysical questions plus the most recent theories of contemporary physics, Heim examines the Newtonian world picture and finds that it too is in the state of collapse.

When the ancient world picture fell, the decentralized universe was not just accepted. Substitutes arose in place of the old stabilities, three in particular.[2] The first was the *Absolute Object*. Heim is talking especially about the atomistic materialism of the Encyclopedists, and he finds a gradual breaking away from this doctrine in the nineteenth and twentieth centuries. Kant's analysis revealed such materialism to be concerned about a *Ding an sich*. From 1900 on, Planck, Bohr, Heisenberg, and others pioneered a now familiar departure from the old materialism with its " absolute objects." Heim, however, does not see even quantum mechanics or probability theories as final solutions, but rather a stage of scientific probing that has arrived at some perplexing dilemmas. The attempt to retreat from them is seen in positivism with its reduction of the function of science to operational description alone.

Absolute time and *space* comprise the second substitute for the ancient stabilities, and like materialism these have served as quasi-religious doctrines in so far as they gave man a " place," satisfying the need to be at home. Copernicus' heliocentrism provided only a temporary world center before Bruno's denial. The doctrine of ether then served as a stable center that provided at least something in the universe at rest where bodies could move and be located. While Newton accepted an empty space and time, he found a fixed geometrical structure in which things could live, move, and have their being. This mathematical objectivity proved ultimately to be the source of the downfall of absolute space and time. Both Newton and Vaihinger sought some ultimate norm by which movement could be measured, some coordinate system of axes in which it could be set. The outcome of this kind of questioning was, of course, relativity theory, and the breakup of absolute time and space.

The third substitute according to Heim was that of *absolute cause* or determinism. This absolute depended on the former ones and the total picture was that of a mechanism on the basis of which determinism could be stated, Laplace being the classical example. The collapse came when Planck questioned the possibility of simultaneous knowledge of both the location and momentum of a corpuscle in space, and this is the real root of Heisenberg's uncertainty principle. Of course, the whole matter has been the subject of vigorous debate and several variations of causal theory have been advanced, but so far it seems to be a hopeless riddle.

The important thing to note about Heim's treatment of these three absolutes is that for him they are attempts to fill in with various absolute magnitudes the vacuum left by Bruno. All of history can be seen as a series of efforts such as these along with their subsequent collapse. Heim, therefore, sees such attempts, not as a cultural immanentism like German Faith where a this-worldly power makes unqualified claims and demands, but a metaphysical or cosmological immanentism whereby a this-worldly magnitude is regarded as an absolute foundation or framework of everything else. And this comprises the " metaphysical immanentism " against which Heim's reconstruction is addressed.

c. Via Moderna *and Its Dilemmas*. Heim, as we have seen, uses the development and contributions of the new physics to point up elements of arbitrariness in the world picture of seventeenth- and eighteenth-century mechanism. This, however, does not mean that he regards the new physics as the final substitute or the solution to all problems pertaining to a *Weltanschauung*. It too, as we have seen, has its yet unsolved dilemmas. More important for Heim, however, is the major dilemma or either-or which characterizes any strictly immanental world view. To bring it out he asks some rather traditional metaphysical questions. Why, he asks, does the world have the characteristics it has? How may Reality be explained? Citing some *early* cause in the process does not solve the riddle, yet in the world as we know it, this seems to be the only answer forthcoming. Yet the question is not just *mal posé;* the search for an ultimate reason or cause is not merely nonsense. This leaves two alternatives. We can regard the whole series of causes and effects as an interminable regress, " a totality out of which every particular thing emerges as from an omnipresent matrix," and hence end up in a type of pantheism. Or we can do our tracing back to some particular point in the series, drive in our nail, hang the rest on that. Something in the series itself is regarded as its cause, in which case we have some form of idolatry.[3]

This dilemma is not one that holds just at the level of metaphysical questions. Each person who asks, What shall I do? faces the same dilemma. To answer by referring to some preceding or present series of norms and authorities is to come face to face with the arbitrariness involved in choosing one of them, hence relativism.[4] Yet decisions must be made, and the nail driven in somewhere. Thus when something is *posited* as an authority (such as German National Faith), we have a kind of positivism.

In the first case the question is really not answered, although it remains a real question. In the second case an answer is given, yet arbitrarily and with an absoluteness that the particular " nail " cannot really support. This is the dilemma of both cultural and metaphysical immanentism, or in Heim's language, the life and thought of the " polar " world. The polar aspects being objective entities and relations on the one hand, and the world of subjects and their relations on the other.

d. *The Final Either-Or*.[5] This pushes us to the final either-or. The choice must be made between secularism in one of its forms and faith in one of its forms. By secularism Heim means the satisfied immersion in the thought and action of the polar world along with the perplexing dilemmas pictured above. In particular, it turns out to be some form of arbitrary absolutism or else relativism. Whichever form of secularism is embraced, it is always a monism. For whatever " world " means and whatever " God " means in secularism, there can be no line between the two. Heim recognizes the many attempts to compromise this either-or, but he feels that consistent secularism must end with Heidegger, marching out to meet the night.

Therefore, instead of embracing the new physics as a substitute *Weltanschauung,* Heim uses it to point up the arbitrariness of the old, and then brings to it certain questions which as a world view it does not solve. He feels that what is implied here is that the more recent world views, limited as they are to polar space, have now moved to a point where their problems are not solvable in terms of that space. In other words, physics has reached an impasse and is crowding over into metaphysics.

In summary, Heim gropes for some transcendental emphasis that will counteract the immediate threats of German National Faith. But in so doing he finds that the collapse of the ancient world view has undercut the meaning of the quasi-spatial vocabulary of transcendence. This collapse has issued in a series of substitutes — absolute objects, space and time, and cause — and while new movements in physics and mathematics have reduced these insights to a relative status, even the new theories face what seem to be unsolvable dilemmas. The major one, the either-or of relativism or positivism, pervades the whole polar world, and it is from various horns of this dilemma that both nihilism and fanaticism have come. Therefore, the real " problem of transcendence " is not just to find a transcendent God in whose name the absolute claims of a Hitler can be countered. Rather, it is to meet the total world view Hitler and all contented secularists assume by presenting an alternative world view. This alternative will do two things: it will serve as a challenge to both cultural and metaphysical immanentism, and it will enable the traditional doctrine of God's transcendence to be *meaningfully reconstructed*.

2. The I-Thou-It World (Intramundane Transcendence)

a. *The Problem of Nonobjective Relations.*[6] The particular problem Heim isolates as the central starting point of reconstruction is the possibility of a non-three-dimensional differentiation. If monism is to be challenged by some kind of dividing line, how can this be done without falling into the usual, three-dimensional way of differentiating? It is clear from the beginning that Heim, like Tillich, stands within the philosophical tradition of a reconstructed idealism. However, while Tillich is closer to Hegel and Schelling, Heim with qualifications is nearer Kant.[7] With Kant, Heim is more concerned to mark out the gulfs than the continuities. Like Tillich he rejects the whole debate concerning the Ego versus objective reality and takes their correlative and polar relation as his starting point. Thus he stands in the philosophical tradition that made the I-Thou philosophy possible, namely, a tradition that said the Ego was real but not capable of objectification.[8]

In his search for a nonobjective way of differentiation Heim begins with an analysis of certain kinds of experiences and relationships in what he calls the intramundane world, assuming all along the subjective-objective nature of that world. He attempts to establish the nonobjectivity of three basic relations in that world as the first step of his analysis.

First of all, can the relationship between my objective world and your objective world be understood in terms of two objective entities? What is "my world" and in what way is it distinguished from "your world"? "My world" is the world that I see from the perspective of which I am the center. It requires little interchange to realize that this is not the same perspective as that of another "I" looking at the world, nor does this other "I" receive the same picture. Each "I" has the experience of being the center of the world, at least of his own world, yet not everyone can truly be *the* middle point or have *the* central perspective, hence the tension that arises when these worlds are represented to each other by various proponents. The problem then is, there *are* different worlds, for "world" is never some objective thing apart from the observing Ego, yet these worlds are clearly not stories, compartments, or adjacent spheres side by side. "Both worlds are infinite. There is no wall or partition at which my world ceases to be and the world of the other person begins."[9] The problem then is, How can we make any sense out of the distinction or differentiation between these infinite "worlds"?

Secondly, can the relationship between the "I" and the "it" be described in objective terms? This would hold only if what we call the Ego is an objective "thing." If it is, then it can be objectively "in" the objective world and related to it as other "things" are. But the Ego is not an objective "thing" if this means something we observe or can describe in the same way we would observe a house or even the contents of consciousness. The Ego is not "in" the world as an olive is "in" a jar. The Ego is that to which all these are presented. Granting this hidden and elusive nature of the Ego, what is it about the objective world that fosters a gulf between the two? At this point Heim follows Bergson and Spengler in finding the objective world to be a *stopped* world. The reason it is a stopped world is that it is a *past* world, a world already become.[10] Each "objective" picture is that of a reality that requires an interval of time before it is heard or seen, and by the time it registers, that which is the source of the image or sound is past. Heim admits that in one sense becoming can be applied even to this, for objective pictures can be seen as a series of past events. The point, however, is that the Ego is not a past or stopped Reality. As that to which objective reality is presented, there is no interval between the Ego and itself. It is immediately, directly known in the Now or present. "I" immediately *am* my Ego and no interval takes place. All of this is not to be interpreted in the context of the old Ego-centric predicament. Heim denies that the Ego is cut off from the world, and even attacks the idealistic notion that the Ego is cut off from time. His only point is that because the Ego does not have the same ontological status as the objective world, there is a gulf between them and they cannot be related by ordinary spatial terms. The Ego and the world do not confront each other like two houses or two mountains. Each has its own reality and content, yet each is infinite in the sense that it is not a spatial area (in the *three*-dimensional sense) that can be marked off.

Thirdly, can the relationship between "I" and another "I" (Thou) be expressed in objective terms? The answer is implicit in the terminology of the question, for Heim in using the I-Thou framework stands within one of the de-objectivizing philosophical traditions of present-day thought. He explicitly expounds Buber's *I and Thou* to establish his point. I and Thou refers not to a type of being but to a relationship of mutual dealings. The *what* of the relationship is an Ego-being (*Ichwesen*), and while the medium of the relationship is the objective world, the two " I's " that meet are themselves not objectifiable entities. We have seen previously that the " I " is that to which objectivity is presented. But when two " I's " meet in relationship, they are not themselves objective things. Yet they are not the same. How then can they be differentiated? There are no boundaries in the I-Thou world, at least in the three-dimensional sense. A " thou " is not a neatly marked off object even though it may have an objective, bodily bearer. Also, there is meeting in some sense, yet the meeting of I and Thou cannot be reduced to the reception of sensations from another body, or " experiencing " in Buber's language. There is a meeting but no " place " of meeting in the three-dimensional sense. Another difficulty arises when each " I " realizes that only itself is an " I," the other " I " thus is " a ' Not-I,' which is an ' I.' " Neither " I " can be the center even though each experiences itself as such in the context of three-dimensional, objective differentiation. Such is the problem. I and Thou are differentiated, yet the boundaries are not geographical. There is a meeting but no locatable " place " of meeting.

To summarize Heim's argument then, he maintains that even in the intramundane world of ordinary experience there are three basic relationships that cannot be understood by means of simple three-dimensional distinctions and boundaries. My world and your world, each one infinite, are not related like my yard and your yard, nor am " I " related to " Thou " like an object to another object. Furthermore, " I " am not related to the objective world in the same way that an object is. There are real relations here and real distinctions. The realities involved transcend one another but not in a three-dimensional way. In what way, then?

b. *Boundaries of Content and Boundaries of Dimension.*[11] At this point Heim begins to use insights gleaned from the new physics, especially in so far as the new theories have helped in breaking up the older and simpler block universe and its structure. The objective universe with its entities that are located in an absolute way comprises a continuum in which things are arranged. Even then it is not so simple as it might appear at first sight, for it is comprised of one, two, even three, dimensions. In addition to the objective world there are other " worlds " or continua of data and experience. Besides the objective way of differentiation, there is another basic method of marking out boundaries. The objective world on the one hand is a world of three-dimensional contents, and these contents are exclusive of one another, for they are " things " in a common space, such as two chairs in a room. As finite entities such contents are " bounded " and thus are related to one another either by an interval of common space, such as between two chairs, or by *contiguity* (actual contact) in the common space, in which case the chairs would touch. Thus we have differentiation (and transcendence) by means of boundaries of *content*.

This objective way of looking at things falls short, however, when we attempt to do justice to the relationships involving the " I." As we have seen, these are real relationships, and they denote realities truly differentiated from one another, yet they are not bounded or marked out in the same way as chairs or stones. Here Heim introduces the concept of dimension to denote a nonobjective way of differentiation. Such dimensions are, of course, found within the objective world itself, although as we know them they embrace one another in one basic continuum. If they could be isolated in such a way that we could imagine a one-dimensional or two-dimensional continuum, the relation of another dimension added on would not be one of content or a " bounded " reality, for each dimension is an infinite plane or magnitude. The two would not be two things in a common space, but rather two infinitudes that together transform the continuum into which they have entered. Further, Heim believes that " dimensional boundaries " have definite characteristics and, therefore, we can actually check whether or not a particular differentiation is one of " content " or " dimension." [12]

Having distinguished between the two types of differentiation, Heim now comes to the crucial step in his argument, the actual application of this analysis to the nonobjective relations of the I-Thou-It world. His claim is that the kind of experience and reality denoted by I and Thou and their relations is not an objective reality " in " objective space along with other things. " I " in relation to a " Thou " is not a spatial-temporal entity in the same sense as an apple. Rather, it itself is a " space." Therefore, it is related to objective space as any space is related to another space, by means of boundaries of dimension. Heim thus attempts an analysis in which he asks whether or not I-Thou-It relations can be conceived in terms of ordinary "boundary" distinctions. His conclusion is in the negative; hence he feels that only " dimensional " differentiation is applicable to them.

The success of Heim's attempt to reinterpret the Ego philosophy of German idealism and the I-Thou philosophy according to the categories of dimension and spaces depends in part on the intelligibility of his concept of a " space." But a clear exposition of Heim's doctrine of spaces is not without its difficulties for the interpreter. Heim's use of space is, of course, broader than the " absolute space " against which he has spoken so sharply. A space, rather, is " every interminable continuum within which a manifold of different contents may be distinguished according to the special law of its structure." [13] Although he has rejected Kant's treatment of space, the Kantian influence is clearly present. Heim is unwilling to admit that space is merely " a subjective condition of our intuitions " ; nevertheless, it is a certain form by which reality is received, and the receiver plays a formative role in the reception. Hence, persons with physical sight have a different space from those who are blind. In spite of this formative role, Heim would deny that a space depends for its existence on the subject, yet there is no space *an sich*.

Space, then, in Heim is a term very similar to the concept of perspective except that it refers also to that particular continuum and its basic structure which a particular perspective grasps. The closest parallels to Heim's " spaces " in contemporary ontological analyses would be the levels or fields that structure the cosmos in J. E. Boodin, the " spatial frames " of Lloyd Morgan, and the " Wholes " of Jan Smuts. All these concepts are attempts to challenge the picture of reality as an over-all unified continuum as found in either idealism or reductive naturalism. In the light of these parallels one wonders why Heim chooses the term " space," and his justification is rooted in the use of space in modern physics. The plurality of spaces there arose from the attempts of mathematicians and physicists to show there is no absolute geometrical or physical system that provides the only possible system of co-ordinates or the only possible system for calculation. Euclidean space is not Einsteinian space, though neither may necessarily be invalid concepts. What is important for Heim is that space here is used pluralistically, referring to many spaces or space systems.

If we grant this concept of space, in what sense then can it be used to illuminate nonobjective reality, especially that of I and Thou? The strongest reasons Heim gives are negative, namely, the difficulties that arise when I-Thou-It relations are seen three-dimensionally and objectively. However, he is more positive when he describes the Ego experience in terms of the Heideggerian notion of being thrown-into-the-world (*Geworfenheit*). This means for Heim the experience of having a place that is " my " place, a world center, and with it a whole system of co-ordinates. This is inevitably involved in being an " I." As a reference system it is a space with definite dimensional structure, and thus it is related to other systems of reference and their structures.

c. *The Polar World*.[14] The total picture arrived at from this scheme of spaces is what Heim calls the polar world. For although he uses *space* quite pluralistically at times (each angle or perspective of a certain object is called a space), they can all be organized within two major types: objective and nonobjective space. Objective space, as we have seen, is that stopped world of the immediate past. It is the world of three-dimensional objects and intervals and is known by sense observation and inference. Nonobjective space like objective space is a continuum of a " multiplicity of entities . . . arranged in order according to a definite principle," [15] but its sphere is that of direct cognizing and the meeting of subjects. As in Buber it is not limited to human subjects, but is extended to all of nature. At this point Heim espouses a type of panpsychism, although not by that name.[16] Superficial encounters with organic and inorganic realities leave the impression of inertness, and the usual procedure is to posit a Thou or inner life only in realities that structurally resemble the human body. Heim rejects this and posits a " psychic substratum " in all natural structure.[17] Therefore, similar to human beings, natural entities at all levels are comprised of exteriors behind which something akin to life, will, or consciousness (*Ichwesen,* Ego-being) dwells. And this nonobjective something behind all outward appearances is the locus of real becoming in the present. It is present with us and passes through the Now with us, unlike the objective world that is both a *past* world and the medium of the I-Thou meeting.

Both objective and nonobjective spaces comprise what Heim calls the polar world, for they are in polar relation to each other. Thus like day and night, male and female, the two spaces are interdependent like positive and negative poles. The name given to this over-all polar unit is polar space, and all relations in this polar world, both objective and nonobjective, are governed by its laws. For instance, reciprocal relations reflect the law of polar space as in the fact that there is no " I " apart from " Thou," or the fact that a point is a point in space only in relation to another point.

But having described the world in this way, the problems are only beginning, says Heim. Even if we are successful in deriving objective and nonobjective spaces and relating them together in one polar world, the question then arises, Does this archetypal principle of polarity solve the problem of ultimate meaning and the origin of all things? Is polar space the ultimate background of all there is? Heim's answer, as we would expect, is negative. Rather than solving problems, polar space leaves us with the most difficult one of all. To set it forth, Heim in later volumes of *Glaube und Denken* uses the Heideggerian picture of being (*dasein*), which is "thrown into the here" (*Geworfenheit*).[18] One finds himself here, having experienced the passive reception (*Urempfang*) of himself.[19] Heim's question is, Why this particular here? What is the original act (*Urakt*) of decision that placed the "I" into its particular center? Polar space can answer this question only by reference to a "placer" who is also in a space, but this in turn would rest on another decision, and the problem of *ultimate* origin is still left open.

This way of putting the problem stresses the destiny side of human experience, for it asks why a particular "I" was cast into a particular boundary. A second way of putting it stresses the freedom side, for though bounded, the "I" is confronted with a great variety of alternatives. The second question comes then, How will I at this moment decide what to do? These questions recall the dilemma described above. We can answer them by arbitrarily selecting some one entity in the polar world and regarding that as the key to the problem of origin or the problem of action (positivism), or we can regard every entity and series in the whole gamut of causes and actions as equally legitimate candidates for the key, and thus look to the whole as its own ultimate clue (relativism).[20] Heim, of course, is not content with either. He feels that the ultimate problem is a real problem, but these alternatives do not solve it. This is the peculiar dilemma that the polar world fosters upon us.

What, then, has Heim done at this stage of his reconstruction? Two things: one positive and one negative. Positively, he has tried to isolate a type of transcendence not reducible to objective, three-dimensional relations by analyzing intramundane experiences and realities, therefore showing the possibility of a transcendence not dependent on the quasi-spatialism of pre-Copernican world views. Negatively, however, he has tried to show that the polarism that pervades the intramundane sphere gives rise to dilemmas that are unsolvable in a purely intramundane framework.

3. THE SUPRAPOLAR WORLD
(SUPRAMUNDANE TRANSCENDENCE)

a. *Traditional Aspects of the Reconstruction.*[21] In *God Transcendent,* which is Heim's most explicit treatment of the doctrine of the transcendence of God, he summarizes the sense in which God is transcendent in two quite traditional terms, God as Creator and Lord. With these terms he addresses the problems and dilemmas of the polar world. Actually, the doctrine of creation is the more basic of the two, for this establishes the dividing line by which Christianity and its alternatives are distinguished. Heim's summary of the doctrine of creation is in the framework of orthodoxy. " The universe, including all causal relations by which it is bound together, and including all laws of nature on which the necessity of causal interrelations rests, is, both as a whole and also in every individual part, not something self-subsistent, but something made to be — at every successful moment made anew to be — by a Power other than itself."[22] Also, rather traditionally, Heim relates the doctrine of God the Creator to the problem, Whence comes this universe? Heim puts this question less cosmologically and more existentially in *Christian Faith and Natural Science* and *The Transformation of the Scientific World View,* where he asks, Why am I this particular " I " in this place and not another " I " in another place? In the framework of the polar world there are only two possible ways to deal with this question: either some member of the series is the ultimate cause, or the whole series is itself ultimate. Heim sees the doctrine of God the Creator breaking through this either-or in the form of a *Tertium Quid*. Thus God is not even a *Primum Movens,* which is the first member of the series, but rather "the One through whom alone it exists and is from moment to moment ordained anew." Because as its Creator he is distinct from the series altogether, he cannot be apprehended in the categories of our experience, which, of course, are polar categories. In spite of the similarity, however, Heim's view is not reducible to a mere *argumentum ex ignorantia*. The unknown X factor serving as a world ground is one possibility, but Heim rejects this and all impersonal categories that might be used to refer to the ultimate background of the polar world. They especially do not solve the existential way Heim puts the question of origin. To answer that, he says, the *Tertium Quid* must be a suprapolar, personal Reality who cuts across the vacillation between an indifference to one's personal existence and an absolutizing of it. When this happens, the "I" is seen under the guise of a gift, and God in this sense is affirmed as the Creator.

The second question that posed a dilemma within the polar framework was that of a sanction for activity. We must act and make decisions, but for what and on what basis? The same dilemma arises when we answer it in terms of available authorities in the polar world. Some one entity or power is made the authority, or else we drift among all authorities regarding each one equally valid and invalid in its claims. The transcendent God enters as the one beyond this either-or. His transcendence means that he is no member of the series, nor is he the series itself, but rather its

Lord. Thus authority traced to his command is not caught in the arbitrariness of either idolatry or pantheism.

b. *Nontraditional Aspects of the Reconstruction*
Intramundane and Supramundane Transcendence.[23] So far Heim has remained in a traditional framework in his language of God as Creator and Lord addressed to the problems of origin and authority. But new ground is broken with the question, How can this be conceived? And here we must carefully mark out exactly what Heim is trying to do. How is the preliminary stage of the argument, the analysis of transcendental intramundane relations, related to the transcendence of God himself? This is the knottiest of all points for the interpreter of Heim. The expected answer is that Heim marks out nonobjective, dimensional transcendence in order to show how God transcends the world. But such is not the case. Heim vigorously denies any simple application of intramundane transcendence to God. God is not transcendent in the sense that intramundane realities, even in nonobjective relationships like I and Thou, transcend one another. In *God Transcendent* he even seems to deny that dimensional boundaries and the relation between spaces can be applied to God. " When we distinguish between Creator and creature, between transcendent and immanent, between God and the world, we are not marking out a boundary line between two worlds or two departments of life, which lie adjacent to each other. Nor is this a *boundary of dimension such as may be drawn between two ' spaces.' "* [24] Such passages are definitely more cautious than the analogical tone of later works where God is described in terms of a suprapolar space. Yet there is no serious contradiction. The point here is that *intramundane* spaces are not applicable to God, and he does not transcend in the same way that *intramun-*

dane spaces transcend one another.

But this raises a serious question, and one that Dorothy Emmett poses for Heim: "But if no intramundane relation throws any light upon the relation of God to the world, then if we are to know anything about it at all, we are thrown back on some revelation *ab extra* which is entirely unrelated to any ordinary modes of apprehension. . . . In this case, we are left wondering what the elaborate discussion of 'dimensions' has in fact achieved."[25] The answer must be in terms of what Heim is basically trying to do and how he proposes to do it. It is not too simple to say that *au fond* the purpose of this reconstruction is *conceivability*. When Heim, for instance, tries to use the nonobjectivity of I-and-Thou relations as a support for a personal God, his stress is that "belief in the personal nature of Power . . . is at any rate conceivable."[26] More important, in *God Transcendent* when he sets forth the purpose of the whole work, he says: "We are not yet required to lay the foundations of a belief in transcendence or to buttress the walls of such a faith by any philosophical structure. We are not asked for Apologetics in the old sense of the word. Our task is a much more limited one. It is just to arrive at a clear definition. We are required to indicate what we mean by the words which we are constantly using in this connexion. We must show how far men are justified today in speaking of a world beyond; and how it is possible in so speaking to avoid relapsing into pre-Copernican views. If we are unable to show what meaning can be attached to those words, recurring as they constantly do in all the creedal statements, then our testimony concerning God is not something which can be conveyed from one mind to another, but only a sequence of unintelligible sounds."[27] This paragraph summarizes Heim's problem and intention. Pre-Copernican and Copernican world views can no longer serve as vehicles for any meaningful demarcation of God and the world. What is needed is a mode of thinking where such a demarcation is at least conceivable. " Conceivable " for Heim does not mean observable or directly knowable, but rather a type of thinking in which transcendence is not merely inconceivable or nonsense. It may not establish such a God, or successfully demonstrate (in any sense) the actuality of his transcendence. It may not even describe in any detail how such a God transcends the world. What it might do is to provide a *Weltanschauung* in which a nonobjective transcendence is at least " rendered intelligible." [28]

God Transcendent and Suprapolar Space. But how can intramundane transcendence help render God's transcendence intelligible if God does not transcend in any intramundane way? In *God Transcendent*, Heim cautiously tries to establish a metaphorical relation between the two. Older spatial metaphors worked as long as " transcendence " was at least a logically framable idea, but now such are inadequate, and another kind of metaphor is needed, a metaphor that will make a non-three-dimensional " beyond " conceivable. But in *Christian Faith* and *Transformation,* Heim is much more willing to draw the analogy in an explicit way. There supramundane transcendence is described as a " suprapolar space." [29] Objective and nonobjective spaces transcend one another in a polar relation. God as source of the whole is thus suprapolar, but Heim goes even farther than this in the analogy. As a " space," God, like other spaces, is an all-embracing archetypal space (*Urraum*) " able to span the difference of the spaces in which we are enclosed." [30]

One of the criticisms of Heim has been that God for him was exclusively transcendent, thus not immanent at all.[31] Actually, the doctrine of the all-embracing and present God in Heim is a strong expression of the immanence of God. "It is only when this mysterious law which governs relations between spaces is applied to the connection between the polar and the suprapolar space that we can understand the paradoxical fact to which the Bible repeatedly refers, that God, whom no man can see, and who, as the Creator, is distinguished from all created things by an infinite qualitative dissimilarity, is nevertheless at the same time, everywhere and at every point in the world, inescapably near."[32] Even in the later works Heim retains his earlier caution, for he insists that the Reality of God himself is not a space. For this reason he denies the Scholastic doctrine of *Analogia Entis,* which for him means that the mode of being of God and the mode of being of the world are placed at the same level. God in his mode of being is neither the world, nor anything in it, nor even a transcendent space. Suprapolar space refers not to God himself but "only to one aspect, a side which is turned toward us, the only side from which God can be accessible to us."[33] Suprapolar space is not the reality or substance of God (which for Heim is always the *Ens realissimum*) but the form through which he is represented. Thus we have a positive and a negative side to Heim's suprapolar spatial analogy. Positively, space is an aspect of God by which God reveals himself, but negatively, God in himself transcends even the form and this is the point where the analogy is broken.[34]

God as a Transcendent Thou. We have asked in this section, *How* can God's transcendence as Creator and Lord be conceived? So far the answer has concerned the view of God as a suprapolar space. To complete the picture we must at least touch upon Heim's view of God as a transcendent Thou. He is aware of the difficulties involved in ascribing personality to God, especially the overtones of a bounded being such as a human person. He therefore says that God is not a Thou in the polar I-Thou sense. God " confronts us neither as an object, in the way in which solid objects are disclosed to us, nor as a Thou, in the sense in which the I and the Thou confront one another in the polar space." Nevertheless, both metaphysics and the practical life demand the personal nature of the suprapolar reality. Metaphysically, Heim feels that an It can never generate an " I." Either I am my own origin, he says, or another Thou is. If the source is a suprapolar Reality, it must itself be a Thou. Practically, Heim says the basic question of our everyday life is whether or not there can be dialogue (prayer) between ourselves and the ultimate suprapolar Power. Granting the need for the personal God, Heim says this is conceivable only if we can distinguish the realm of Ego and consciousness from the objective and the measurable. And this is possible only if at least one aspect of God can be seen as a space. Thus the divine can be a Thou, yet so structured as to be available to us in all our relations, including I and Thou. Thus God is a Cosmic Ego (*Weltall-Ich*), a *suprapolar* Thou, differing from polar Thou's because he is not walled out from them as they are from each other. He is, rather, the meeting point of such beings by which they communicate and in which their relations are transformed.

c. *The Existentialist Conclusion.* If we stopped this characterization at this point, a serious misunderstanding would be encouraged. In describing the dilemmas within the polar world and the either-or between secularism and Christian faith, the impression can easily be gained that for Heim these choices are theoretical, one picture of the world over against another picture of the world. This interpretation runs aground, however, on Heim's admission that none of this can be proved if proof means either calculated observation or deductive inference. If this is true, what *is* Heim talking about? How can it be known at all? This question introduces us to the existential level of his reconstruction. There we find Heim more than any other theologian in this study tying the doctrine of transcendence closely to epistemology and soteriology.

Heim asserts that God's suprapolar transcendence is something grasped only by entering into or discovering the new space. As we have said, all his talk about *Weltanschauung*, including his whole reconstruction, does nothing more than establish the conceivability of a nonobjective transcendence, thus opening the way for an existential receptivity in which content can be communicated and a new existence can be received. Thus the dilemmas of polar space are dilemmas of life and decision, and the *Tertium Quid* Heim speaks of, which breaks the either-or of relativism-positivism, is a transforming power, " a new suprapolar space pertaining to the presence of a higher all-powerful 'I' who knows about us and our destiny and who is concerned about everything which may cause us anxiety." [35] Transcendence is, therefore, not grasped in the theoretical stance of the spectator. " When we turn to God it is not a case of a new relation being disclosed, as when we turn in any other direction. No, the Reality of God invades the structure of all relations, disclosing, as it does, a direction which is 'beyond' both the two alternatives of the immanent sphere. As soon, therefore, as we conceive the bare possibility of this new direction, along which we may look for the self-disclosure of God, there must come a complete change of attitude, such as to involve not only a widening of our horizon, but a drastic new orientation of our whole existence." [36] This new orientation is described as entering a new space. As a space (like any space in Heim's sense) it will have surrounded us previously even if we have not been aware of it, and its disclosure comes about by some event in which man "comes to himself." Only then do such problems as Heim has been analyzing become matters of concern: Whence come I? What am I to do? Any synthesis of the subsequent dilemmas that arise comes as a third way of existence and as a gift, although as an unforeseeable *Tertium Quid*, it will seem paradoxical and even nonsense to the either-or's of the polar world.

In summary then, Heim is saying that while the *doctrine* of God's transcendence can be theoretically embraced, *God's transcendence* is grasped only in personal existence. As something absolutely unique, God's transcendence cannot be grasped in the metaphors, not even in the talk about the suprapolar space or a suprapolar Thou. At the theoretical level it is important to try to remove the stumbling blocks in the way of conceiving *some* non-pre-Copernical transcendence and this is Heim's purpose. But the transcendence of God, God's aspect as a suprapolar space, is grasped only by entering that space. What Heim is talking about is repentance and salvation, or moving in the new direction with one's whole existence. Heim even goes so far as to say that such terms as transcendence, gulf, world, originator, etc., still denote the realm of immanence when they are at the level of "terms." Political speeches, autosuggestions, and value theory can all appeal to God transcendent in such terms and the transcendence of God is not grasped at all. Thus Heim's "final either-or" is not a theoretical one, although, of course, it involves theoretical elements. It is *either* existence under the shadow of death with the accompanying *Sorge* and *Angst, or* the new existence.

V
GOD
AS DYNAMIC WHOLE:
Charles Hartshorne

Charles Hartshorne (born 1897) is an American philosopher who has taught most of his life at various American universities. As a holder of several fellowships, he was able to do research at both Freiburg and Marburg, which enabled him to sit at the feet of Edmund Husserl. Most of his training, however, was undertaken at Harvard, where he was associated both as student and later as teacher with the man who has been his chief philosophical inspiration, namely, Alfred North Whitehead. Other influential teachers include Raphael Demos, C. I. Lewis, and W. E. Hocking. After a brief period of teaching at Harvard, Hartshorne took a position at the University of Chicago, where he spent the bulk of his teaching career, until he accepted a position in the department of philosophy at Emory University.

Basically, Hartshorne should be thought of as a philosopher rather than as a theologian. However, the chief concern of his philosophical writings is the metaphysics of theism. More specifically, this means the traditional problem of relating " the God of the philosophers and the God of Abraham, Isaac, and Jacob." Hartshorne wants to treat this problem within the framework of philosophy; hence, the relation of his thought to Christianity and revelation is, at the most, indirect. While he follows a philosophical, ratiocinative method rather than a theological method, his thought is directed at a problem that theologians have always struggled with, the problem of God's absoluteness and relatedness.[1] In this sense Hartshorne might be thought of as a "philosophical theologian." As a philosopher his chief background is American philosophy especially as it reflects the traditions of Peirce and Whitehead.

1. POLEMICS AND THE PROBLEM

a. *Traditional Theism and Its Problems.* Hartshorne's description of the rise of traditional theism is reminiscent of Harnack and Hatch, for he sees Christian orthodoxy as a mixture of Biblical faith and Greek philosophical postulates, the latter corrupting the former. While the Biblical tradition asserts a religiously adequate God of love and concern, the classical tradition asserted a set of nonreligious assumptions that posited the timeless and self-sufficient nature of whatever made up the ultimate backdrop of the world.[2] All along, of course, the Christian tradition claimed that its God was ultimate in the sense of being "the everlasting and ungenerated controlling power of the universe." So far there is no problem until "ultimate" comes to mean a self-enclosed, self-sufficient, timeless Perfection. When this happens, an idolatry of the infinite over against the finite pole of reality arises which Hartshorne calls *ontolatry* or *etiolatry*.[3] The result is a doctrine of God which is both religiously and metaphysically inadequate.

Religiously speaking, a God who is the *Actus Purus* outside of time, change, and potentiality is incompatible with a God who can fulfill the needs of a religious relationship. The Perfect-in-all-respects is essentially an unrelated and unresponsive being. Existing in the absolute bliss of eternity, he needs nothing outside himself and can be affected by nothing outside himself. Although Hartshorne does not explicitly mention Scotus Erigena (Thomas Aquinas is the more frequent target), the *De Divisione Natura* would exemplify the kind of theism against which Hartshorne speaks. There, God in his highest, most ultimate nature (creating but not created) is even above Being (super-esse); and prior to the creation of the levels of forms, God does not even know himself. Hartshorne's point is that this undercuts any possibility of a God who "loves," "sympathizes," or even "wills." If God is such that nothing can affect him, the traditional view that God "wills" some things and not others, yet is unaffected by and indifferent to the outcome, is sheer nonsense. Such a doctrine further undercuts religious concerns by nullifying such notions as sinning against God or positively serving God. If God is absolutely unrelated, timeless, and immutable, nothing that happens in time affects him; hence, both sin and righteousness are matters that never attain significance for God but concern human relationships alone. The practical result is a religion that harms more than it helps human relationships. If God is the only one who creates, works, and bestows blessings, and man merely receives, unable to "serve" God in a way that makes a difference to him, egoism is encouraged. If God is an immutable absolute, Dewey and the humanists are right in saying that orthodoxy's otherworldliness not only is an irrelevance but positively encourages ethical indifference.

Furthermore, such a God is not religiously adequate, for what is there worshipful about him? The very definition of "God," after all, is "a name for the uniquely good, admirable, great worship-eliciting being." But why worship or even admire a being whose closest human type is the tyrant on whom all depend and who depends on none? Complete independence is not an admirable trait at the human level; thus "the father that as little as possible depends upon the will and welfare of his child is an inhuman monster."[4] Even worse is the fact that a consistent assertion of an independent Deity will result inevitably in admitting that God is merely unknown. If God is absolutely out of relation (self-enclosed), we can know and think nothing about him, which is the reason the *via negativa* shipwrecks. If God is merely not this and not that, what differentiates him from nonbeing? The seriousness of this difficulty is the religious irrelevance of a merely unknown God.

Hartshorne is aware that orthodox theism cannot be identified simply with the position described above. It is filled with references to the God who is known, who loves, cares, wills, creates, and knows entities beyond himself. His point, then, is that these elements can be added to a metaphysics of static perfection only by sheer contradiction. If the religiously relevant God is still to be asserted, the result is metaphysical nonsense. The orthodox doctrine that God is omniscient is a case in point. God is affirmed as one who knows, yet whose knowledge is immutable while the objects of his knowledge constantly change. This must mean that God knows about things, but not the things in their concrete changing actuality; hence, he apparently is not *all*-knowing. If God knows contingent happenings, one would expect his knowledge to be dependent for its concrete content on such contingencies. If it is admitted that God's knowledge is contingent but his being is not, further problems are introduced, for how can an entity's knowing be separated from what the entity is? The being of an entity does not *exclude* but *includes* its relationships; hence, another contradiction arises. The orthodox answer is in terms of the doctrine of God as the *totum simul*, where God transcends past, present, and future as an Eternal Now. But Hartshorne feels this is a contradiction, for it annihilates the meaning of "now" and time itself. If God knows what is future to man as a Now, in what sense is it really future, and what would prevent the whole experience of process from being mere illusion? If time is real, future cannot be reduced to the state of present, for the very meaning of present depends on the open possibility of actualizing future states.

Other contradictions arise when such a theism attempts to say how and why the self-contained creates. "Cause" is the usual category brought in to show how God creates, but in the usual meaning of cause, the total concrete reality is cause-effect and one cannot be isolated from the other. For orthodoxy the situation remains the same for God whether he does or does not create; thus the effects do not "follow from" the cause. *Why* God would create presents another problem. The altruistic motive is the usual answer, but if this is so, does not altruism include a value experience of joy or satisfaction that adds something to the altruist? But how can anything new be added to the experience of the Absolutely Complete?

b. *The Humanist Alternative.* There is one very simple way out of this maze. Reject it altogether as nonsense, and this in fact is the alternative that has arisen in contemporary humanism. Logically speaking, this position is the opposite pole from the above theism that seeks a God who is in all respects perfect and independent. For humanism's faith is in a reality (man) that is in no respects perfect. Humanism thus is the second alternative against which Hartshorne sets his reconstruction.[5]

Hartshorne's relation to humanism, however, is not simply a negative one. He agrees wholeheartedly with many of the humanist criticisms of traditional theism. Yet, in the final analysis, humanism will not do. Its major goal, "the integration of human personality," is a high one, yet it shipwrecks on the following dilemma. What is the total basis of taking seriously human values and achievement? Whatever it is, Hartshorne feels that such hopes cannot stand up under the threat that ultimately all such values and achievements come to nothing. Belief in a racial immortality is a possible basis, yet the eventual uninhabitability of our planet is now practically a certainty. How do the humanists meet such a threat? One way is by saying that whether or not values will ultimately cease being generated, at least we know good in the present and can remember it in the past, and what comes after cannot cancel this out. The need then, as Hartshorne sees it, is some means by which past value can be retained. If it is retained, it will be in the same way any past is retained, by memory. But if man's memory is the only receptacle, it will itself in the end be annulled. The only answer forthcoming, then, is merely to "be brave." But bravery is one of those values under question, and we cannot be intellectually alert, and still escape the paralyzing effect of the fact that it all comes to nothing in the end. For reasons such as this, Hartshorne feels that by and large humanism has a disintegrative effect upon its adherents, and this is supported by the kind of effect the great humanistic novelists produce; namely, one of cultural disintegration and decadence.

The root problem Hartshorne is digging at here is humanism's attempt to stake itself, as Max Otto put it, on man alone, apart from any cosmic background or view of nature except as an object to be controlled for man's purposes. In this framework it ignores profound metaphysical problems that cry for solution: the nature of passage, the relation of past values to time, the problem of origins and their conditions, and the nature of nature. Thus, ironically enough, Hartshorne's criticism of humanism is that it is an archaism. In so far as it allies itself with reductive naturalism and materialism and remains within the old debates concerning supernaturalism, it shows itself unaffected by the growing criticism of older views of nature, and immune from the increasing devotion to nature made possible by new visions of its expansiveness and depth. In so far as humanism is willing to admit that man's attitude to nature can be something akin to " love," it is bordering on the *deus sive natura* of Spinoza, which is the essence of the religious attitude toward the world and the beginning of theism.

c. *Beyond Humanism and Orthodoxy: The Problem.* Hartshorne's analysis, therefore, is one that accepts the humanist criticisms of orthodoxy, but that would go " beyond humanism " to a revised theism. This brings us to his central criticism of both. Neither has left open the possibility of a *Tertium Quid* between or beyond the either-or each poses for the other. In other words the analysis of the theistic problem as one that involves the two alternatives — absolutistic theism or humanism — is inexhaustive, and both sides err in assuming the matter settled. Dewey is " unscientific " in dismissing the problem as closed, which is a difficulty with most humanism. The supernaturalistic theism it rails against is not the most recent or respectable view that presents itself. Orthodoxy's error is the same, although the either-or within orthodoxy is somewhat different. It assumes that unless the metaphysics of a Changeless Ultimate is retained the only other alternative is pantheism. Its either-or, then, is God sheerly independent of the world or God as a name for the total collection of entities in the world. Part of the problem is thus vagueness and ambiguity. Humanism in its attacks and theism in its defenses agree that the God in question is "absolute," "perfect," and "the greatest," but the relative grades of these terms are never considered. And it is in the relative grades that Hartshorne would look for a third alternative.

Hartshorne never tires of finding new ways of working out classifications of theistic and nontheistic types.[6] One of the earlier analyses is found in *Man's Vision of God*. Here he gives a minimal definition of God as an "entity somehow superior to all other entities," and then proposes to discuss superiority in terms of two types of perfection: *absolute* perfection, which says the perfect has no potential states, and *relative* perfection, where no entity is superior to the perfect except the perfect itself. He then adds to this twofold analysis three grades of superiority: in all respects, some respects, or no respects. And when these are applied to the two types of perfection, we have a scheme of classifying possible doctrines of God that breaks down the old either-or. Orthodox theism would thus say that God is absolutely perfect in all respects (*AA*). Atheism, humanism and polytheism, would describe God in manlike terms or like some other imperfect thing; thus God would be perfect in no respects (*RR*). Yet there is an alternative not yet included. God may be absolutely perfect in some respects and relatively perfect in others, which is Hartshorne's proposed "panentheism" (*AR*).[7]

Such is Hartshorne's attempt to open a third alternative[8] "beyond humanism" yet avoiding the problems of orthodox theism. His "problem," then, is to establish his alternative by elaboration and evidence. But how is all of this relevant for the problem of transcendence? In one sense this is Hartshorne's central concern. It is true that he does not see the problem the way Heim does, namely, that of a cosmological construction that will give new meaning to the *trans* in transcendent. Yet he is one with Heim, Tillich, and Niebuhr in seeing hopeless contradictions and ambiguities in orthodox theism, and like them, he does not want to pay the humanist price of solving the problem. He too wants to retain a God who is eternal, absolute, and the creator. Yet the central assertion of religion is *deus est caritas,* and how can this be held along with ultimacy without contradiction? *In what sense* is God absolute if he is also love? Immanentism for Hartshorne, then, would be that doctrine of God which lost the absolute side completely. A polytheistic or humanistic doctrine of God would illustrate such a loss as well as pantheism, which sees God as the name for the collection of entities called the world. Although he does not use the term " immanentism," it seems he would also apply it to *AA,* the absolutistic theism, for there we have God limited just to one abstract aspect, and God in his unique, full, transcendent relativity is lost.

2. Hartshorne's Cosmological Metaphysics

So far Hartshorne's proposal to combine absolute and relative aspects in God solves no problems. Even traditional theism " combined " the two, but, according to Hartshorne, at the expense of contradiction. What prevents his own alternative from being merely a composite of two contradictory elements? In Hartshorne's language the absolute and the relative are two " aspects " of the one being, yet this is reminiscent of the " God out of relation " and " God in relation " of patristic times and even the *deus nudus* and *deus revelatus* of Luther. Is Hartshorne's " two aspects " doctrine in any sense distinctive? To answer this we are pushed beyond Hartshorne's specific reconstruction of the doctrine of *AR* to his total organismic philosophy in which his reconstruction is set and in which it must be understood.

a. *Alfred North Whitehead.*[9] Whitehead was a metaphysician in the grand style, consciously identifying his work with both Plato and Aristotle. His view of the nature of metaphysics is more Aristotelian than Platonic except that the result in Whitehead is of a far more synthetic nature than Aristotle. The synthetic nature of Whitehead's work is reflected in his definition of philosophy as the " critic of abstractions." The distinction here is that of abstract-concrete, and an abstraction is an " omission of part of the truth," the concrete thus referring to the full, most inclusive reality. Philosophy as criticism of the abstract in the name of the concrete will thus tend to be synthetic in nature. Whitehead's search for generality is not in his terms mere speculation or verbal abstraction, but a search for a concrete vision and the total setting of all the partialities which are filtered through by experience. Hence, the " fallacy of misplaced concreteness " is *the* basic fallacy against which all of Whitehead's philosophy is leveled, and this is the key to his rejection of both materialism and idealism with their search for bits of matter or mind.

What, then, results from Whitehead's own attempt to escape the abstraction fallacy? In the first place, a total *theoria* of the universe arises. Nature is not a " system " in any narrow sense, but it does have enough unity to enable us to assert "the same general principles of reality, . . . stretching away into regions beyond our explicit powers of discernment."[10] Whatever else it is, nature is one, vast, interwoven fabric, not *en bloc* but an inexhaustive passage or process. But fabric of what and passage of what? Process philosophy has often been accused of evading or ignoring the problem of substance, but Whitehead at least has an answer. The *what* of process is "structures of activity," which are enduring patterns emerging as the outcome of process and comprise its character and continuity. The make-up of such structures is events or "epochal occasions," and the passage of these events is described in terms of a perpetual actualizing of possibilities inherent in the events themselves. The resulting picture is not one of a multiplicity of unrelated events each going its own way. An occasion is not something real plus its relationships, for an occasion is its relationships. Reality, therefore, means the concrete totality of events interlocked in relation and proceeding in passage via a synthesis of former events with their eternal objects out of which comes the actualized new event. Nor is the whole an entity within which processes occur. The whole (nature) itself is a process.

But the metaphysician cannot stop here, according to Whitehead. What condition is necessary by which there can be a process, by which some and not other potencies are chosen for actualization? Out of the infinity of eternal objects how can we account for the actualization of some of them? In answer to this, Whitehead posits a primordial aspect to the universe, akin to Plato's *Receptacle* and Leibniz's *Chief Monad*. The universe as Whitehead sees it is not just a multiplicity. As process it has a unity or identity running through it in terms of an eternal condition by which concretion takes place. This "reservoir of potentiality and coordination of achievement" for Whitehead is God. When Whitehead wrote *Science and the Modern World,* the term "God" referred to this primordial aspect, or at least to the primordial function of serving as the "principle of limitation" by which some potencies were restricted and graded for actualization. However, the year after *Science and the*

Modern World he began to speak of God as *actual*, " includ-[ing] in himself a synthesis of the total universe." [11] Nevertheless, this was still a hesitating stage of Whitehead's developing doctrine of God, for here in *Religion in the Making* he still defined God as the " nontemporal entity whereby the indetermination of mere creativity is transmuted into a determined freedom," [12] thus God primordial is still dominant. By 1929, however, the former hint of a God who was also actual and the synthesis of the total universe was elaborated into the Consequent Nature of God, and God as the " principle of concretion " (*Science and the Modern World*) became the " Primordial Nature of God." Whitehead had apparently perceived the boundaries of dualism and bifurcation he was skirting when he spoke of a nontemporal, nonconcrete, ground of concrete actuality. Such a deity would be almost a sheer abstraction, and there is little place in the Whiteheadian universe for *sheer* abstractions. The final picture, therefore (*Process and Reality*), was that of one deity who embraced the growing world of actualized events (The Consequent Nature of God) and who also served as basis of " the order in the relevance of eternal objects to the process of creation." [13]

What we have here, then, is an organismic interpretation of God and nature. The infinite God and infinite universe can thus be related not as two " spaces " (Heim) but as one infinite, everlasting organism, which in one aspect is a primordial creativity by which as a total fabric the universe continues to grow and by which its values and events are preserved.

b. *The Nature of Nature*.[14] Hartshorne has said that a type of theism is needed that will without contradiction combine relative and absolute characteristics in one deity.

But if relative and absolute characteristics are *in* God (change, process, relation), it is clear that God in some sense will embrace what we term nature. In *Beyond Humanism* he illustrated his position in Spinoza's phrase *deus sive natura;* thus the nature of nature is a crucial issue in Hartshorne's thought. As a serious metaphysician in the Whiteheadian sense of searching for categories of the widest generality, Hartshorne from the beginning assumes the unity of nature in some sense. There are, however, several notions of unity that he rejects. Following Whitehead, he repudiates all preorganismic views of nature, especially those of reductive naturalism and materialism. Nature's unity is not even found in a system of unchanging laws, for even if there are such " laws," they too will be in process. He also rejects nature's unity pictured as a sheer aggregate or " collection of natural entities." Pantheism, according to Hartshorne, occurs when God is identified with nature in this sense, and he is definite in rejecting it. On the positive side, Hartshorne's view of nature is practically identical with that of Whitehead's outlined above, for he also sees the world as an all-inclusive organism in process. In this phrase we have the two basic concepts around which Hartshorne's metaphysics revolves: process and organism (society), or *in toto,* " social process."

Process as All-Inclusive. " Reality as social process " is the best summary phrase for Hartshorne's metaphysics, although he labels his view panpsychism and " organic monism." One way of expounding it is by recalling the traditional philosophical problem of being and becoming. In *Beyond Humanism* he saw being as almost synonymous with reality, for he defined it as " the total system of all cosmic dimensions of continuous variation." However, his later and more typical view is that being is " the abstract fixed aspect of becoming," or the "fixed constant of a process."[15] The key to this way of using "abstract" is Whitehead, for whom abstract meant the omission of part of the truth and concrete referred to the full reality. Therefore, it is in a whole-part context that Hartshorne relates being and becoming, with becoming or process the whole (concrete) and being a part (abstract). His justification for this is that if a totality is fixed, no part can be changing, while a changing whole can "contain" an abstract part. In Whiteheadian terms he would say that the enduring character or pattern is part of the more general process. Hartshorne follows Whitehead here in that *what it is* that becomes is a new totality or togetherness; thus becoming is not something that occurs within a larger, fixed entity, for if such does occur, the entity itself is changed and as a "whole" is different.

The whole point, however, is that for Hartshorne becoming is the all-inclusive category, and this lays the ground for an organic monism and the view of the total universe as a growing whole. One assumption here is the notion of Whitehead and Bergson that time is accumulative and nonsymmetrical, expressed in Whitehead's phrase "the immortality of the past." For Whitehead an event is not just a present entity totally divorced from the past. An event in the process is comprised of data of antecedent events out of which the "specious present" emerges. In the total process, therefore, what we call the *past* is not lost but gathered up in each subsequent present, for the present event, "the unit of things real," by definition includes the actualization of *antecedents* and their *possibilities*. Time thus is nonsymmetrical in that any particular present contains more content than any stage of its past. This analysis of process is applied by Hartshorne to the universe, which is seen as a totality in process growing more and more complex due to the accumulation of events and past values. Therefore, the first answer to the question of the unity of nature is that it is an all-inclusive process or a growing whole.

The World Society. To complete the question of the unity of nature, we must ask, What kind of whole is it that is in process? How is it structured and what kind of relationships does it include? The answer is that the all-inclusive process is structured after the manner of a society where relations are reciprocal and take place in the context of "shared experience." Nature, in other words, is an organism, which is why it is never a mechanism or a mere aggregate. It is easy, of course, to envisage various societies within the totality, but on what basis can it be said that the whole is an organism? Only if we can defend the existence of certain variables that extend to every level of a scale running throughout the universe.

Hartshorne has isolated a number of such "variables" or "ultimate categories of reality," and three especially characterize the world as a society.[16] The first is the element of *chance*. Hartshorne is a zealous antideterminist who insists on some element of spontaneity throughout nature. However, he rejects any thoroughgoing indeterminism. Necessary causal connections are still to be maintained, he feels, although only in some aspects of an event. Thus there is no absolute predictability in nature. *Incompatibility* or conflict is a second cosmic feature. It arises inevitably due to concretion, which means the actualized stage of reality is particular and thus exclusive, not only of other possibilities not actualized but of other particulars. Such incompatibilities have their place, for their presence serves as the ground of the world's beauty, preventing it from being either a dull monotony or mere chaos. This brings us to the third and most important feature of nature, that which raises nature to the level of a society, namely, love or *harmony*. The basic meaning of harmony is " unity in contrast," and the type of unity Hartshorne has in mind is organic. This means that as an organism the universe is not harmonious in the democratic sense of a composite of mutually co-operating members. There can be harmony at the most general level because the universe is a " monarchical society " with order imposed by " a single, dominant, all-ruling member."

Underlying this view of harmony pervading the universe is Hartshorne's panpsychism, which he owes in part to Gustav Fechner.[17] Harmony, therefore, is not merely order that has been " pre-established " or built into impersonal parts. Since society means " shared experience," a minimum of such experience is posited for each member, and *feeling* is the minimum characteristic of that experience. Hartshorne, of course, admits the presence of impersonal composites, " organic wholes," such as stones or buildings, yet he would insist that while these are not organisms as wholes, they contain or include organisms. At the level of the smallest units and the largest (the universe itself), there is subjecthood.

Such is Hartshorne's *theoria* of the universe. He sees it as one vast unified and eternal process covering a wide scale where complexity increases toward the top and toward the future. It is flexibly unified by the presence of both process and the presence of unity-in-contrast made possible by the all-pervading life and subjecthood of its members and the monarchical control of the organism as a whole. However, the fact that nature is a world society in process does not mean that Hartshorne is blind to all elements of tragedy and discordance. In fact, such tragedy is a corollary to Hartshorne's analysis of process. For real process carries an element of contingency or chance, which means that "tragedy is inevitable in some degree." Yet such tragedy is definitely limited, for it is always embraced by "a divine beauty of synthesis," a providence that "furnishes a maximal ratio of chances of good to chances of evil."

3. God Absolute and Relative

In the light of such a metaphysics we must put the question again: How does Hartshorne combine relative and absolute aspects of God and yet avoid the contradictions that he rejects in orthodox theism? How does Hartshorne avoid merely a verbal composite in his doctrine of God as *AR*? The answer brings us back to *Process and Reality* and Whitehead's doctrine of the two "natures" in God. In Hartshorne's language there are two "aspects" or "poles" in God, and it is clear that he is trying to reproduce Whitehead's theism at this point. These aspects are fundamentally the absolute and relative. Or to put it in other terms, God is perfect in some respects and imperfect in others, both independent and dependent, abstract and concrete, subject-for-all-objects, and object-for-all-subjects, cause and effect, creator and created, and changing and changeless.

a. *The Absolute Aspect: God as Primordial.* Hartshorne relates being and becoming by means of such distinctions as concrete-abstract. Being is that abstract constituent which persists through the changes of a larger whole. He sees change as comprising three aspects: the concrete history of past experiences, the rise of novelty adding to this history, and an abstract character common to all states. Because for Hartshorne the whole changes, and God as relative embraces the whole, there is an abstract element in God common to all his states. This holds for every organismic reality. There is an element of enduring identity in all process, including that all-inclusive process, God. This enduring element is Hartshorne's version of Whitehead's Primordial Nature of God. " Although nothing is additional to God, everything contingent is additional to God considered only in his ' essence,' meaning by that, what is common to God in all alternative possible states — or that by which God is himself, or again, that which is referred to in saying ' He ' exists necessarily. His essence is his very individuality, by which ' He ' is identified. Contingent predicates, by definition, are nonidentifying. God would be God without them."[18] Thus Hartshorne retains the traditional doctrine of God's essence or substance. This is the aspect that makes God God, namely, what is common to God in all his states. This is also the basis of the unity of God by which he is not reduced merely to relative states. We must remember that it is not all of God, nor was there ever a time when God was merely his absolute aspect. It is the *abstract* aspect of God, but it is important to remember that " abstract " in process philosophy does not mean merely verbal or general, but rather a cross section of a reality: real but not fully so. Nor does this mean that the relative or actual aspect of God is nonessential. That would be hypertheism, and as we shall see, Hartshorne's rejection of this marks his central disagreement with Tillich. Rather, in this doctrine of essence (that which God has in common with himself throughout all his states), Hartshorne is merely saying that God would be God without the content of certain particular events or states in his experience. His being God does not, for instance, depend on whether or not a particular earthquake or war does or does not occur.

What is it, however, that endures? True, it is God, but what is it that comprises this enduring essence of God which is independent, noncontingent, and absolute? Hartshorne has two answers, although they are not easily put together. First, the noncontingent aspect of God is his *existence*. That is, God will *exist* regardless of what happens; he depends for his existence on no particular world or process. " The ultimate identity of existence, which contingently includes all ordinary things within itself, does not in this fashion include itself, the identity, as a contingent item. This identity *is,* and it ' is ' in another fashion than ordinary things, for it alone is not contingent — if contingency is what we have above supposed." [19]

But Hartshorne goes farther in describing the content of what it is that endures. The second answer follows the analogy of a man's character in relation to his changing states. *Character* with its ethical overtones is what persists throughout. Hence, a man is honest, wise, or good regardless of changing circumstances. That which endures in God is his ethical character. " If, as religion says, God is perfect in goodness, wisdom, and power, then he is unchanging in these respects." [20]

Problems arise, however, when we put together Hartshorne's various descriptions of the absolute aspect with love, goodness, and ethical traits. Hartshorne tells us that in his absolute aspect God is nontemporal, immutable, and exempt from change, and completely independent. As absolute he has only external relations with man and external relations for Hartshorne are nonmutual relations where " the term in no way ' depends ' for its being or nature upon the relations." [21] Such features are easier to reconcile with God's existence as that which endures noncontingently than with his love and character. If it is God's love that is absolute, in what sense can love be nontemporal, immutable, independent, and nonmutually related to the loved? The

GOD AS DYNAMIC WHOLE   149

difficulty, it seems, lies in the ambiguity of these terms, and Hartshorne is using them in a special way at this point. Independence can mean total lack of dependence in any way on anything else. But Hartshorne's definition of independence is, "A thing will be itself whether or not the thing of which it is said to be independent exists or has a certain character."[22] God will love, in other words, regardless of circumstances. The absoluteness of love thus means the fact of love rather than its nature, else the old contradictions would have returned. The importance of this is that Hartshorne is using absolute, independent, etc., in a somewhat different sense from his attacks on such concepts in orthodoxy. Even Hartshorne's "absolute aspect" is a qualified notion, for in one passage he reinterprets absolute in the context of "religious reliability" or adequacy, which is a functional doctrine of God's absoluteness. Hence, Hartshorne's reconstruction has not only involved the attempt to put absolute and relative aspects of God together via a new analogy, but a reconstruction of the very notion of "absolute." There is *no* aspect in Hartshorne's God that is absolute in the sense of a first mover. If so, it could never be identified with just the *fact of* God's existence and moral character, but would also include the nature of such as unrelated, and *unrelated love* is nonsense.

b. *The Relative Aspect: God as All-Inclusive.* We now come to that feature of Hartshorne's reconstruction which gives it the name, panentheism, and which Hartshorne himself stresses untiringly; namely, the doctrine of "divine relativity." The whole matter begins with his insistence on the "religious availability" of God, and the consequences that go along with a God who really knows and loves. If there are such things as contingent happenings, and if God knows them, is not the content of God's knowledge dependent in part on the way novelty works itself out? If God is really God, and is to be worshiped, what is worshipful about a sheerly independent and therefore indifferent being? Are not influencibility and affectibility (passibility) higher responses than sheer reactionlessness? A man reacts to a pillar, but not vice versa; yet no one praises the latter for its superiority. Therefore, Hartshorne concludes, if the traits of God declared in religious tradition are to be taken seriously at all, God is a being who really can be affected, and therefore whose experience will vary with the process. Therefore the passages from the Old Testament that speak of the God who " repents " and changes his mind are not just embarrassing anthropomorphisms. God can really change and he can change his mind, i.e., if he is in real relationship with other beings.

But if God can be affected, in what way can he be related to the world and still retain his absoluteness? Here Hartshorne rejects a number of possible positions. God cannot be just *a* part or process of the world (as in polytheism) else his absoluteness is undercut. He cannot be just sheerly transcendent in relation to the world with a great gulf fixed, else how could he then be affected? Also, if God and the world are two separate entities, God becomes a constituent of a whole greater than himself, and his absoluteness as omnipresence is lost. Nor will the pantheist view do where God is a name for an impersonal world whole, for God as personal and free in relation to the world would be lost.

In place of such alternatives another possibility is already implicit in Hartshorne's scheme of things. A hint is provided by the nature of perfect knowledge. In perfect knowledge the knower is not externally but internally related to the known, which means that the knower is not a constituent to which a relation is added, but a total relation embraces the two and comprises part of their being. The situation of knower-known, then, is that of a whole within which each participates. In short, perfect knowledge includes its objects, and in perfect knowledge the knowing is not separated from the being of the knower. Thus if we are objects of God's knowledge and care, we are in this sense included in his being. Secondly, if Hartshorne's organic monism holds up, with its picture of reality as an eminent, all-inclusive social process, God will be neither a bifurcation within nor a reality beyond. Since it is an organism, God can include it without its being a name for a mere aggregate of parts.

The conclusion, then, is that God is the all-inclusive reality. "God in this doctrine is the supreme *socius,* the all-dominating member of the cosmic society, the ideally and universally social being, as contrasted to beings locally and defectively social."[28] Therefore we can explain how God can be *affected* and yet his absoluteness not be imperiled. As all-inclusive God embraces all changes within himself, every change makes a whole a different whole. Hence, as a concrete, all-embracing whole, God is relative, for process is the widest category. And this undercuts neither his personality nor his absoluteness, for the analogy here is that of an organism, and God is the all-inclusive organism that contains an abstract enduring identity that persists through changes and depends on none of them.

As an all-inclusive being, what is God's specific relation to the parts? It is a mixture of control and flexibility. There is enough control so that the world society is a monarchy, yet the individual parts, like cells in a body, are relatively free. They are free enough to rebel against the harmony imposed by the cosmic organism, but not free enough to imperil its goodness or existence. Because of such freedom, God is not responsible for everything that happens in his "body" although he suffers and endures it all. This is why God does not have pure bliss but is, to use Whitehead's phrase, "the fellow sufferer who understands."

c. *Some Implications.* Hartshorne's final picture of God, then, is that of an all-inclusive organism embracing every happening in nature. This is a dynamic, not a static, inclusiveness, however, for God functions by constantly receiving and being enriched by new events and values, by setting limits to evil and serving as a condition by which possibilities are graded and values actualized, and by storing such values in his "memory" so that they are not lost but continue accumulating and serving as the seedbed for new gains.

From this reconstruction Hartshorne is ready to revise and solve the contradictions surrounding the traditional attributes of God. Immutability is kept but limited to the absolute aspect, and then in revised form. Omnipotence is lifted out of whatever notions of tyranny were implied in the traditional doctrine, and is pragmatically redefined as "causal adequacy" or God's ability to give the cosmos what it needs. The most decisive revision occurs at the point of the doctrine of God's knowledge and experience. Hartshorne's God is omniscient in the sense that he knows everything for what it is. He perfectly remembers the past, clearly perceives the present, and also envisages the future, but *as future*. If time is not an illusion and future is really future, God does not know it as a present, or even as that which "will be." The status of the future is that of possibility; hence, as future it is a "may be," and it is as a "may be" that God knows it. Also, if future is really future, God too has a future and is not Pure Act in which all potentialities are actualized. Hence, as the universe increases in complexity, and novelties continue to be actualized, such increases are additions to God's life so that his experience at one point of time is always filled with more content than in any previous period.

God as personal is retained in a quite literal sense, and the personal is identified with the relative or reflexive aspect of God. This, however, raises some difficulties. If the personal has to do with the *R* aspect, in what sense is the *A* aspect of God described as his character, love, and goodness? Are not these characteristics features of personality? Possibly Hartshorne's distinction is the following. The *A* aspect is *the fact that* God is love, and this fact is independent of any change in the totality, but *how* he loves and relates to multiplicity, the conditions necessary for love such as consciousness, personality, and effective organs, comprise the *R* aspect of God's total being.

4. Transcendence as Unrivaled Superiority

It is not surprising that Hartshorne, like Whitehead, has again and again aroused the suspicion that he does not do justice to the transcendence of God. In a review of *Beyond Humanism,* Robert L. Calhoun felt that Hartshorne's " God or Nature " identification omitted the unfathomable depths in God,[24] and John Wild reacted to *The Divine Relativity* by saying, " There is an element of sharp transcendence in the object of religious adoration to which Mr. Hartshorne's conception simply fails to do justice." [25] Nevertheless, Hartshorne has always been conscious of the problem of transcendence-immanence, and although these terms do not carry the chief burden of his reconstruction, he has been willing to define and use them. In *Beyond Humanism* his estimate of "transcendence" was a low one, for he saw it as a vague concept denoting a sheer "beyond." And this vagueness is the reason Hartshorne does not use the term more. For his problem is the narrower one of *how* God is transcendent: as sheerly dependent, or dependent-independent, etc.? Hartshorne's answer is in terms of his *AR* formula, and as his philosophy has developed, he has been willing to use the term "transcendence" to denote something in both sides of the formula, the reflexive and nonreflexive.

a. *The Meaning of Transcendence.* But what does Hartshorne mean by the term "transcendence"? What does a thing do when it "transcends"? His answer is in the framework of value rather than cosmology. Transcendence for Hartshorne thus does not mean mystery, otherness, independence, or beyondness, but rather, superiority. "Also, instead of 'perfection' it might be safer to use the term 'transcendence' for superiority-to-all-others, since both word and phrase suggest relation to other beings." [26] Other concepts that are almost synonyms in Hartshorne's vocabulary of transcendence are *incomparability, unrivaledness,* and *uniqueness.* One of the most frequent statements Hartshorne makes about God is a declaration of his uniqueness: "God is the *only* being who . . ." "God, for both old and much new theology, is the being whose uniqueness consists in his unrivaled excellence, or whose amount of value defines a necessarily one-membered class (and so in a sense not a class)." [27] But in what sense is God's transcendence a superiority? To answer this question two sets of distinctions are necessary. One concerns that over which God is superior. Hartshorne's answer is that God surpasses *everything,* including himself; hence he is the self-surpassing surpasser.

The other has to do with the degree of God's superiority. The answer here is a notion of central importance to the whole reconstruction of transcendence in Hartshorne. God is "categorically supreme." Because God is all-inclusive and the most general, he is the one individual who can be conceived in purely a priori terms. Man and all other entities illustrate only partially the general metaphysical categories in which they participate. God as the most general perfectly exemplifies them. God thus is not "other" or superior to man or world in the sense that in God all characteristics are canceled out. Rather, they are *perfectly* realized, and *this* is what comprises God's infinite uniqueness. "In spite of, indeed because of, his infinite difference from man, God repeats in himself all positive qualities and qualitative contrasts that are present in man, including the quite positive contrast between actualization of potency and potency itself, as this contrast is unified in change."[28] One result of this is God's relation to the polarities, and here Hartshorne differs from the rest of the men in this study. God is not "beyond" the polarities as suprapolar (Heim) or as ground (Tillich). As all-inclusive God is supreme in all the polar aspects of metaphysical analysis; actuality and potentiality, cause and effect, absolute and relative, etc. This, therefore, becomes the central issue between Hartshorne and Tillich in their exchange.[29] In Tillich's language God "grounds" the polarities; thus, though real, they only symbolically express the ground-itself. Hartshorne, on the other hand, feels that God "contains" the polarities and is their chief exemplification. Several assumptions pervade Hartshorne's position here that should be noted. One is the philosophical analysis of the relation of the polarities to one another. Following Morris R. Cohen, he says the polarities do not exist as pure states, but as mutually interdependent. God therefore could not be purely cause without also being effect. Another assumption is Hartshorne's basic premise that God "literally" knows and cares for us, and that our decisions and potentialities are not illusions.[30] This being the case, our potentialities are real for God; hence, he must embrace effect, potentiality, and createdness as well as their opposites.

Such is the meaning of the term "transcendence" as Hartshorne applies it to God. God is transcendent as an incomparable being without rivals, whose supremacy is the perfect instance of all the categories and polarities that pervade the world society.

b. What *God Surpasses*

Man. In Hartshorne's most frequent descriptions of God's superiority, man is the contrasting pole. The basic contrast between God and man is that between a total organism and one of its parts, the usual metaphor being man in relation to a cell in his body. Such has many consequences that set God and man apart. Only God knows with perfect clarity all events and their relations. Only God sees the whole and this has important consequences for his holiness. Because he does see the whole and knows all, he acts rightly. This is why God is righteous without the help of rules and why man needs them. Right action means decision on the basis of knowledge of the full, concrete situation. "There could not be a wrong decision which thus took account of this situation; for a right decision can be defined as one adequately informed as to its context. Omniscience in action is by definition right action."[31] But man knows only a part, hence has many "ethical blind spots," and needs rules to protect himself against his own bias. God's full knowledge plus his right decisions and motivations make up his holiness, and in that sense only God is holy. God's love also surpasses man as the complete surpasses the partial and deficient. Only God literally loves others, for only God literally (completely) experiences his neighbor as himself, and knows what such love would involve. Our love is qualified by the fact that *our* happiness and ideals are not identical with our neighbors'. Not knowing our neighbor fully, we cannot love him as ourselves. Thus there is an element of pretension in our designs to promote the welfare of others. Because of God's righteousness and love, he can transcend man in the sense of serving as inspirer to man's love and humbler of man's pretensions. God also surpasses man in being "eternal" and not just "everlasting."[32] Hartshorne means by eternal, ungenerated, and by everlasting, undying. Man is everlasting in the sense that at death the individual as an individual becomes fixed though not destroyed, for as a person he and his values are stored in God's memory. God, however, is eternal in that there is never a time when he comes into being. One consequence of this is that while both God and man create, man always uses materials (events) prior to his existence while God has no antecedent material that is not also himself.

The World. Hartshorne has made it clear that God is all-embracing and that there is nothing outside of God. If the world thus is not a "more" to God, is God in any sense "more" than the world? The answer is yes in the sense that a man is "more" than his body, and "body" is not a synonym for man. In spite of Hartshorne's early *deus sive natura* language, nature or universe is not for him merely a synonym for God but for God's body. Hartshorne uses the term "universe" pluralistically, and thus he can say that any particular universe is "inside God," but "outside" his essence. This is the central issue, for it is the presence of God's essence that is the basis of God's transcendence of any particular world. However, God in his essence does not transcend "world as such," for it is God's essence to have a world. There was no time when the world was not and God was. In other terms, there never was a bodiless God. That would mean to Hartshorne an abstract and mutilated God. Yet he feels that he retains the basic intention of the traditional doctrine of *creatio ex nihilo*. His version is that God does not create by using material antecedent to his own existence. "Divine acts refer only to antecedent events which like themselves also embodied divine acts. Anything which God in a given phase requires has also required him in a previous phase of his life."[38] Thus God transcends the world first as its primordial creator, not in the sense that he initiated an "absolute beginning" or first state, but in the sense that he was a necessary condition for every particular universe, and no universe antedated this condition in time. Secondly, he transcends the world as an enduring identity who flexibly controls it, and who persists throughout all its change.

God. God is transcendent in that he is an unrivaled Superior over all others. However, as a God whose one aspect changes and is in process, such superiority is not *absolute* in the sense of completion or finality. As a dynamic whole, God also surpasses *himself* in the process. What does this mean? Surpassing can be in some, none, or all respects. God's self-surpassing is not in all respects, else there would be no absolute aspect at all, nor in no respects, else he would be *Actus Purus*. God surpasses himself only in some respects. In the process his experience is richer and more complex, his knowledge fuller, and his love more content-filled since he continually has more objects to love. God thus is superior in that at no time is he rivaled by any other entity, yet at any future time he can be his own self-surpassing rival.

c. How *God Transcends: Dipolar Transcendence*. Hartshorne has defined transcendence not only as superiority but as categorical superiority, in which God is the complete exemplification of the categories. But how does God transcend (surpass) in this exemplifying role? What are the main ways he surpasses? The answer is twofold, and it comprises Hartshorne's most original contribution. God is a supereminent case of both absolute and relative poles. " The supreme in its total concrete reality will be the supereminent case of relativity, the surrelative, just as, in its abstract character it will be the supereminent case of nonrelativity — not only absolute but *the* absolute." [34]

Ens Necessarium. Most traditional versions of transcendence place the stress on God as Unconditional, Unoriginated, the Fountain of Being, and the *Ens Realissimum*. Hartshorne too has retained transcendence in this sense in his retention of an absolute aspect in God. Several connotations comprise the content of this aspect. In one sense it refers to God the primordial creator, the condition of all creativity and process. In another sense it refers to the independence of God from the various changes in his total being: that which gives God a unified identity as God. Basically, it means (and herein is God absolute in the unrivaled sense) that God is the one *necessary* being. Only God self-exists and is the source of his self-existence. God cannot fail to exist as himself even though he can change. Only God is the unconditioned, necessary existence whose essence makes it impossible for him not to exist. This doctrine of God's noncontingency (in one aspect) contrasts God to ordinary individuals whose existence depends on the way events work out; hence, their existence is uncertain. This aspect of God's transcendence makes the world wholly extrinsic to *something in* God. This is why God as all-inclusive does not transcend the world merely as a whole transcends its parts, because there is a necessary element beyond any particular world-whole or any of its parts.

The Surrelative. Those doctrines of God which have admitted anthropomorphisms into the divine character have often done so with embarrassment. The "real" God is the "God beyond God" who is absolute and not relative. At this point Hartshorne's view of transcendence veers sharply from any such treatment. If God-alone is superior to God-with-the-world, then God degrades himself by creating. Hartshorne feels if a value judgment must be made at all, it is God-alone that is the inferior aspect. But in what sense is the reflexive aspect of God transcendent or superior? The answer is that God's relativity is not an ordinary kind of relativity. Following the "way of eminence," Hartshorne says that God is supremely or maximally relative, from which notion comes one of the labels of his position, *sur*relativism. Why is God as maximally relative superior or transcendent? The answer is clearly stated thus: "To be relative in the eminent sense will (accordingly) be to enjoy relations to all that is, in all its aspects. Supreme dependence will thus reflect all influences with infinite sensitivity registering relationship to the last and least item of events." [35] A partially relative being will be related to only a portion of the totality of being, thus will love partially, and be insensitive to vast, unknown portions. As social beings the partially relative will be only "locally and defectively social," but as surrelative God will be the universally social being: knowing all, loving all, and enduring all. Another way God's relativity is absolute (contrary to man's relativity) is that he will be completely relative regardless of circumstances, but the extent of human relativity varies accordingly. The final picture, then, is that of an all-inclusive deity in whom occur all changes and relationships, who "senses" them and can thus "adequately" work for the harmony of the whole.

VI

GOD

AS SUPRAHUMAN EVENT:

Henry Nelson Wieman

1. THE IMMEDIATE BACKGROUND

a. *Philosophy of Religion in the 1920's.* In spite of their many diversities, the men in this study are united on one matter. All are reacting to some degree against various kinds of "immanentism" which dominated religious thought in the preceding generations. Henry Nelson Wieman is no exception. The immediate background of his philosophy of religion is the dilemmas that American liberal theology faced in the 1920's. Because liberalism's methodological mood was essentially that of *rapprochement,* it was pushed more and more to square the content of Christian faith with the methods and results of science. Some did this by retaining the Kantian and Ritschlian heritage of former decades of American theology, thus relating science and faith by a bifurcation: scientific method and " religious experience." However, the scientific challenge had more radical results for others, and the consequence was the humanist movement in the 1920's and 1930's. Between liberals and humanists was a group of men Meland called " humanistic theists " who were willing to use the word " God " within a basically humanist framework. Thus in some circles religious thought was characterized as an exodus from theism toward antitheistic humanism, with the stopping place of liberalism a very unstable point.

Since the turn of the century a " new theism " had been emerging in America with evolutionary theory the basic framework. In the 1920's this philosophy of religion was the order of the day at Chicago, and the tone was that of an " immanent theism "; antisupernaturalistic, anti-orthodox, and antitranscendental.[1] Both Gerald Birney Smith and Shailer Mathews represented the " Chicago School "[2] at this time, and they marked early roots of an " empirical theism." The mood was also anthropocentric. If God was not actually identified with human ideals and values, he was seen as that in the cosmos which lent support to them. Smith was critical of humanism for not providing such cosmic support, and God for him was " a quality of the cosmic process akin to the quality of our own spiritual life."[3] For Mathews, God was the " personality evolving activities " in the universe, a " Person immanent in process itself."[4] But it was the more humanistic Edward Scribner Ames who represented the identification of God with human ideals. In his central work, *Religion* (1929), God was seen as the symbol of " reality idealized," in the same class with Alma Mater or Uncle Sam.

b. *Henry Nelson Wieman.*[5] The kind of theism just described comprised the backdrop against which Wieman arose in revolt. To understand his revolt and his own reconstructed theism, a brief survey of Wieman's " intellectual autobiography " is needed, with special stress on his intense religiousness and on the philosophical influences that lay behind his radical modernism. Wieman's religious training came from a home pervaded by a genuine but moderate piety especially mediated by his mother. A " religiousness " was thus implanted in Wieman that never left him. It was this religiousness which lay behind his sudden experience at Park College through which Wieman determined to devote his life to religious inquiry. While at Park he also came under the first of many important philosophical influences. In this case, it was the passion for philosophy itself that was generated, especially for the idealism of Royce.[6] After three rather rebellious years at San Francisco Seminary, Wieman spent a year studying in Germany under Eucken, Windelband, and Troeltsch, although he was impressed with none of them. A two-and-a-half-year ministry in Davis, California, followed during which he read Bergson for the first time. And in 1915 he returned to graduate study, entering Harvard, where he worked under Hocking and Ralph Barton Perry. Due to Perry, the problem of value became central for Wieman at this time, and although Hocking had a great impact upon him, he says that his Bergson studies prevented him from embracing an idealist metaphysics. Also at Harvard he discovered and read Dewey, and during the next ten years in which he taught at Occidental College, he read Whitehead; both of whom have been lasting though qualified influences. From Occidental Wieman went to the University of Chicago, where he spent the bulk of his teaching career. More recently he has been teaching at Southern Illinois University.

In summary, Wieman's thought must be seen in the light of both the intense religiousness, if not even mysticism, that has marked his life and teaching and his persistent restlessness with orthodox doctrine. In this last characteristic Wieman is like many liberals of his time, except, unlike them, he fully identified himself with the philosophical currents that were challenging American idealism: the pragmatism that Dewey and Mead were dispensing from Peirce and James, the process metaphysics of Bergson and Whitehead, and the axiological theories of Perry and more recently Pepper. All of this well fitted Wieman to take his place in the Chicago School as an inheritor, a rebel, and an elaborator. As an inheritor he took over the modernism of the group (especially in the stress on empirical method), the polemic against orthodoxy, and the social understanding of religion. Yet as a rebel and elaborator he became the critic of the school's halfway empiricism and the anthropocentric orientation of its theism.

2. The Problem: Cultural and Philosophical

Like others in this study, Wieman's reconstruction is addressed to concrete individual and cultural problems. However, the background of such concern is not so much an immediate cultural crisis such as Tillich and Heim experienced as the general claim of American pragmatism that ideas be culturally relevant and workable.

What is the "cultural crisis" as Wieman sees it? Essentially it is the development of great blocs of power without the co-ordinate development of a "creative interchange" that would make sure that power is employed for man's total good. Furthermore, since Hiroshima the wrong use of power may well mean the death of civilization. What is needed then is some "directive in history" that will tap the source of human good as a concrete channel of power.[7]

But where shall we look for this answer? Science, at least in its technological aspects, is an ambiguous source of good, which means it helps increase power but to no particular end. Will religion traditionally conceived then be of help? Wieman feels not, for the simple reason that such religion is in a crisis of its own, and the outcome of this crisis is that traditional religious myths and doctrines seem unable to provide this needed direction. The crisis of religion is the story of the impasse between skepticism, which attacks traditional doctrines, and belief, which merely defends them.

One alternative that arises at this point is that of religious liberalism. For it was liberalism that was discontent with traditional orthodoxy and tried to reconstruct it and adapt it to the modern world. However, Wieman feels that this adaptation was only " piecemeal." Thus some particular doctrine (like evolution) was squared with some religious doctrine. But in all this there was no real reconciliation with science as a method of inquiry, thus the dualism of scientific (objective) knowing and religious (subjective) experience remained. Furthermore, when there was adaptation, it was merely a cultural synthesis in which the real distinctiveness of religion was lost. For such reasons Wieman felt that liberalism, linked as it was with idealistic philosophy, offered no solution to the religious crisis.

Wieman recognized that another alternative, however, was presenting itself, an alternative critical of both orthodoxy and liberalism, namely, " neo-supernaturalism," which was Wieman's term for " crisis theology," " neo-orthodoxy," and such movements that included Barth, Brunner, and in America the Niebuhrs.[8] Wieman appreciated certain features of this alternative, especially its critique of liberalism and its attempt to preserve the distinctiveness and integrity of religion. Yet this alternative is not a live option, for neo-supernaturalism has rejected the one means of distinguishing truth and falsehood, and also good and evil, namely, the scientific method of observation, inference, and experimentation. Because these new movements reject the one avenue of knowledge and certainty, they must be seen as a passing fad.

In place of these alternatives Wieman advances the program that he labels " naturalistic theism." This program is basically a method of " religious inquiry " (philosophy of religion) that will investigate two main problems. *What* is the source of human good by which we can direct our lives? Wieman attempts to answer this in his doctrine of value coupled with his doctrine of God. *How* can we be certain of it and commit ourselves to it? Wieman answers this in his " broad " view of scientific method by which even religious inquiry must abide. We might well ask what such a program has to do with transcendence. On the surface and in comparison with Niebuhr or Tillich, the emphasis of Wieman's thought seems to be immanental. However, Wieman himself sees his " naturalistic theism " as a protest against immanentism, and on two counts. First, against the religious humanists with their stress on the " God-idea," Wieman wants to " make the actuality of God himself, and not our ideas about God, the object of our love and devotion." [9] He wants an actual, not merely a theoretical, deity. Second, he wants to avoid making subjective, human preconceptions about God normative. The God we need, in other words, is not one that can be merely established, shaped, or controlled by man's ideas or ideals. Wieman may or may not stick to this, but at least such is his intention. Thus in both epistemological and ontological senses, Wieman wants a God who is really transcendent.

3. The Philosophy of Henry Nelson Wieman

Wieman's insistence on the scientific method as the one way of knowing should make it clear that his is a *naturalistic* theism. Both his method and metaphysics are intended at least to express a certain type of naturalism. It is also clear that this will have important ramifications for the way Wieman conceives of God. Therefore we must first attempt to set forth the salient features of his total philosophy. Wieman's philosophy is made up of three interwoven strands, each in some way dependent on the others. They are the theory of value, the understanding of truth and knowledge, and the contextualist and operationalist view of reality. Because Wieman's method of religious inquiry is one that emerges from within the framework and norms of a developed philosophy, all three themes are determinative for his understanding of God. His value theory aids him in isolating the function that God as " most worthful " plays, or, in other words, what the term " God " minimally means. His theory of knowledge governs the total method by which " God " is approached, experimented with, and ultimately known. And his theory of reality governs his treatment of the region or kind of reality " God " must embrace if he exists at all. What we have in Wieman, then, is a mature philosopher engaging in religious inquiry on the basis of his philosophy. This does not mean that Wieman is essentially a philosopher and peripherally a religionist. At the level of his own experience, the two have always been mutually influential on each other. But at the level of conceptual inquiry, Wieman's philosophy is in a normative relation to his religious thought.

a. *Theory of Knowledge*.[10] One of the most distinctive and controlling features of Wieman's thought is his attempt to bring liberalism's empirical or experiential emphasis into accordance with scientific method. This program necessarily involves the narrowing of " empirical " and the broadening of " scientific." Therefore Wieman's theory of knowledge is not a scientism in any reductionist sense. He insists on the importance of extrascientific matters such as intuition, art, faith, etc. His only plea is that none of these things be identified with knowledge. There is no *sancta sanctorum* which must be protected from investigation and verification. Furthermore "knowledge" involves the same basic elements wherever it is found, namely, the elements of scientific method. But what is knowledge?

Wieman's simplest answer is that knowledge is "truth captured by man and domiciled in his abode."[11] It is appropriated truth. What, then, is truth? In Wieman's early writings truth was described in terms of the results of the truth-seeking process; thus it was "the correct designation and description of features of the world," and to the degree that concepts are needed to communicate truth, concepts constitute truth.[12] As late as 1943, Wieman stated that truth includes a perception plus the propositions that come out of it.[13] In *The Source of Human Good* (1946), truth is relegated to the realm of possibility in regard to knowledge, for it is "any specifiable structure pertaining to events and their possibilities."[14] The important elements in the definition are the facts that truth must be specifiable and testable, that what truth is about is events and their possibilities, and that it is not the full complex reality of a process but an abstract version of reality. Thus there is "full disjunction between the true concept of a concrete reality and the concrete reality itself."

What, then, is knowledge? Knowledge is what happens when the specifiable truth inherent in structure becomes specified and verified. "Knowing is correspondence between a structure specified by a system of signs and some order of events determined by reactions of the organism and distinguished by selective attention."[15] But where does the correspondence occur: *in abstracto*, or in actual human awareness? Wieman apparently means the latter; therefore we can say more simply, knowledge occurs when operative and designative concepts are verified by an actual experiment of some kind.

This brings us to Wieman's conception of the verification of knowledge. The first stage has to do with the data of knowledge, which is experience of some kind, and the type of experience is what governs the breadth and accuracy of the subsequent knowledge. All knowledge is "scientific" for Wieman in the broad sense that a method of observation, inference, and experimentation is involved. But not all knowledge is reducible to laboratory methods of scientific testing. This is the narrowest and most accurate kind of knowledge and thus involves narrower bits of experience, for in laboratory knowledge we operate with controlled methods and with closely designated and detailed areas of experience. Yet there can also be a "scientific" knowledge that works on everyday bulk problems such as fixing a car. Scientific method in this sense can be applied to all major interests of life: morals, religion, art, education, etc. Actually, Wieman is talking about ordinary common-sense intelligence of the kind needed to find an address or cook a meal, for such things involve observing, inferring, and trial-and-error experimentation. This twofold approach to the verification of knowledge is thus a basic one for Wieman's thought, and the underlying unity of the two ways is the pattern of observation-experimentation. In so far as there is differentiation of "kinds" of knowledge, it involves a spectrum of various degrees of selected detail and the subsequent accuracy involved.

b. *Theory of Value.*[16] Wieman began work on value theory in his doctoral dissertation under Perry and Hocking. His later reading of Whitehead apparently was permanently influential, for like Whitehead he makes the experience of value metaphysically prior as well as normative over all other matters. Metaphysical theories, aesthetic, and even cognitive endeavors must all serve ends more basic than themselves; hence they are rooted in value, not vice versa. Wieman's own theory of value can be summarized around three fundamental questions: What are the ingredients or raw materials of value? Where does value itself reside? What is the highest value?

Wieman's answer to the first question shows his starting point in human experience, and misleadingly has a hedonistic ring. The "raw materials" of value are "enjoyments," or activities that yield enjoyment (appreciable activities). The role of enjoyment is that of a test by which we know whether a value is operating or not, but the enjoyment itself is not the value, nor do all enjoyments necessarily promote value. What, then, is value? This drives us to consider the second question.

What is the locus or bearer of value? Where does value reside? Wieman is certain that values are not to be identified with any particular thing, enjoyment, state of consciousness, or even ideal. The word for such things is "goods," which means any fulfillment of interest. To find value we must search for the conditions that are necessary for such an interest or enjoyment to be fulfilled. Any particular good comes about only because many antecedent conditions operated together to make it possible. Thus, values are located in an actual process along with its possibilities, or as Wieman expressed it in one place, value resides "in the total complex context." Value thus is the make-up of a particular context that makes appreciable activity possible.

But can value be graded? Are not some enjoyments better than others, and thus is there not a value that can be called "best"? Yes, says Wieman, for obviously two "goods" are better than one. And the situation where two goods exist side by side without destroying each other is "better" than the situation where one exists as a parasite on the other. "Better" is a situation where two goods actually support and even enhance each other. "Best," then, refers to the situation in which processes function in such a way that maximum mutual enjoyment is produced for all. "Highest value," then, could be identified with the process or context that promoted such a situation. And this is Wieman's notion of "mutual interaction" promoting "maximum mutuality," or his philosophy of integration.

Although Wieman had come to this basic position by the time of *The Wrestle of Religion with Truth,* the concept has become more and more refined through the years. In the first place it has become more of a dynamic concept; thus Wieman sees the maximum good as a continual and creative enhancing of goods in relation to one another ("creative interaction"). Secondly, it has become more and more limited to *human* good with various types of communication defining the meaning of mutual enhancement. The most developed concept here is that of qualitative meaning. Wieman first related value and meaning in 1936 when he described "mutual meaning" as one of the five principles of that "connection between activities which is value."[17] At that time "meaning" was that which made possible the experiencing of something faraway through the mediation of something here and now. But what is *qualitative* meaning? Wieman has always highly valued a delicate sensitivity that perceives rich and more subtle shades and dimensions in the events and processes of the environment. Sense experience is, of course, quite limited in this respect, but if it takes place within a system of meaning, certain sights and sounds can call up a host of otherwise forgotten associations, connotations, memories, and anticipations that can *immensely* enrich a given experience. Thus what would be an ordinary sense experience can become the means of embracing a larger world of rich and intensive qualities and events. Thus "qualitative meaning is that connection between events whereby present happenings enable me to feel not only the quality intrinsic to the events now occurring but also the qualities of many other events that are related to them." [18]

"Good," then, in the fullest sense is a vast process of activities that promotes the mutual enhancement and creative enjoyment of its members. "Enjoyment" at the top of this society (human beings) means the maximum possible reception of qualitative meaning. Value is that context in which events converge to produce such.

c. *Theory of Reality.*[19] The terminology of the above value theory should enable us to anticipate the kind of metaphysics that is its framework. Wieman himself calls it a new naturalism,[20] and with some qualifications, contextualism.[21] The place of metaphysical endeavor in Wieman's philosophy has grown more and more minimal through the years. In the beginning he enthusiastically expounded Whitehead and the more cosmological dimensions of metaphysics, but more recently he has announced a shift of focus from metaphysics to anthropology, from inquiry about the universe to inquiry about man.[22] Yet he has never given up metaphysics in the sense of an inquiry into "structures common to all perceptual events whatsoever."

Like other naturalists Wieman rejects any recourse to "transcendental grounds, orders, causes, or purposes." His is a metaphysics of the foreground, but of what is the "foreground" constituted? As a *new* naturalist he denies that it is the bulk world of matter, matter being "that statistical average of their (electrons and protons) impact which we experience in the form of a clod and stone, dust and wind, earthquake and fire." [23] The make-up of the foreground is events, qualities, and their relations, all interwoven together into contexts, and all in process. In Wieman's earlier Whiteheadian orientation, the key categories for describing existence were process and structure. Whatever existed was a process of some kind. Later, however, although process is retained, it is filled out with events, qualities, and their conjunctions.

What is an event? The simplest definition is a "unity of passage" that perception is able to isolate and distinguish. Compared to Whitehead's doctrine of events, Wieman's concept is in a more nontechnical and common-sense framework. In one of his examples a "dinner" is described as an event; thus, event means a happening, a doing, an experiencing, and here his operationalism becomes evident. "We know a reality by the way it works. The reality is its working." [24] But what is included in a "happening"? According to Wieman an event is comprised of two elements: qualities and strands. One or the other dominates the reception of an event depending upon the selective function of perception. If the event, dinner, is seen in terms of units of calories, in other words with the aspect of an analyzed order and sequence lifted out, then we have isolated a *strand* of the event. But if the event is perceived as a totality, a conjunction of all the strands, we have its quality,[25] which is why Wieman says that, experientially speaking, event and quality are synonymous.[26] "Ultimate reality" for Wieman is this total complex of event or quality for such is "the ultimate substance of the world out of which all else is made." There is no background in relation to this. Whatever exists, exists either as an event or a complex of events. This whole treatment of event and its breaking up into qualities and strands follows Pepper's distinction of quality and texture in his exposition of contextualism. "Now what is quality and what texture in this event? Its quality is roughly its total meaning, its texture roughly the words and grammatical relations making it up. Generalizing, the quality of a given event is its intuited wholeness or total character; the texture is the details and relations which make up that character or quality." [27]

Such events are in process; therefore, the same event never occurs twice. But if an event is a never-repeating "unit of passage," is there any continuity or identity at all in the process? At this point Wieman separates himself from contextualism and attempts to construct a doctrine of substance. In one sense process is as far back as we can go for explanations. There is no "power" or "cause" back of process, which itself is not a process. Yet the process has an unchanging aspect. In his exchange with Calhoun in 1936, Wieman was willing to answer to a degree Calhoun's question about what-it-is that is in process. There are still several senses in which we can retain the notion of substance. Substance might mean the one fundamental activity underlying all other activities. It might refer to that total though hidden system of activities which overarches all particular activities. And it might refer to the eternal and abstract aspect of process which is form, structure, order, etc. In *The Source of Human Good,* Wieman identified substance with the *structure* of process that persisted through changes. And while structures come and go, there is one uncreated and unchanging structure: " that minimum structure which energy must have to be creative." This " primordial order of creative energy " is that minimal structure which retains identity and unity through process.

Such is Wieman's philosophy, embracing the three themes of knowledge, value, and reality. " Nature " as a whole thus is a plurality of processes and events. As a " world " it is one in the sense that there is nothing beyond this plurality of events, yet it is not a total harmony as Hartshorne would have it, but a plurality of processes, some working for good, some for evil, but none serving as an over-all controlling unity that would guarantee the outcome.

4. Wieman's Philosophy of Religion

We recall that the basic problem Wieman addresses in his program of naturalistic theism is that of providing empirically certain means of finding the Source of human good, which will thus transform both the individual and the culture. We have also seen that Wieman puts the problem this way partly because he speaks from within a particular philosophical tradition and partly because of his own experiments in " private religious living." The general program, therefore, is one of a new inquiry (philosophy of religion) that will isolate concepts by which actual experimentation can take place, and it is especially the God-concept Wieman has in mind.

a. *The Establishment of the* General *Region of Deity: Axiological.* Wieman realizes that for many the very existence of deity is problematic, but like many contemporary theologians, he by-passes the usual attempts to argue for the existence of God. For this involves the impossible endeavor of jumping from argument (concepts) to existence. He prefers to say God's existence is demonstrated in the same way any other existence is established, namely, by actual interaction. What Wieman wants to do in his writing is to set up an

GOD AS SUPRAHUMAN EVENT 177

operative conception of God by which others can make the same experimental verification he has made.[28] The first step in the quest for such a concept is the establishment of the *general* region of deity where we can look for data.

Wieman begins by asking what is the minimal meaning of the word " God " throughout all times and places, and hence what is the essence of at least high religion? His procedure, at least in one article, is to survey what he feels are the best lives in the history of (Christian) religion in the West, searching for the kind of commitment, though not beliefs about that commitment, such lives had in common.[29] Over against the humanists, Wieman concludes that religion is at its best, not when it furthers man's ideals, but when it provides revolutionary impetus against them. Religion then is commitment to whatever is the source of this perpetual transformation. Since " God " has always been the term referring to the agent of highest good for man, " the supremely worthful," we are justified in using the term about whatever we find today to be the source of supreme worth. Therefore, the general region of deity is the axiological. In prescientific ages the mode of conceiving God was by a God-myth, but if we can now find what it is that makes for highest value, we will have a minimal but accurate God-concept, stripped of all burdening traditional apparatus. Thus for Wieman, " God is that in the universe which will yield maximum security and increase of human good when lives are properly adjusted to him." [30]

We must point out, however, an element of ambiguity in Wieman's attempt to establish God in this way. For the most part he seems to be saying that God's existence is established not by the conceptualizing of philosophy of religion but by the experimentations of actual persons. Therefore, his own definitions are instrumental and tentative until such verification takes place. However, there are passages in Wieman that seem to indicate that he has by his analysis established the unspecific *fact that* God exists at least in a minimal sense. The argument goes thus: We inevitably seek some things and not others; hence, we make a better-worse distinction in relation to ourselves and our culture. This means that somewhere along the scale there is a maximum " better " or " best possible." Man alone cannot approximate this best possible without help, for even an ordinary good, such as breathing, takes place only by means of many complex processes co-operating together. Those conditions and processes, whatever they are, which enable man to actualize his own " best possible," are God. Whatever " greatest good " means, man depends on some " pattern of behavior " in the universe for its realization, and that pattern is God.

b. *The Establishment of the* Specific *Region of Deity: Axiological and Ontological.* It should be clear by now that Wieman's approach to God is via God's functioning, for " the reality is its working." And God's functioning as that which brings about the greatest good for man is the general region of inquiry. But if God as " highest value " is the general region, we yet know little about God. At this stage D. C. Macintosh's caricature of Wieman's God as the " Wonderful-What-Is-It " holds true. For the God-concept to be operative it must be more specified and this involves " ascertaining what are the essential criteria of value," then " seizing on the knowable reality which displays these criteria." Such is Wieman's avowed method and it shows how his philosophy works itself out in his philosophy of religion. The theory of knowledge determines the basic procedure of defining a general region in which to inquire for data (" bits of experience "), namely, the region of value and value experience.

Wieman's theory of value determines more specifically how God functions as "highest value," and his theory of reality describes *what* God is.

When we approach the problem of what kind of functioning is this highest value, we come face to face with Wieman's many and controversial definitions of God, which Richard Kroner once termed "blasphemous." There has been a constant development throughout these definitions, and generally speaking, it follows Wieman's pilgrimage from an organismic naturalism dominated by Whitehead to a contextualist naturalism dominated by Dewey, Mead, and Pepper. This has meant, for the most part, a gradual narrowing in two senses. First, Wieman's interest in metaphysics itself, especially at cosmological levels, has become narrowed to the amount and kind of metaphysics necessary for a value theory. Therefore, while metaphysics dominates the definitions of God in the early writings, value theory dominates the definitions of God in the later period. Second, Wieman has progressively narrowed his God-concept both at the level of the reality that is God (such as creative event) and the product of his functioning (such as qualitative meaning).

Tracing the different stages of this narrowing is an almost impossible task, for while there are many terminological changes, they do not all denote points of departure from former positions.[31] Rather than attempt a history of the terminology of Wieman's theism, we shall merely isolate four changes toward a more specified God-concept. However, because the fourth concerns Wieman's doctrine of transcendence, it will be dealt with in the following section.

The first trend in the development of Wieman's theism is explicitly due to his metaphysical development from Whitehead to contextualism. In the early period Wieman designated reality in terms of existing processes and their possibilities. In *The Wrestle of Religion with Truth,* Wieman enthusiastically expounded and employed Whitehead's doctrine of God. In his next book Wieman defined God as an integrating process,[32] which was his elaboration of Whitehead's notion of concretion. The following year Wieman published his *Issues of Life,* in which God was spoken of not as a process but as an "order." And in subsequent articles Wieman spoke of God as an "ordered process," and an entity embracing both process and possibility (structure).[33] Since that time Wieman has become more and more a contextualist, first seeing reality as a type of interaction and then as made up of events, their qualities, and conjunctions. Therefore, his later definitions of God have been in terms of a type of event rather than process and structure.

The second trend is also a metaphysical one. In this development Wieman's God-concept culminates not only in an event but a certain type of event, a certain way the event works. In the early writings we have noted that Wieman's categories are process and order. Within this metaphysics God as process and order functions by *organizing* reality. God is "that persistent order of all being by virtue of which their reorganization constantly occurs."[34] The way God organizes is by integration thus "increasing interdependence and co-operation in the world." Later he described this divine function after the manner of "growth of living connections." What seems to be happening is a narrowing from the concept of organizing reality to a certain kind of organizing, namely, integrative interaction, and the final stage is that of *creativity.* Wieman first identified God with creativity in his reply to Bernhardt in "The Power and Goodness of God" (1943). In *The Source of Human Good* this concept is fully elaborated in the notion of creative event, and it is creative because the results of integration turn out to be a whole new structure of interrelatedness within and without the individual. This is elaborated in *Man's Ultimate Commitment*. This trend in Wieman's theism has been from ordinary notions of process, structure, growth, and interaction to the notion of creativity, which qualifies and further describes all of them.

The third trend is more in the axiological setting, for it concerns the *products* of God's working. Wieman's God is never just event, process, or interaction, but always an " event which. . . ." That is, the full definition of God for Wieman includes both the bearer of power (process, event, etc.) and the way it functions. This too has undergone narrowing and further specification as Wieman's doctrine of the good has become more specified. In the early years Wieman's value theory was quite vague. The " best possible " situation for man was a situation where interests were fulfilled for individuals and also integrated into one another, which means they mutually supported and enhanced one another. " Maximum mutual enhancement " was Wieman's program, but what involves " enhancement "? Calhoun sensed this vagueness when he observed that such terms as " growth of connections " are not normative terms and not necessarily " good." Wieman apparently was aware of this problem, for he narrowed his concept to " growth of meaning." But meaning too is a broad and evasive concept. Wieman thus continued his narrowing by drawing on C. W. Morris' work on signs, symbols, and myth.[35] And the full elaboration comes in Wieman's concept of the growth of " qualitative meaning." God here is the most worthful, for as creative event he produces the situation of highest value, an enjoyment of qualitative meaning in which men are transformed. This third " trend," then, is from the broader characterization of human good as mutual enhancement to human good as a transforming and communicative interchange in which felt qualities are progressively increased.

In summary, Wieman's more specific designation of the region of God fully utilizes his objective theory of value and his contextualist metaphysics. For " God " refers to an existing event that creatively produces man's good. The impression must not be left, however, that Wieman's " stages " of development are disjunctive. They not only overlap, with a continual returning to the terminology of former " stages," but there is a definite unity running throughout. Wieman thus has always attempted to characterize the divine by natural categories that denote existence as we experience it anywhere.

5. God's Transcendence: Metaphysical and Functional

Wieman has said that the problem of immanence and transcendence is basic to all other inquiry concerning God. Such a statement may surprise many of his critics, for in no other area has Wieman been so much a target as that of the transcendence of God.[36] In the light of such criticisms, some justification may be needed for including Wieman in a study of contemporary reconstructions of the doctrine of transcendence. Of course, if transcendental stresses are by definition limited to those critics of liberal theology who are influenced by the Continental theological revolution, the case is settled. Not being of that fold, Wieman does represent a new liberalism and as such represents an immanentism in two important senses. Methodologically, his approach is nontraditional and nonrevelational, but rather " rational." Thus he assumes God is the kind of reality (like all reality) that can be discovered by broad scientific methods. Second, following from the first, God's make-up is the make-up of all existence, hence he is one process (or event) among others even though he may have a distinctive pattern. Nevertheless, we must remember that Wieman like Niebuhr arose in sharp criticism of liberalism especially at the point of the doctrine of God. His program has not only been theocentric. Central to it has been the endeavor to find a method of inquiry that would open the way for the operations of an objective God who is reducible neither to man's ideas about him nor to man's ideals. Because of this, Wieman has also been a "prophet of God's transcendence" in several important respects.

a. *Wieman and Transcendence.* The multiplicity of passages in Wieman's writings attacking transcendence should be explanation enough why he is understood as the prophet of immanence. These attacks, to be sure, are all marked by resistance to certain definite types of transcendence. One type that Wieman opposes is any claim that God is totally unknowable at the level of the only way of knowing: observation, reason, and experiment. Hence his constant polemic against Barth, Tillich, Reinhold Niebuhr, and others. Wieman's point is that if the divine does transcend reason, then we are lost, for man is left without any way to find the source of human good. A second type of transcendence that he rejects is the ontological transcendence of a God who is beyond time and events. This is one side of the Hebraic-Christian tradition that Wieman says he rejects. That God works in history but resides beyond history is a contradiction to Wieman. If he resides beyond history, this means he is something else than an event or process and thus cannot *do* anything. It is also a contradiction because the only thing that could "exist" beyond events and processes would be more events and processes. A third type of transcendence

Wieman rejects is God as sovereign over evil. Wieman means by this the doctrine of a final and ultimate victory of good, which he says reduces evil to illusion. Wieman's conclusion, then, about these versions of transcendence is that they serve as useful myths. By myth Wieman means "that concrete body of stories and legends preserved in the popular memory which is the unconscious creation and inheritance of the common life,"[37] an example of such being the folklore gathering around a Civil War hero. As myths they do have a function, serving as ways of demanding absolute commitment to God, showing up the darkness of man's evil against God's righteousness, etc. Yet, this way of understanding transcendence is a myth and must be reconstructed so that the intentions of the myth at least are retained. It is this reconstruction of Wieman that we must now consider.

b. *God as Source of Cosmic Integration: Metaphysical Transcendence.* Wieman's treatment of transcendence like his total theism has not been a completely static affair. It has especially involved one major change of emphasis, a change that reflects his total movement from Whiteheadian and metaphysical interests to contextualist and axiological ones. The work that reflected Whiteheadian influence more than any other was *The Wrestle of Religion with Truth* (1927). Here Wieman enthusiastically expounds Whitehead's theism and defends it as both scientifically and religiously adequate. As this was antecedent to the full development of Whitehead's own theism (*Process and Reality*), "God" was a term limited to the metaphysical function of explaining concretion. The important thing to note here is Wieman's interest in this kind of problem and his willingness to elaborate a God-concept within such a framework. For this is what is behind Wieman's early willingness to describe God as a power that played an important role in the order and movement of the universe. The universe is both running down (entropy) and winding up, and God is that "cosmic cause" countering entropy and making for maximum richness and novelty. "God is the process which works to make the whole universe organic." [38] As a power cosmic in scale, God embraces both an actual existing process and possibility. "This order which is God is partly an order of existence and partly an order of possibility." [39] Thus he both exists (as process) and transcends existence (as possibility). "God is not merely an abstract order that does nothing. Neither is he the process of nature that does everything regardless of value. But he is the structure of supreme value viewed as possibility of existence, and also that kind of process in nature which most nearly approximates this order of supreme value and promotes further approximation to it. Thus God is both the most beneficent actuality and the supreme ideal." [40] Thus, in Wieman's early period, God is not transcendent just in relation to man but is "metaphysically" transcendent. This does not mean he is independent of nature or the universe, which for Wieman are all-inclusive terms and denote realities vaster than God. Yet Wieman would never regard God *sive natura,* for God is neither nature nor the order of nature, nor any "level" in nature such as matter or mind, nor any particular process such as the biological process. Rather, he is a "higher synthesis" working through all levels as a creative order. The emphasis on God as a cosmic synthesizing order in which all things participate in all other things is clearly Whiteheadian, but after *The Wrestle of Religion with Truth,* Wieman grew more and more critical of Whitehead and thus of "metaphysical transcendence," finally announcing the end of this stage of his thought by saying that Creative Good is " not metaphysically transcendental but it is functionally transcendental." [41]

c. *God as Source of Human Good: " Functional Transcendence "*

God Transcendent in Relation to Man's Working: *Functional Transcendence Proper.* Wieman has always said that God works (or the " working "termed God) in an entirely different way from man. The reason for this is that only God is the creator. By creator Wieman of course does not mean a *primum movens* or cause of everything that happens, or even the ultimate source of existence. Wieman's feeling about such doctrines is that they are contradictory and speculative. But he retains creation in two basic senses. The first is that of " growth," especially the growth of organic connections. And man cannot work in this way. Man can construct a mechanism such as a house, which is merely the putting together of a " system of external connections," but he cannot grow a tree or even his own body except by assistance from the grower. God also works at wider levels than man can work, thus he generates both the appreciable world and man's appreciating mind. " Appreciating mind " raises the matter of the top level of the working of the creative event that is the " innovating use of symbolized meanings." Such is the second sense in which creation is retained, and there are many reasons why man cannot work in this way either. The main one is that he can work only within the limits set by the present order, that is, the limits that are involved in the structure of the human mind, its tools, and total resources. But the creative event transcends such limits because " it is the order of the existing world as created to date, plus the order of creative energy as it operates in the world, plus the range of relevant possibilities as determined by this structure or creative energy and the world with which it must work."[42] In summary, man's working depends upon antecedent and complex conditions and processes that must structure the world in a certain way before he can work at all. In so far as man finds meaning in the world, especially qualitative meaning, it is the result of an incommensurable event producing such and not his own work. For this reason God is "qualitatively different from man," and transcends man's working.

A corollary to this notion that God as creator works in a way that transcends man's working is Wieman's doctrine of God as suprapersonal. Man's working is by abstraction, by selection within present limits, and by external construction, and this is all the work of mind and personality. It is clear, then, that God is "more than mind." The ambiguity of the term "suprapersonal," however, is evident here, and a comparison with Tillich will help bring it out. Tillich too feels God is suprapersonal in the sense that he is "the ground of everything personal." For Wieman, God is suprapersonal, not because "being includes personal being," but in the sense that personality is annulled. But this annulling of divine personality is not a loss but a gain, says Wieman, for functionally it means God can do what personality can never do. Hence God is not subpersonal. Such, then, is the first way God is transcendent, namely, as a suprahuman and suprapersonal creator whose way of working is qualitatively different from man.

God Transcendent in Relation to Man's Needs: *Soteriological Transcendence.* "God" for Wieman has always been that creative power in nature which operates to transform man for his total good. It is in such a soteriological context that Wieman's doctrine of God's transcendence is most strongly expressed. At this point Wieman's role as critic of liberalism is quite apparent. He has no illusions about human goodness and the human condition. But what does Wieman mean by human evil? Here his value theory is central. We recall that the highest good for man was a situation in which man was maximally receptive to the creative event that produced in man maximal appreciation of qualitative meaning. Human evil occurs when this is hindered. When man responsibly resists such creativity (whether he is conscious of it or not), it is "sin." But when man absolutizes some creat*ed* good like truth, beauty, or goodness, without subjecting it to creativity, it is "demonry." The particular results of these evils in human life are inner conflicts of the self, the sense of futility and despair, guilt, and loneliness. At this level "sin" arises when the individual refuses to commit himself to the power that can overcome these evils.

The relation of God to this situation is a transcendent one, and it is the transcendence of God as Judge and God as Good. God is transcendent Judge because as creative event he condemns man's evils (the symptom of which is despair), and also his goods, and not only his goods but the best goods man can even imagine, namely, his ideals. "The holiness of God means that his good is antagonistic and destructive of our cherished goods, because and when our cherished goods are exclusive of the good that all can desire to conserve." [43] Apart from the judgment of this creativity which is at work in the world, man will identify value either with some particular good, or with his own vision of what good *ought* to be; hence, fixation will result, and there will be no possibility of the situation occurring whereby the goods of all mutually enhance one another, perpetually lifting the total society to a higher pitch. What is needed is for man to be constantly *transformed,* which means commitment to and openness before the transforming power that is at work. As a transforming power it judges and crushes man's goods, desires, plans, and even ideals.

The reason God can be the transcendent Judge is that he is the transcendent Good over against man's evil. "God is hidden and transcends 'our world' because the full riches of God's goodness in each concrete situation of the natural world are largely inaccessible to the human heart by reason of habits, attachments, pride, envy, greed, grouches, and other predispositions, in considerable part unavoidable by reason of the social order in which we live."[44] Because God is good, man must fit his way — not vice versa. Therefore it is God's initiative that dominates and not man's. God's goodness is transcendent because herein lies God's absoluteness. God is unqualified good, and absolutely trustworthy in the sense that he always works for the best possible results. He is good in all circumstances and conditions; it is always good to commit oneself to the creative event; and the value of the creative event is infinite. Such is God's soteriological transcendence. The creative event is set over against man as the righteous and transforming judge preventing any realized or envisioned ideals or goals in the time process from being regarded as a final resting place.

God Transcendent in Relation to Man's Knowledge: *Epistemological Transcendence.* Because of Wieman's stress on knowledge and experimentation with respect to God, one might wonder if this leaves any room at all for traditional assertions concerning God as the *deus absconditus.* Yet the doctrine of the hidden God is an important strand in Wieman's theism. We recall that his attempt has always been to uncover a minimal definition of God giving a point at which we could be certain *that* there was a divinely functioning process in the world but promising little about its specific nature. It is here we must look for Wieman's doctrine of the mystery of God and hence God's epistemological transcendence.

God is transcendent in relation to man's knowledge partly because of the nature of man and partly because of the nature of God himself. In the first place man himself is not exactly fitted to comprehend God. Because the human organism has great limitations, man's "conscious awareness is only a peephole compared to all the riches and all the horrors that are in this world." In addition, because man in his sin resists creative changes of habits, there are many degrees of sensitivity to the divine, therefore, while God is in nature and can be "naturally" known, he is not immediately discernible by everyone. Hence, epistemological transformation is one of the conditions of knowing God.

But there are two characteristics about God himself in relation to man which serve as the ground of his epistemological transcendence. The first characteristic follows from man's epistemological limitations and it concerns God as the *Unspecific*. Wieman explicitly says that to regard the traditional symbols as references to detailed characteristics of God is to deny his transcendence. "To be transcendent means to be beyond the reach of our specific knowledge but not beyond the reach of our knowledge that such a reality has being. They who claim to know by revelation or faith or speculation or intuition or analogy, or in some other way, the specific nature of transcendent reality, do thereby deny its transcendence."[45] God thus for Wieman transcends as "The Unspecific Objective," unidentifiable with *any* particular thing: institution, social program, ideal, etc. He is, rather, that "undefined and unexplored totality of what is best as it emerges sequentially in concrete situations where choices must be made."[46] However, God is not wholly unspecific. If he were, no knowledge of him would be possible at all, and this is the error of Barth, whose God is wholly vague. God transcends as the partly unspecific, unknown to a degree but not unknowable.

The second characteristic of God that makes him epistemologically transcendent is a characteristic common to all existence, namely, *concreteness*. Wieman has always defended the view that God, whatever primordial realm he may include, was an actually existing objective reality. Thus he is a " reality which is here all about us waiting to be perceived and interpreted when the social and psychological order of our minds is appropriately transformed." [47] This is one basic reason why he cannot be reduced to man's subjective desires, which would dictate what he ought to be. As an objective and creative reality, God cannot be controlled, shaped, or predicted by man. Wieman's later way of saying this was to deny that God as creative event was of merely instrumental value. As concrete, God especially is not identifiable with any idea about him or any system of concepts. Wieman is well aware that even his own definitions of God, even if they are " true," are only abstractly so, and God in his full concrete reality as the creative event eludes them. This is true because " every concrete reality is more than, and in some respects different from, any statement which the human mind can make of it." [48] Therefore, when we speak of God, " the depth and fullness of the Being in which we find our ultimate stay and trust may be far beyond anything covered in any account which can be given of creative interchange." [49]

VII

THE TRANSCENDENCE OF GOD

We have reviewed several very different ways of speaking about God's transcendence. One feature, impossible to ignore, has been the presence of radically different metaphysical traditions in these reconstructions. None of these men would be satisfied with an abstractly transcendent God; hence all in some sense want to speak of the God who redeems. Yet all utilize philosophical tools that help them describe the being of the one who redeems. God thus is the ground and power of being, a dimensionally conceived Other, and an all-inclusive organism. Such transcendence apparently is based both on the kerygma and on a metaphysical legacy. This is, of course, what bothers the kerygmatic or confessional theologian. What business, Barth would say, does the theologian *qua* theologian have of speaking on any basis other than the Word, and in any concrete framework other than that provided by the Word in its written form, the Scriptures?

This question merely voices one side of the "theological impasse" at which neo-reformation theology has arrived in recent decades. Barth, Otto Weber, Hermann Diem, Arthur C. Cochrane, and Hendrik Kraemer are examples of the purely confessional side of the impasse. Tillich, Bultmann, and from Barth's viewpoint, Brunner, are examples of the "correlation" or "apologetic" side. The famous controversy of Brunner and Barth over natural theology is a classic representation of this "dilemma of the Protestant mind" as Paul Lehmann once called it.[1] When we consider transcendence, the question becomes, What can be said about the Transcendent on the basis of human capabilities, or in older language, on the basis of a *theologia naturalis?* Does human experience in and of itself arrive at a Transcendent? If so, what is its nature? Or on the other side, What can be said about the Transcendent on the basis of the Transcendent's revelation of itself? The purpose of this chapter is to isolate these two questions, in so far as they can be isolated, and then pose the problem of their relationship, hoping thus to find a way to at least gaze beyond the impasse, even if we fail to resolve it.

1. The Transcendent as Limit

One of the frequent myths, if not even travesties, that one hears about philosophy concerns its remoteness from the concerns of concrete human living. Philosophy's "speculations" about ultimate matters supposedly introduce us merely to bloodless categories and irrelevant abstractions. In spite of philosophy's frequent setting in an academic institution, its origins, purposes, and issues have not been those of a "purely academic discussion." Philosophy's questions, whatever else they are, are *human* questions, and therefore carry with them the burdens, perplexities, and anxieties of human questions. Essentially philosophy's questions are about being which means those features of man and his world which are so general that we may not be aware of them in ordinary decisions, or in particular experiments on cross sections of that world.[2] Tillich appears to be right in pointing out that the shock of the possibility of nonbeing is behind man's questions about being, especially his questions about his own being.

It is our thesis that philosophy throughout its history has described human existence as it lives before the Transcendent. This "living before the Transcendent" is not merely the prerogative (or peril) of the philosopher, but of man *qua* man. Many are the traditions that have voiced this experience. Terms such as First Mover, *mē on,* the One, *Ungrund,* and the Absolute, all witness to that variety. Such traditions can be analyzed in terms of four types of experiences in which man lives under and becomes conscious of the Transcendent. The first two, the Beginning and the End, follow temporal imagery. The second two, the Depth and the Height, follow the imagery of spatiality.

a. *The Transcendent as the Beginning.* Man, from the time he could ask questions at all, has, it seems, asked about the Beginning. From primitive myths of beginnings, such as the Babylonian *Enuma Elish,* to sophisticated arguments about a First Mover, man shows that the human (way of) being is being that lives from the Beginning and that turns back in perplexity to the Beginning. Man's myths of an Eden of innocency or of a Golden Age in the past indicate a nostalgia that is part of his being, a nostolgia for the Beginning.

Furthermore, in spite of " scientific advances " we seem no nearer to penetrating the mystery of the Beginning. The curtain is not open even a crack. To be sure, man now knows a great deal more about the past, that which at one time was present. He may use radioactivity measurements to calculate the age of his planetary system or even the universe, but the events such measurements record are events among other events on a temporal line of secondary causes. They are not the Beginning. One might even say that such calculations bring us no nearer to the Beginning. The Beginning is just as much a mystery when we are speaking of events that occurred two billion years ago as in speaking of events that happened yesterday.

What this amounts to is that we are for some reason cut off from the Beginning. Man has his being in the post-Beginning, and the Beginning thus eludes his grasp. In Dietrich Bonhoeffer's words: "Man no longer lives in the beginning — he has lost the beginning. Now he finds he is in the middle, knowing neither the end nor the beginning, and yet knowing that he is in the middle, coming from the beginning and going toward the end." [3]

A perennial testimony to man's state of being cut off from the Beginning are the debates over the classical "proofs" of God. Versions of Thomas' five ways, Anselm's ontological approach, or Kant's moral argument always seem to be with us.[4] However, if and when they are successful, the most they tell us is that contingent nature with its secondary causes is best explainable by a noncontingent reality. They tell us that there is a Beginning, but they tell us nothing of *how* being came to be, nor do they give us the content of the nature of the Beginning. They especially do not transport us to the Beginning where we might find an end to the perplexities and insecurities of existence. Thus when the proofs do arrive at the Beginning, they find the curtain closed. Therefore in the sense that counts, they do not arrive at the Beginning.

The proofs, of course, are not undisputed. To many they are not successful. Thus the "tough-minded" empiricist victoriously displays the fallacies that like skeletons in a closet he discovers in the proofs. But little comfort is his if he supposes he has substituted the "real" and final explanation. Infinite regress is, of course, merely a confession that we know nothing about the Beginning. One might deny that there is a Beginning, yet the question, Whence? is not a nonsensical question. Thus the alternatives, a noncontingent Reality, an infinite regress, the Void, all picture man aiming at the Beginning but hitting only . . . nothing.

b. *The Transcendent as the End.* Man lives not only in the aftermath of a Beginning that nevertheless remains a question mark. As a temporal being aware of his temporality, man's life is a rushing away from the Beginning, toward . . . What? This too has been a question of man since he first began to question. In his optimistic moods man hopes it is toward *something.* In his hopeful moods man anticipates something for himself in the future. The religions, mythologies, and ever-recurring dreams of mankind picture westtern paradises, islands of the blessed, and solar immortalities. Less other-worldly hopes transport such heavens to the plain of history and anticipate utopias. Contemporary cultural versions of this " nostalgia " toward the future include both Communist utopianism and the American dream. Individualistic versions of this attempt to live toward the End and expect something at the End may be immortality, or to settle for less, a time in the future when our basic problems are really solved and the bluebird of happiness alights. A rationalized and " scientific " version of this hope that mere temporality will produce *something* is the trust that immanent forces in nature are working toward this something. One metaphysician, Samuel A. Alexander, felt that in the next emergent level of evolution, God himself would be born!

Such are the hopes that there is *something* at the End. Unfortunately, they remain mere hopes. For even as we are not at the Beginning, neither are we at the End. We are rushing

THE TRANSCENDENCE OF GOD 197

toward that which we do not know, and when we would answer the question, How can I be sure about the End, we find ourselves face to face with another curtain.

But in his less hopeful moods, man fears that at the End lies *nothing*. Man is *homo viator*. His being is transitional, and that toward which he goes, lying in wait for him, is nothing (*le néant*). Here we have the End as it is portrayed in Existentialist metaphysics. This End is given a name, and its name is death.[5] This too can be seen at both individual and historical levels. Individual being is transient being, which means that every present is perpetually dying, and also man's total being finally dies. But historical being also is transient being. We are all well aware that human history is a tiny notch on planetary history, which is another tiny notch on a universe that is passing away. Albert Camus has described the transiency of existence by likening death to a persistent breeze blowing from the future leveling everything in its path, rendering to everything what Rilke once called the "falling sickness." Yet this less hopeful mood is still only a mood. There is no certainty that the End means nothing. Not living in the End but toward the End, our hopes remain hopes and our fears remain fears. The End like the Beginning is therefore the dark.

c. *The Transcendent as the Depth*. We have said that the former two questions reflect man's encounter with his finitude temporally considered. But man as *dasein* (being-there) finds himself in *a* place in the world that is neither the foundation of the world nor the total world. In short he encounters his finitude spatially considered.

This fact becomes part of man's awareness when he asks the simple question, What is the nature of this "place" in which I find myself? He seeks an explanation, not in terms of the *whence* but in terms of the *what*. Yet when he sets out on the road toward an explanation, he finds the road an endless one. Explanation is a relative term. It is a matter of degree. That is, an explanation is given whenever a particular set of demands is met. It is relative to that set of demands. Therefore one may " explain " how a car had a flat tire by citing preceding conditions that " caused " the incident. Or one may explain the make-up of a chemical by listing its component parts or by citing the experimental conditions that when followed will elicit certain operations or behaviors.

All these explanations are explanations within a projected and delimited framework. Even when they are finished, and finished successfully, they do not bring an end to all possible questions. They merely offer a tiny peek at something not available to ordinary, superficial experience. Therefore, we have actually said very little when we say that an entity (or complex of entities) " caused " an event to happen. All the terms of the explanation: entity, cause, event, are highly abstract and vague. What actually goes on in the relation we call causality? Do the powers or contents of an entity somehow become another entity, or leap over an abyss to affect a totally separate entity? Even if these Whiteheadian types of questions are answered (and few are sure that they are), we have only settled the matter at another level according to another set of demands. The tiny peek is widened only slightly.

What we have found then when we ask about the nature of the present is that after only a few preliminary questions, we are floundering in the unknown. To be sure, we can quite successfully " explain " the present by not raising these questions. But even if we can cajole or threaten our minds into avoiding improper and silly questions, our very being

THE TRANSCENDENCE OF GOD   199

will ask them. For we inevitably make assumptions about the nature of our world and of ourselves in the very act of avoiding such questions, and in fact in the decisions by which we live. What is it about nature, world, or process that eludes our probing? We are calling it the Depth. This is not at this point to adhere to any particular philosophical position. Almost all philosophies have in their own ways portrayed the Depth. Plato pictured a Receptacle (ὑποδοχή), which served as the matrix of the forms or patterns after which the universe was made. Whitehead saw a primordial element in all process explaining how possibilities were graded and actualized. Heidegger speaks of the "Being of being" (*Sein des Seienden*).[6] Even naturalism speaks of contexts of events, qualities, and relations that are more concrete and complex than reality seen at first glance. The Depth we might say is neither the Beginning nor the End, but rather the power in being that holds the Beginning and End apart, therefore preventing all from coming to nothing. Thus man surveys his place and asks, What is it? When no answer is forthcoming he is merely perplexed. When " answers " appear, they provide only glimpses. Here too we find the curtain drawn.

d. *The Transcendent as the Height.* Man's question about the Depth is also a question about himself, about *his* Depth. It is a questioning after the *what* of things in which he has his own being. In a sense he is removed from it in that it eludes him, yet as *his* Depth, it is in him and he in it. In addition to this man's being is also being lived under that which is over against his being, or *other* than his being.

This Other is not so much the object of a perennial question, since before it man's questions cease, and the noise man makes becomes silence. Ultimately, the nature of things, in spite of the confident portrayals of such men as Lucretius and Hegel, is a mystery. Furthermore, it is probably more of a mystery to modern man than to primitive man, for now it remains a mystery after and in spite of the sophisticated questions we have put to it. But the Height is not mere mystery but rather the *alienum*. The Height, in other words, is that about the world, something man in spite of himself finds in the world, which is alien and strange to his being.

Here we have the Transcendent in its most "religious" sense. If Rudolf Otto is right, the essence of religiousness is a "creature feeling" of awe or shuddering before that which is Wholly Other.[7] Something of the sort might be found in William Blake's portrait of a terrible aspect of nature symbolized by the tiger and its "fearful symmetry." The young Schleiermacher also knew of this when he spoke of "strange, dread, mysterious emotions, when the imagination reminds us that there is more in nature than we know."[8] Man, be he a native Polynesian or a modern physicist, is constantly coming onto something that produces a response of awe. Such awe is not of the Depth. Man wonders about the Depth and investigates it. But the Height is too alien and too strange for either curiosity or inquiry. Man has responded to the Height in many ways. In magic he tries to protect himself from it, or he tries to tap its power for his own use. If he is more sophisticated, he may try to protect himself from it by "rational magic" in which he "explains" and catalogs it. Or in fascination (*fascinosum*, Otto) he may be drawn in his awe to worship it, or sacrifice to it.

We call it the Height because it is primarily the Other, the strange. Thus many religions have come to associate deity with such heights as mountains or the sky. *Zeus Hypsistos* (Zeus Most High) of Greek religion and Heaven

THE TRANSCENDENCE OF GOD 201

in Confucianism are examples. Even as man is not the Depth, neither is he the Height, nor does he enter or possess the Height. He may wonder about, worship, or try to avoid, the Height, all of which are signs that when man would enter the Height by way of his ever-growing and ever-collapsing towers of Babel, he finds only the dark.

And now, three clarifications. First, these are not four transcendences but four modes of the Transcendent. Nor are they neatly separated but are related in polarity and by overlapping. The Beginning and End are polarities that surround man's existence in the middle, a middle that grips on to being by means of a power of being, the Depth. In a sense all three connotations are gathered up in the Height as man "awfully" faces his finitude in the light of these several modes of infinitude. What man faces in all of these is his Limit, and in a sense, the Limit of everything. Man's being, in other words, is being between the Beginning and the End, between the Depth and the Height. Thus the nature of man's being as limited being is not due to a subjective projection on the part of man. Man does not invent or imagine the Limit. His being, rather, is rendered as limited. Something limits it or "finitizes" it. This something under which man exists as transient in time and as a particularity in space is the Limit, the Transcendent.

Second, we should be clear that the Transcendent in this sense does not arise out of a particular world view; that is, it is not a postulate put forth to help metaphysics give a coherent explanation of reality. Certainly, it has appeared in some form in almost every world view. But it would be more accurate to say that the Transcendent is something encountered, or by hook or crook avoided, at the edge of every world view. Thus it is not a "tenable" notion in the sense of a theory that we substantiate by evidence. Rather, it "encompasses" (Jaspers) and limits all such procedures.[9] This is why it is the Transcendent.

Third, we should clarify that this Transcendent is not necessarily God. As we have seen, theologians often utilize these modes of the Transcendent to say what they mean by God, and this may be inevitable. The Transcendent thus may be " God " in the generic sense of *theos*. But this Transcendent has no specific name. It has not " placed " itself. We who are not at the Beginning do not know whether the Beginning is God. Because the Transcendent is the Limit and *our* Limit, we can say nothing more. Thus to speak of God in this sense is not necessarily to speak of the God who does " place " himself, who gives his name, and who himself provides the possibility of such speaking.

2. The Transcendent as God

We have just considered the Transcendent as "natural man" experiences and portrays it, or rather, we have considered that which is grasped at the edge of every " experience " and every " portrayal." It may or may not be " God," since the term " God " can be and often is applied to almost anything. But when we ask, Is it *our* God? we must face the fact that the Christian tradition means something almost embarassingly specific when it speaks about God. It insists, first of all, that only God himself can be the basis of speaking about God. His Speaking provides the possibility of our speaking. We then must ask, Where has God provided such a basis? If our method is an attempt from some superior viewpoint to explicate all the logical alternatives, and on some basis that transcends all of them to choose one, then the answers to the question are many and probably quite arbitrary. God may speak in nature, mind, trances, moral experience, or religious genius.

However, such a method is not a live option, for we do not have our existence at a superior point *in abstracto*. We have our existence *sub specie Christi*. This means that our embarrassingly specific affirmation about God is that God is the one who was " in Christ reconciling the world to himself " (II Cor. 5:19). As Carl Michaelson says: " The God of Christianity is not simply *Sein*. He is *Dasein*. His reality is not abstract, but concrete — a reality of which one can say, ' It is *there*.' "[10] *There,* in Christ, we meet God. There we know God, or rather God allows himself to be known at that point. This means we do not decisively know him at other points. We may know something, but *God* we know from and in the Christ-event, which as an event is a nexus of both the past and the present. To speak of the Transcendent as God in this specific sense is to speak from the situation of redemption. For this is what we mean in particular when we say, " The Word became flesh." This God we know in and from an inscrutable act of grace. Therefore the Transcendent as God is simply the one who redeems. His name thus is not merely I AM THAT I AM (YHWH) or even the proposed revision, I AM WHO CAUSES TO BE, but rather, I AM WHO REDEEMS. His name is *Agapē* (I John 4:8) or we might even say his name is *Charis* (grace).

From this act of grace which is the content of the " good news " (εὐαγγέλιον), we may become aware of other matters such as the facticity and radicality of human sin. But we become aware of sin as sin only from the act of grace. In this sense God is the Transcendent in that our existence has status only by means of a gift. Apart from the gift, we have no status. Our name is *nihil,* the nothing, the void. Apart from the gift, not even our sin is recognized. To be recognized as sinner against God is possible only in an act of grace. But within the gift, we have all status, for "who can separate us from the love of Christ?" We share, amazingly, *his* glory. The Transcendent as God, then, is the one from whom we have everything: existence, recognition, judgment, and redemption.

All of this is, of course, simply a way of elaborating the characteristics of "kerygmatic" transcendence mentioned previously.[11] The question of the Transcendent is first a question of how the Transcendent is known and only after that a question of the nature of his being (the epistemological priority). Also it is transcendence grasped at the point of our *existence,* for it is grasped as we stand under that act of grace which is both judgment and forgiveness (the *existential* priority). But can we go farther to speak about the ontological nature of the Transcendent as God? To put it another way, Is the Transcendent as God in any sense absolute? Is he in any sense the Beginning, the End, the Depth, and the Height?

a. *The Transcendent as the Creator.* The phrase "In the beginning God created . . ." is not a cosmological but a revelational assertion. It does not mean, "Our calculations show that the Beginning is God." Rather, it means, "The Word that was made flesh came not into an alien world but into *his own* world." In other words, the power of the God who redeems the world extends over the world. One implication of redemption is power. Redemption may be rooted in *agapē,* but if it really redeems, it is a powerful *agapē* or sovereign love. Redemption is inevitably a struggle with other "powers" (especially sin and death). Thus the God who does redeem is *the* power. Nor does his redemptive power concern merely the human sphere of being. Redemption is addressed decisively to man, but "man" is neither angel nor Platonic form. Man's being is being rooted in nature, which means that his being partakes of spatial-temporal particularity, process, and the ever-moving events of nature. If God's powerful redemption extends to the human sphere of being, it also extends to all being. To put it more specifically, the God man knows in the incomprehensible act of grace is the God from whom all being has its being as a gift.

We spoke previously about man's limitation or finitude in terms of both temporality and spatiality. But if the Transcendent as God is really the Redeemer, his power will extend in and through both temporal and spatial planes. If this is so, God as sovereign love will surround and embrace that dark moment, if it is a moment, and even if it is a perennial moment, when being comes forth out of nonbeing. The Redeemer thus is "maker of heaven and earth." His sovereignty extends to the *Whence*.

However, the "maker of heaven and earth" is not the Beginning. The Beginning is merely the limit at which man arrives when he asks, "Whence?" The kerygma does not dispel all the mysteries connected with the transition from nonbeing to being. We might even say it dispels none of them. What it does say is that the *Whence,* that from whom we have our existence, is none other than the one from whom we have forgiveness. Not only redemption but existence itself is given to us. Existence is an act of grace. This is what we mean by God as Creator, namely, the one who in grace enabled being to be.

b. *The Transcendent as the Fulfiller.* We have said that the Transcendent as God essentially means the one who freely gives. The Beginning is thus seen as an act of grace.

Obviously such a God is not limited merely to the Beginning, for we know his gift only because he has invaded the "middle" (καὶ ὁ λόγος σὰρξ ἐγένετο). Such an invasion can be a decisive redemption only if God is Lord of the middle. More specifically, this means he can freely act on the middle, or history, which is a more frequent term for the middle. Therefore, there is no period or phenomenon in the middle that is secure or immune against such acts. Everything in history stands under the possibility of a judgment or a redemption from God. The "future" theologically interpreted is not, therefore, merely the realm of possibilities waiting to be actualized (Hartshorne) nor the unguessable creativities that the *élan vital* might produce (Bergson). The future means what God in his freedom has in store for us. In Bultmann's terms, God is the one who comes.[12] Or to put it another way, God as Redeemer is Lord of the End. His sovereign love extends not only to the *Whence* but to the *Whither*. For such reasons, J. A. T. Robinson has said that "every statement about God is *ipso facto* an assertion about the end."[13] The future *ultimately* considered is simply what God ultimately has in store.

It should be clear that this "end" is not the End conceived as Limit. Again, the contrast is not between that which is hidden and mysterious and that which is clear. When we say God is the end, we mean the future is in his hands and we are rushing into a future that has its existence as a gift of grace. But this does not clear up the mysteries and even insecurities of the future. The freedom of God is even more inscrutable than the End as our Limit. Thus we have mystery, but we also have more than mystery. For if God is the end and Lord of the end, it means that that toward which our transient being is heading is none other than the one who acted in the middle for our redemption. In this sense we might say the end is none other than Christ. Coexisting alongside the mystery of the end is an illumination of the end. The end as God is neither a nothing nor the "something" of projected human hopes. The end is the end brought about by the God of the end. The end too is an act of grace.

c. *The Transcendent as the Preserver.* So far we have said that the power of the God who is Redeemer extends to and through temporality, and thus he is Lord of both the Beginning and the End. Does his sovereign love also extend to and through that plane of finitude called spatiality? We have seen that out of his freedom God acts on the middle, but is this his only relation to the middle? Is God sovereign over the middle only in the sense that he brought the middle into being and acts on it as the one who comes? Are we to say that apart from these, the middle (history and nature) exists of itself? To put it another way, is the *power* of being, which somehow prevents being from collapsing into nothingness, a self-made, self-derived power? At this point, we must say — we are, in fact, driven to say — that the middle is not autonomous in relation to him from whom everything exists as a gift. It is the power of the Redeemer that prevents all from collapsing into nothing.

Thus the world is not only his world in that he made it. It is his world in that it *remains* his world. We must stress that "remaining his world" is not an inevitability that flows automatically from the fact that God is "maker of heaven and earth." God in his freedom is not enslaved or bound to his own work. In his freedom he may choose to detach himself from his work or to repudiate his work. We know he has not so repudiated it only from the fact that he has chosen to redeem it. Because God acts in the middle for its redemption, we know God has chosen to remain with his work. And this " remaining with his work " is like creation an act of grace. Some theologians prefer to call this simply God's *creatio continua* (continuing creation), but we would prefer, following Bonhoeffer, to call it *preservation,* which is the act of grace in which God chooses to recognize and confirm being.

It is God, therefore, in his gracious, preserving work who holds the Beginning and End apart. This does not mean that God and the Depth are synonymous. The Depth is the limit we arrive at when we probe into the *What* of being and there is no specific answer forthcoming from itself as to its nature. But when we confess that being continues as being only because of a continuing grace, we are affirming that God is sovereign in relation to the *What*. This means again that the power that keeps nonbeing from engulfing being is none other than the one whose Word became flesh. Thus *our* Depth theologically interpreted is not merely a primordial condition of process (Whitehead) or an Encompassing (Jaspers), although these in themselves may be legitimate ontological analyses. Our Depth is the one from whom we have grace, which means the Depth itself is grace. Thus we are his and remain for him in the depths of our being regardless of the radicality of our rebellion. There is nothing we can do to annul our status of having our continued existence from his grace.

d. *The Transcendent as the Holy.* So far we have said that God the Redeemer is also and inevitably absolute in the sense that his power extends to the Beginning, the End, and the Depth of the middle. We have also stressed that in all of these God remains hidden (*absconditus*) as well as revealed as creator, fulfiller, and preserver (*revelatus*). As hidden, the

THE TRANSCENDENCE OF GOD 209

Transcendent as God is also the *alienum*. In relation to us he appears as the strange, the other. He is "strange" as creator, fulfiller, and preserver, not primarily because there is mystery connected with the Beginning, the End, and the Depth. The strangeness of God is a strangeness not of mere mystery, but the strangeness of an inscrutable grace. We mean by this that all our attempts to get behind the act of grace with "explanations" collapse. Our efforts to assign reasons for grace, to show why God "ought" to act in that way or why he did act in that way, all run aground. For those who see God *sub specie Christi,* behind every act of God, behind every so-called "attribute" of God, is the one attribute that is not an attribute because it is God himself, grace. This and only this can be the basis for saying God is strange, or Holy, i.e., for saying God is God.

Recent phenomenological studies of the Holy [14] have stressed the original, nonmoral connotations of the Holy, the time when Holy meant the *mysterium tremendum,* an "awful" and fascinating power. The Old Testament illustrates this, for there the original meaning of holy (*qadosh*) was separateness or set-apart-ness. Later the term took on connotations of moral purity, so that the Holy was also the righteous (*tsedeq*). But once we admit that the name of God is grace, we must go farther. How does grace affect our way of seeing God as separate in his "awful" being and as righteous? In the kerygma God's righteousness is not merely a characteristic of God by which man is threatened. God's righteousness is something he freely and astoundingly shares with man, the unrighteous.[15] In short, God does not cling to his righteousness but gives it, which is to say it is righteousness interpreted through grace. For this reason God's righteousness is inscrutable. We can comprehend a righteousness that follows the punishment-reward structures of legal justice. Such is the nature of our righteousness. But a righteousness that breaks that framework eludes us. This inscrutable righteousness, this mysterious righteousness, is what the Holy means *sub specie Christi*.

Such a holiness not only eludes us, it also threatens us. For implied in the righteousness that comes only as a gift is a negation of all other bases of righteousness. Before this righteousness we in and of ourselves have absolutely no status. Against this righteousness we cannot even sin or rebel unless in grace our sin is recognized as sin. As we said previously, in and of ourselves our name is *nihil* (nothing). This is why God, as Holy, is not merely the Height. The mystery and awfulness of the Height is comfortable compared to this inscrutable Grace apart from whose free gift we are *nihil*. It is also different from the Height in that it breaks forth from the Height, comes into the middle, suffers, and dies. As Barth has said, " The highness of God consists in his thus descending."

In these senses God the Redeemer is absolute. His power does extend to beginning and end, depth and height. Here too we are radically limited but in a different way. Here our limit is not a nameless infinite or unknown. Our limit is the one who placed himself and whose name is grace. Here too our existence is an in-between existence, but " in-between " refers to existence on the receiving end of a gift. Such limitation thus is positive in character. We might even say it is a " blessing," for this limit is a gift, an act of grace. We live between the beginning and the end only by means of a gift. We live between the depth and the height and are not destroyed by either only because he so chooses.

In the light of these things, we must object to any view of God's absoluteness as the " unrelated " or the " unchanging," which thus must see God in two paradoxical and conflicting modes of being, absolute and related.[16] This method is apparently one that takes the Transcendent as Limit, probably conceived in a particular metaphysical tradition, and identifies it with the Transcendent as God, as if the kerygma had no place in establishing the nature of God's absoluteness. We are not denying the problem of relating the Limit and God. We only want to say now that when we are speaking about God on the basis of God's speaking, God's absoluteness is defined in terms of his redemptive act of grace. There is no "absoluteness" behind this which we bring to this, and in the light of which this is interpreted. There is no "unrelated" God or aspect of God. Rather, there is a mystery of an unfathomable grace that is a depth we can never plumb. But it is a depth of *grace*, not an ontological abyss that exists only in conflict or paradox with grace.

Here, of course, is where we must depart from Tillich. For Tillich comes to the kerygmatic act of grace from a philosophy in terms of which the act is interpreted. This is why his is a *hyper*theism and why the real God is being-itself that grounds the symbolic "God" of theism. Thus in spite of himself, he does not allow his philosophical concept of being-itself to be judged, transformed, and interpreted by the God who is grace. Rather, the reverse is true. His "answer" merely answers the philosophical question but apparently does not transform it.

3. The Analogy of Grace

We can no longer delay the difficult and perhaps unanswerable question, How are the Transcendent as Limit and the Transcendent as God related? We must insist that this is a valid theological question. A theological question is defined essentially in terms of its intention to investigate and clarify the kerygma. Any question that would further that end is a theological question. And this question, like all questions about the relation between the divine and the human, Christ and culture, or theology and other disciplines, is a crucial one, for the way it is answered determines the controlling principles of theological method, and more concretely the principles by which the church relates itself to culture. So we ask the question from faith. We do not leave the " circle of faith " to ask it. But we do ask it.

a. *The Theological Impasse.* We have several times referred to an impasse that has developed between apologetic and kerygmatic theologies of our time. Both Tillich and Barth have seen the situation in Protestant theology as one constituted by these two basic alternatives. It was this issue which originally split the " crisis theology " group of the periodical *Zwischen den Zeiten* (*Between the Times*). In the 1930's many interpreters saw Barth, Brunner, Bultmann, Tillich, and even Reinhold Niebuhr all participating in one more or less solidified movement called neo-orthodoxy or neo-supernaturalism. Barth and Brunner especially were always seen together. Actually Tillich's *Kairos* Circle was from the beginning separate from the Swiss theologians.[17] And in 1934 the growing tension between Brunner and Barth became a rift, reflected in their two pamphlets *Natur und Gnade* (Brunner) and *Nein* (Barth).

However, while many agree that these alternatives are the basic options for postliberal Protestant theology, there is little agreement as to what the precise issue is between these options. For some it is a matter of emphasis, with Tillich and Bultmann stressing the " common ground " that must exist between the kerygma and the situation before the kerygma can be relevantly communicated, and with Barth trying to speak from the Word and only the Word. Others like Cushman see the Tillich-Bultman side as one that "takes man as starting point and finds God a co-implicate of the properly interpreted human self-consciousness," deriving "the knowledge of God from a prior and self-confirming knowledge of man,"[18] while the Barth side basically grounds anthropology in Christology.

We feel, however, that such statements do not really do justice to the principle that Brunner, Bultmann, and Tillich as apologetic theologians have in common. None of these men wants to "derive the knowledge of God from the knowledge of man." We have pointed out previously that radical existential estrangement as one of the presuppositions of Tillich's correlation principle forever prevents such a derivation. Estrangement cuts across any common structure or identity that would enable man to make such a derivation. There is no question of the priority or givenness of revelation for Brunner or Tillich. Granting we can speak of God only on the basis of God's speaking, how is that speaking to be related to man who hears. Barth's answer to this question is radically Christocentric, or we might better say, following Althaus, Christomonistic (*Christomonismus*). Revelation comes in Jesus Christ and in Jesus Christ alone. Thus there is only one possibility and one basis of any true theology and any valid speaking about God. That basis is God's act in Jesus Christ, which God in his freedom miraculously enables to be communicated in human words. There can be a correspondence or analogy between such words and the Word, but such correspondence is due entirely to God's act. Thus it is an analogy of faith (*analogia fidei*), which means that God's Christological act and nothing else is its basis.

Correlation theologians agree that God's revelation and man's response in faith are the defining essence of the theological standpoint. Even Tillich insists that revelation is something *independently* given. But again, what is the relation between that independently given revelation and man who hears? According to the apologetic theologians man who hears is man who " needs " and has a " negative knowledge " of God preceding this revelation (Bultmann);[19] or man who hears is man estranged from his own essential being and whose questions still reflect that essentiality (Tillich); or man before and outside of revelation is *humanitas,* a person, capable of language (*Wortmächtigkeit*), and thus capable of at least being addressed by God (Brunner). The common element here is the attempt to set revelation in creation. They see revelation occurring within, though not on the basis of, some preceding structure, be it creation, the *imago dei,* the mystical a priori, or man's situation. This preceding structure does not make revelation possible in the sense of producing it, but it does serve as a necessary, preceding condition without which revelation could not occur. Such a " condition " is not autonomous (although every theology is in danger of making it so) in relation to revelation, but it is that in which revelation occurs.

The methodological implication of this is that wherever the event of revelation is translated into human language, the result is a mixture of the content that comes from the " preceding structure " and the content of revelation. Kerygma itself is always this mixture. This situation has at least two consequences. One, the concrete media of revelation such as Scripture must have their " symbols " interpreted (Tillich), or they must be demythologized (Bultmann). Two, the " preceding structure " of creation, reason, or language capacity plays a positive and legitimate role in the theological task; hence existential analyses, historical methods, and metaphysical traditions have a valid place in the discipline that tries to clarify the kerygma. Revelation can thus be " correlated " to the situation not because of a preceding identity that makes man autonomous and revelation superfluous, but because of a preceding structure that has its being from God and that comprises that into which revelation comes. Revelation is an act of God in and affected by that structure. All interpretation (hermeneutics) thus takes both into account.

We said before that kerygmatic theology gave priority to the epistemological question, What is the basis of our speaking? Now we can see the opposite principle in apologetic theology, for its stress is, *what is* revelation, especially in relation to creation or the orders of being? Here an ontological question is given priority. After that question is answered, a method then arises that operates according to a context of norms. There is a valid sense in which such apologetic theology is a continuation of Schleiermacher, for he too saw theology reflecting universal structures (such as universal religiousness), which then had a particular and unique realization in Christian religiousness.

We have called this situation an " impasse." This implies that an unsolved problem occurs on both sides. Obviously, if one of these theologies has definitively solved the problem, the situation is not an impasse but a victory. On the correlation side, the difficulty is what seems to be a denial that the basis of theology is *sola gratia*. If " preceding structures," " needs," and " necessary conditions " enter into the theological discipline and the result is a context of norms, is not the Lordship of the only possible norm, the Word become flesh, denied? Hence is there not an autonomy subtly hidden in this alternative? Nor is the kerygmatic side without its problems. First, granting the point that revelation is in the Christ (which also and in some sense means the Scriptures), granting that formal principle, we still have the problem of ascertaining the *content* of that historically given event. It is clear that many disciplines with their respective norms engage in that endeavor: linguistics, archaelogy, history, etc. Thus the kerygmatic theologian inevitably works with a plurality of norms when he utters any human word about the content of the revelation under which he stands. Nor are these disciplines merely innocuously present in this enterprise. They are present in determinative ways, for their results do affect what the theologian says. Furthermore, if such disciplines were not somehow present in theology, it would mean that the theologian could " obey God " but in good conscience speak ethical, philosophical, or scientific nonsense as he pleased. Theology in short would be obscurantist.

Secondly, the endeavor to see the theological norm monistically implies that it exists alongside and completely outside of every human and cultural enterprise that does not have the Christ-event as its standard. This not only results in a dualism that sounds suspiciously like Kant (a position that the so-called " later " Barth has tried to avoid), it leaves the spheres and disciplines of culture autonomous. Furthermore, it results in a kind of neo-Marcionism. For if revelation is identified with the Christ-event, does this mean that the mighty acts of God in Israel's history were merely human inventions? This is where Christomonism seems to leave us. On the other hand, if revelation really occurs in some sense prior to the Christ-event, if the Christ-event occurs in a *Heilsgeschichte* that anticipates it, we do have in the picture the " preceding structures " of which the apologetic theologians speak. Such is the theological impasse.

b. *The* Analogia Gratiae. The dilemma just outlined may not be a problem peculiar to contemporary theological currents. Possibly this is *the* ever-recurring theological problem; the issue between Tertullian and Origen, St. Francis and St. Dominic, the Confessional Church and Schleiermacher, and the issue today. If so, we hope for no " solution." If we can illuminate the dilemma itself, showing why it is a valid dilemma in which to stand, that must suffice.

The issue, more specifically, centers around the relation between the Christ-event (including Christ's birth, death, and resurrection) and grace. Is grace something this event makes possible? To answer " yes " would commit us to the crudest of forensic theories of the atonement where Christ's death is a ransom " paid " to God enabling him to satisfy the demands of his own justice and thus forgive us. And of course a paid forgiveness is not forgiveness. We would rather say that the Christ-event reveals God's grace, and the God who is *always* grace. It does not make it possible for him to be gracious. This, however, is not a " timeless truth," for that event is the decisive moment in which we know and receive to ourselves that redemption. It is the mightiest of God's mighty acts, but it is not his only act.

The truth in kerygmatic theology is that in the *ordo cognoscendi* (order of knowing), the Christ-event is the one act through which the other acts are seen and interpreted. But in the *ordo essendi* (order of being), it is one act among many acts. Kerygmatic theology is thus correct epistemologically, but apologetic theology is correct ontologically. To put it another way, grace is not limited to that act, though we receive grace decisively through that act. All God's acts are acts of grace, even his judgment, for in judgment God is God in relation to us and is not ignoring us. The act of grace in the Christ-event reveals that all existence, every sphere of being, every human reality, has its being not from itself but from God. Some might object that this preceding structure of grace binds God, thus preventing grace from being rooted in a *free* act of God. However, God's freedom need not be interpreted so nominalistically. True, he may grant his grace in particular " free " acts. But we dare not rob him of the freedom to establish a structure of grace in which the acts take place.

We would say then that revelation, in the sense of the Christ-event, comes into and is surrounded by " preceding structures." However, the principle of these structures is not nature or creation. Neither is it *humanitas*. Brunner's language about nature *and* grace, creation *and* redemption, is unfortunate. There is no such nature or creation existing alongside or outside of grace. For creation is one of God's gracious acts. Creation and history, which precede and frame the particular revelation in Christ, do have a status. It is not a self-derived status nor does it take place outside of grace. It is the status of a *donum gratiae* (gift of grace).

This is not an analogy of *being* in the sense that the common element between God and the world, revelation and creation, is *esse* or being. What holds in common between God and the world is grace: the analogy being between God who is *gratia ipsa* (grace itself) and natural and human structures, which are *esse gratiae* (being of grace). Grace is the basis of this analogy; hence an analogy of grace comprises the structures into which the decisive revelation comes. This principle differs from Tillich, however, in that it is not based on the philosophical claim that all being ontologically participates in its ground. The basis of this principle is not ontological but soteriological, for it is rooted in the notion that all being is *esse gratiae*.

This does not undercut the radicality of human sin and

the doctrine that man can do *nothing* to produce or even set up conditions for his redemption. What the analogy of grace means in relation to man is that God redeems *his own* creature, the creature of his grace. Redemption thus is not sheer creation in the sense of bringing being from nonbeing. It is, rather, the forgiveness and transformation of a corrupted and rebellious creation. In short, it is a restoration of God's own to himself.

The analogy of grace has, of course, many implications as to how theology, the discipline of the kerygma, is related to other disciplines. Negatively, it means there is no theological basis for relating theology and let us say philosophy as two entirely exclusive entities. This would assume the kerygma exists as a clearly discernible, propositional norm that is parallel to, though exclusive of, human norms. But if the free grace of God is really the norm, it does not coexist with other norms forcing a decision between them. It exists as a forgiving and transforming redemption that transforms and utilizes *everything* human.

The words "transform" and "utilize" are at least two ways theology is related to other disciplines and the sphere of human experience in general. Human insights, experiences, and truths are neither annihilated nor ignored. In redemption they are forgiven-transformed, i.e., given their true status under God. As an illustration we might again ask, What is the relation between the Transcendent as Limit (encountered in the possibilities of human experience prior to the kerygma) and the Transcendent as God? What the kerygma does to this experience is to speak to it and transform it. This is not to derive a metaphysics directly out of the kerygma, nor would we ignore these perennial human questions. The human question itself, along with its norms, insights, and truths is taken into the forgiveness of God and there transformed. The same holds for human morality. Under the kerygma, human morality does not continue unaffected, autonomous, and independent. Our whole evaluation of it and its status is transformed. More concretely such " transformation " means a relativizing of metaphysics and morality, robbing them of any absolute character they might claim for themselves, rendering to them a forgiveness in which they see themselves anew under God.

The second word, " utilizes," helps declare the relation of theology to other disciplines. Because human disciplines and human truths do have status in the analogy of grace, theology's relation to them is inclusive. We said before that this was inevitably so. We say now, it is legitimately so. The consequences of the human endeavors to find truth, tentative though they may be, have a positive and normative status in theology. This does not mean that they replace the theological norm, the Christ. Rather, we would distinguish between a *definitive norm,* i.e., a norm that defines the essence of a discipline, and thus in the last analysis controls its purpose and task, and *subordinate norms,* which make their own contributions to a discipline. For instance, philological studies do have a place in our attempt to ascertain the content of the kerygma. *What* we say does in part depend on the results of such studies. Their norms are listened to, but they do not replace the Norm. Under the guidance of the Spirit they help us ascertain and clarify the content of the Norm. In this sense theology may " utilize " philosophy, metaphysics, history, science, etc. Thus in addition to a " conversionist " relation between the kerygma and culture, to use a term from H. R. Niebuhr, there is also an operational relation, in which subordinate norms function in behalf of and contribute to the clarification of the Norm.

When we apply this "operational" relationship to our problem of transcendence, we find that theology may legitimately employ the insights, the distinctions, the "truths" of human experiences of the Transcendent as Limit. For if there is an analogy of grace, the Transcendent as God is not *totally* other than the Transcendent as Limit. Such has been the story of theology through the centuries; thus, *via negativa,* Aristotelian distinctions between secondary causes and the first cause, and idealist metaphysics have all helped the church witness to the Transcendent as God. True, this story is a story of the distortion of such transcendence, but that merely reminds us it is the human story. The astounding thing, the absolutely incredible thing, is that God by granting to us a historical revelation, has placed himself " at the mercy " of the errors, the sins, and the relativities of human interpretation. He in a sense submits himself and the knowledge of himself to human disciplines. If real incarnation took place, we can say nothing else but this almost absurd thing. This too witnesses to his grace; for in spite of the fragility of the disciplines, norms, and questions we bring to revelation, he by his Spirit uses them to make himself known.

But what does the theologian do when the subordinate norms conflict with the Norm? This question is certainly a legitimate one, yet as a question, it is similar to such questions as, What if the theologian makes an error? Of course, theologians do make errors. Subordinate norms have conflicted, do conflict, and will conflict with the Norm. In fact such conflicts help define the essence of the theological task. Our claim is that the theologian does not have any one principle that will assure him in advance that this will not happen. Therefore, there is no answer *in abstracto* to such a question. We can only say that, *in abstracto,* there will be conflicts, and that the theologian must then take up the struggle. To insist on any more is to insist on a *gnosis* that would make an end to the methodological problem of theology. To this we must say, with Paul, " God forbid."

NOTES

Chapter I   The New Temper and Its Background

1. Daniel Day Williams, *What Present-Day Theologians Are Thinking* (Harper & Brothers, 1952), p. 12.

2. For the breakup of the various strands of the "medieval synthesis," see E. A. Burtt, *The Metaphysical Foundations of Modern Physical Science,* Doubleday Anchor Books (Doubleday & Co., Inc., 1954); A. C. McGiffert, *The Rise of Modern Religious Ideas* (The Macmillan Company, 1915); and John Dillenberger and Claude Welch, *Protestant Christianity* (Charles Scribner's Sons, 1955), Ch. 1.

3. Some good historical studies of immanence are the following: A. C. McGiffert, "Immanence," *Encyclopedia of Religion and Ethics,* Vol. VIII; also, *The Rise of Modern Religious Ideas,* Ch. X; W. M. Horton, *Theism and the Scientific Spirit* (Harper & Brothers, 1933), Chs. III and IV; and J. K. Mozley, *The Impassibility of God* (Cambridge University Press, 1926), Ch. II.

4. H. P. Van Dusen, "The Liberal Movement in Theology," *The Church Through Half a Century,* Samuel McCrea Cavert and H. P. Van Dusen, eds. (Charles Scribner's Sons, 1936), pp. 77–78.

5. A. C. McGiffert, "Immanence" (quoting the *Speeches* of Schleiermacher), p. 169.

6. Hamann, Herder, Fichte, Schelling, Hegel, Fechner, and Lessing are among the great names of immanence in this period.

7. Carl Becker, *The Heavenly City of the Eighteenth Century Philosophers* (Yale University Press, 1932), p. 17.

8. Three quite different yet helpful books on liberalism are: L. Harold DeWolf, *The Case for Theology in Liberal Perspective* (The Westminster Press, 1959); David Roberts and H. P. Van

Dusen, eds., *Liberal Theology: An Appraisal* (Charles Scribner's Sons, 1942); and H. R. Mackintosh, *Types of Modern Theology* (James Nisbet & Co., Ltd., London, 1937).

9. I am following Werner Brock's account in *Contemporary German Philosophy* (Cambridge University Press, London, 1935), Ch. 1.

10. See W. L. Davidson, *Recent Theistic Discussions* (T. & T. Clark, Edinburgh, 1921) for a study of the Gifford Lectures in this period.

11. Some good summaries of American liberal theology are found in W. Burggraaff, *The Rise and Development of Liberal Theology in America* (Goes Press, 1928), and F. H. Foster, *The Modern Movement in American Theology* (Fleming H. Revell Company, 1939).

12. E. C. Vanderlaan, *Fundamentalism Versus Modernism* (The H. W. Wilson Company, 1924), p. 72.

13. Before 1920 some key books in American theology stressing God's immanence were: H. C. King, *Reconstruction in Theology* (1901); W. A. Brown, *Christian Theology in Outline* (1906); F. J. McConnell, *The Divine Immanence* (1906); Paul Carus, *God* (1908); W. E. Hocking, *The Meaning of God in Human Experience* (1912); W. F. Adeney, *The Christian Idea of God* (1912); Josiah Royce, *The Problem of Christianity* (1913); H. A. Youtz, *The Enlarging Conception of God* (1914); G. B. Smith, *A Guide to the Study of the Christian Religion* (1916); and E. W. Lyman, *The Experience of God in Modern Life* (1918).

14. A few such works in the 1920's are: J. M. Snowden, *The Personality of God* (1920); H. A. Jones, *Faith That Inquires* (1922); C. A. Beckwith, *The Idea of God* (1922); G. B. Foster, *Christianity in Its Modern Expression* (1924); J. F. Newton, ed., *My Idea of God* (1926); D. S. Robinson, *The God of the Liberal Christian* (1926); J. E. Turner, *The Nature of Deity* (1927); J. W. Buckham, *The Humanity of God* (1928); Richard Roberts, *The Christian God* (1929); E. S. Ames, *Religion* (1929).

15. For a study attempting to document the charge of "optimism" in the anthropologies of the liberal period, see Mary Frances Thelen, *Man as Sinner in Contemporary American Realistic Theology* (King's Crown Press, 1946), especially pp. 54–59.

16. H. R. Niebuhr, "Religious Realism in the Twentieth Century," *Religious Realism*, D. C. Macintosh, ed. (The Macmillan Company, 1931), pp. 418–419. According to Macintosh, writing in

the same volume, the object in religious realism that is independent is "a religious object such as may appropriately be called God, existing independently of our consciousness thereof" (p. v).

17. Thelen is helpful in pointing up the difference between "religious realism" and "realistic theology." The former is to be identified primarily with the short-lived group writing in *Religious Realism* (1931), while the latter has to do with the more permanent mood that came over American liberals in the 1930's, reflected especially in the "theological discussion group" of that decade. However, there are points at which the two movements overlap. Both were critical of the liberalism of previous decades. Both included to some degree the same persons, and both had the common background of postdepression, realistic temper.

18. Emil Brunner, "Continental European Theology," Cavert and Van Dusen, *op. cit.*, pp. 140–141.

19. The main stages of American fundamentalism are three: (1) pre World War I, from its beginnings in the Bible conferences of 1877 culminating in *The Fundamentals* of 1909–1911; (2) a post World War I resurgence around such names as E. Y. Mullins, F. L. Patton, and J. G. Machen, with William Jennings Bryan and the Scopes trial serving as the central symbol of the fundamentalist cause; (3) post World War II, which saw the rise of "neo-fundamentalism" in its varying shades, especially seen in Carl Henry, Edward Carnell, and C. Van Til, all writing from the 1940's on.

20. See Thelen, *op. cit.*, for an analysis of Marx and Freud as important factors in the background of American realistic theology.

21. McGiffert, *The Rise of Modern Religious Ideas*, p. 206.

22. In addition to the writings of the existentialists themselves, two books are especially fine guides. David Roberts' *Existentialism and Religious Belief* (Oxford University Press, 1957) contains excellent studies of the major existentialists, while Helmuth Kuhn's *Encounter with Nothingness* (Henry Regnery Company, 1949), is one of the best analyses of the major motifs of existentialism.

23. Karl Jaspers, *Reason and Existenz* (Noonday Paperbacks, 1957), pp. 51 ff. Also Martin Heidegger, "The Way Back Into the Ground of Metaphysics," *Contemporary Philosophic Problems*, W. H. Kirkorian and Abraham Edel, eds. (The Macmillan Company, 1959).

24. The writings of Martin Buber are the most relevant examples of this movement. See especially *I and Thou* (Charles Scribner's Sons,

1937) and *Between Man and Man* (The Macmillan Company, 1948). For an attempt to found a " Christian philosophy " on the category of the " singular," see J. V. Langmead-Casserley, *The Christian in Philosophy* (Faber & Faber, Ltd., London, 1951), pp. 177 ff.

25. See especially Ch. IV of his *God and the Common Life* (Charles Scribner's Sons, 1935). For a summary of Calhoun's views on transcendence, see Thelen, *op. cit.*, pp. 129-132.

26. Robert L. Calhoun, " The Semi-Detached Knower," *The Nature of Religious Experience,* J. S. Bixler, ed. (Harper & Brothers, 1937), p. 182.

27. Examples of such metaphysics would be Henri Bergson, *Creative Evolution* (Random House, Inc., 1944); Lloyd Morgan, *Emergent Evolution* (Henry Holt & Co., Inc., 1927); and Alfred North Whitehead, *Process and Reality* (The Humanities Press, 1955).

28. T. E. Hulme, *Speculations* (Kegan Paul, Trench, Trubner & Company, London, 1924), p. 4.

29. H. P. Van Dusen, *The Plain Man Seeks for God* (Charles Scribner's Sons, 1933), p. 104.

30. William Temple, *Nature, Man, and God* (The Macmillan Company, London, 1935).

31. See Rudolf Otto, *The Idea of the Holy* (Oxford University Press, London, 1923).

32. See W. R. Inge, *Christian Mysticism* (1898); Baron Friedrich von Hügel, *The Mystical Element in Religion* (1908); Evelyn Underhill, *Mysticism* (1911); Rudolf Otto, *Mysticism East and West* (1926); and Rufus Jones, *Studies in Mystical Religion* (1919).

33. John Dillenberger, *God Hidden and Revealed* (Muhlenberg Press, 1953).

34. Emil Brunner, *loc. cit.*, pp. 139-140.

35. Walther Eichrodt, *Man in the Old Testament* (S.C.M. Press, Ltd., London, 1951), especially pp. 9-27.

36. See especially John Bennett, " After Liberalism — What? " *The Christian Century,* L, Part 2 (Nov. 8, 1933); Harry Emerson Fosdick, " Beyond Modernism," *The Christian Century* (Dec. 4, 1935); Henry Sloane Coffin, " Can Liberalism Survive? " *Religion in Life* (1955); G. G. Atkins " Whither Liberalism? " *Religion in Life* (1934); and H. P. Van Dusen, " The Sickness of Liberal Religion," *The World Tomorrow* (Aug., 1931).

37. For descriptions of this impasse, see Gabriel Widmer, " Orien-

tations actuelles de la dogmatique réformée," *Revue de Théologie et de Philosophie* (1958, I); Robert B. Cushman, " Barth's Attack Upon Cartesianism and the Future of Theology," *Journal of Religion* (Oct., 1956); Hermann Diem, *Dogmatics* (The Westminster Press, 1960), pp. 80–81; and Hans Frei, " The Theology of Richard Niebuhr," *Faith and Ethics,* Paul Ramsey, ed. (Harper & Brothers, 1957), p. 75.

Chapter II   Reinhold Niebuhr

1. See Reinhold Niebuhr, *Does Civilization Need Religion?* (The Macmillan Company, 1927), pp. 51 and 238.
2. Reinhold Niebuhr, *Beyond Tragedy* (Charles Scribner's Sons, 1937), Chs. 3 and 4.
3. See Reinhold Niebuhr, *The Self and the Dramas of History* (Charles Scribner's Sons, 1955), Ch. 4.
4. Reinhold Niebuhr, *The Nature and Destiny of Man* (Charles Scribner's Sons, 1951), I, p. 14. Quotations from this book are used by permission of the publisher.
5. *Ibid.,* II, p. 66.
6. For Niebuhr's fullest analysis of the " self," see *The Self and the Dramas of History,* especially Ch. 5.
7. Reinhold Niebuhr, *Christianity and Power Politics* (Charles Scribner's Sons, 1940), pp. 182–183.
8. Charles W. Kegley and Robert W. Bretall, eds., *Reinhold Niebuhr: His Religious, Social, and Political Thought* (The Macmillan Company, 1956), p. 299.
9. Reinhold Niebuhr, *Nature and Destiny,* II, p. 299.
10. This exposition of Niebuhr's view of ontology leans heavily on his *The Self and the Dramas of History* and the Niebuhr-Tillich exchange in the first two volumes of the Library of Living Theology on the thought of each man.
11. Reinhold Niebuhr, *The Self and the Dramas,* p. 94.
12. *Ibid.*
13. Charles W. Kegley and Robert W. Bretall, *The Theology of Paul Tillich* (The Macmillan Company, 1952), p. 217.
14. Kegley and Bretall, *Reinhold Niebuhr,* p. 433.
15. Niebuhr's fullest elaborations of this problem are found in two of his essays: " Coherence, Incoherence, and the Christian Faith," *Christian Realism and Political Problems* (Charles Scribner's Sons,

1953), and "Mystery and Meaning," *Pious and Secular America* (Charles Scribner's Sons, 1958).

16. Reinhold Niebuhr, *Christian Realism and Political Problems,* p. 203.

17. Christian Wolff originally coined the term "ontology," and this is his definition. See "Ontology," *a Dictionary of Religion and Ethics,* Shailer Mathews and Gerald B. Smith, eds. (The Macmillan Company, 1921).

18. Reinhold Niebuhr, *Nature and Destiny,* I, p. 86.

19. *Ibid.,* pp. 126, 131, and 165.

20. *Ibid.,* p. 57.

21. For Niebuhr's doctrine of meaning see his *Christianity and Power Politics,* pp. 181–183; *Nature and Destiny,* I, pp. 141, 164, and 168; II, p. 299; *Faith and History* (Charles Scribner's Sons, 1949), pp. 27, 45–46, and 103; *Discerning the Signs of the Times* (Charles Scribner's Sons, 1946), pp. 97, 160; *The Self and the Dramas,* Ch. 12, also pp. 62, 80, 225, and 237; *Pious and Secular America,* Ch. 9. See also D. D. Williams' article on Niebuhr in Kegley and Bretall, *Reinhold Niebuhr,* pp. 206–207.

22. Reinhold Niebuhr, *Faith and History,* p. 45.

23. Reinhold Niebuhr, *Nature and Destiny,* II, p. 299.

24. Niebuhr's most elaborate treatment of history is in his work *Faith and History.* See also *The Self and the Dramas.*

25. Reinhold Niebuhr, *Faith and History,* p. 55.

26. Reinhold Niebuhr, *Nature and Destiny,* II, p. 1. See also his *Beyond Tragedy,* p. 200.

27. For Niebuhr's view of nature, see his *Beyond Tragedy,* p. 95; *Nature and Destiny,* I, pp. 26, 54; *The Self and the Dramas,* Ch. 17, also p. 45.

28. Reinhold Niebuhr, *Beyond Tragedy,* p. 293. See also his *Nature and Destiny,* I, p. 3; II, p. 20; and *The Self and the Dramas,* p. 45.

29. However, we should note a different and nontypical use of the term "nature" when he contrasts nature and grace. (*Nature and Destiny,* II, p. 246, and elsewhere.)

30. Reinhold Niebuhr, *An Interpretation of Christian Ethics* (Harper & Brothers, 1935), p. 17.

31. Reinhold Niebuhr, *The Self and the Dramas,* pp. 28, 33, and 142. See also his *Pious and Secular America,* Ch. 9, where Niebuhr

lists such facts as basic "mysteries."

32. Reinhold Niebuhr, *Christian Ethics*, p. 32. See also Kegley and Bretall, *Reinhold Niebuhr*, p. 10.

33. For passages on God as Source and Ground see the following: "Christian Faith in the Modern World," *Ventures in Belief*, H. P. Van Dusen, ed. (The Macmillan Company, 1952), p. 17; Niebuhr, *Christian Ethics*, pp. 15 and 33; *Beyond Tragedy*, pp. 3 ff.; *Christian Realism and Political Problems*, p. 187; *Nature and Destiny*, I, p. 141; II, p. 299; *Reflections on the End of an Era* (Charles Scribner's Sons, 1934), pp. 183 and 185. This vocabulary of the Absolute, the Ultimate, and the Ground begins in Niebuhr in 1934, a year after Tillich joined Niebuhr at Union Seminary, possibly indicating real influence on Tillich's part.

34. Actually, the two strains in Niebuhr's thought are not neatly separated. Therefore, in several passages he mentions the threefold scheme of transcendence: Creator, Judge, and Redeemer. (*Christian Ethics*, p. 39, and *Nature and Destiny*, I, p. 132.) In attempting to isolate the two strains, the point is not that they are two conflicting views of transcendence, but that in the one case, God's transcendence confronts ethical and religious realities, and in the other, it is used to address a traditional ontological problem.

35. Reinhold Niebuhr, *Nature and Destiny*, I, p. 169.

36. George Hammar, *Christian Realism in Contemporary American Theology* (Lundequistska Bokhandeln, Uppsala, 1940), p. 249.

37. The term "Hellenistic" (or "Platonic") is used here to denote not just any eternal-temporal distinction, but rather the way of distinguishing them by making the eternal a fixed, changeless, realm, classically expressed not by Plato but in Parmenides' *Way of Truth*.

38. Reinhold Niebuhr, *Nature and Destiny*, I, p. 169.

39. *Ibid.*, p. 126 (italics mine).

40. Reinhold Niebuhr, *Faith and History*, p. 137.

41. Reinhold Niebuhr, *Nature and Destiny*, II, p. 61.

42. Reinhold Niebuhr, *Discerning the Signs of the Times*, p. 97. Niebuhr calls this "the transection of every moment by the eternal."

43. Reinhold Niebuhr, *Nature and Destiny*, II, p. 56, also p. 46. Niebuhr's *Discerning the Signs*, pp. 119 and 177 ff.

44. Hammar, *op. cit.*, p. 249.

45. Kegley and Bretall, *Reinhold Niebuhr*, p. 448.

Chapter III Paul Tillich

1. With the exception of Tillich's early theses, some important articles in *Die Religion in Geschichte und Gegenwart*, 2d ed., and his "Religionsphilosophie" (1925), most of his early writings are translated into English. See his *The Interpretation of History* (Charles Scribner's Sons, 1936); *The Protestant Era* (University of Chicago Press, 1948); and *The Religious Situation* (Meridian Books, Inc., 1956).
2. Tillich, *Interpretation of History*, p. 108.
3. *Ibid.*, p. 109.
4. For Tillich's early treatment of the Unconditioned, see his *Religious Situation*, especially the Introduction and Part Three; also pp. 35, 93, 147, 160, and 176.
5. Tillich, *Protestant Era*, p. xx.
6. *Ibid.*, p. 163.
7. At this point we are following John Laird, who defines hypertheism as the belief that "the evidence which leads to God also leads beyond him." In short, God is beyond the "God" pictured in ordinary theism and hence is *hyper*theistic. See Laird's "Theism and Hypertheism," *Harvard Theological Review*, XXXVI (Jan., 1943), pp. 70 ff.
8. For Tillich's characterizations of ontology, see his *Systematic Theology* (University of Chicago Press, 1951), I, pp. 18, 166; *Biblical Religion and the Search for Ultimate Reality* (University of Chicago Press, 1955), pp. 7–8; *The Dynamics of Faith* (Harper & Brothers, 1957), p. 90; and *Love, Power, and Justice* (Oxford University Press, 1954), pp. 19–20, 23.
9. This, too, comes out of German idealism after the fashion of the later Schelling. After Schelling rejected not only Hegel and Fichte but his own early "philosophy of identity," he never again admitted that actuality was reducible to either the subjective or objective side. Both are always necessary. This is found in his dual epistemology in the *Weltalter* where he posits both a knowledge of union and vision as well as that of external norms. See Friedrich Schelling, *The Ages of the World* (Columbia University Press, 1942), p. 89.
10. Tillich, *Systematic Theology*, I, p. 163.
11. Tillich, *Biblical Religion*, pp. 49 and 9. See also "Being and

NOTES 231

Love," *Moral Principles of Action,* Ruth N. Anshen, ed. (Harper & Brothers, 1952), p. 661; also Tillich's *Protestant Era,* p. 85.

12. Tillich, *The Courage to Be* (Yale University Press, 1952), p. 25.

13. Tillich, *Biblical Religion,* p. 49. The original source of this phrase seems to be Leibniz's *Principles of Nature and Grace Founded on Reason.* See Thomas S. Knight, "Why Not Nothing?" *Review of Metaphysics,* X (Sept., 1956). For Tillich, the more immediate source would be Schelling, *Sämtliche Werke,* II, 3:7, and Heidegger, "What Is Metaphysics?" *Existence and Being* (Vision Press, Ltd., London, 1949), p. 380.

14. Tillich's thought has varied somewhat at this point. He first said that "ground" was the term intended to avoid symbolic connotations. (*Systematic Theology,* I, p. 156.) Later, admitting that "ground" was a symbol, he still insisted that being-itself was not. (Kegley and Bretall, *Paul Tillich,* p. 335.) His most recent statement is the most complex where he says such terms carry both symbolic and nonsymbolic overtones. They "designate the boundary line at which both the symbolic and nonsymbolic coincide." (*Systematic Theology,* II, p. 10.) Tillich's point is that such statements are ecstatic" and are made from a participation in being-itself, and this participation is the "nonsymbolic point." The change here is that while no particular term is itself nonsymbolic, they can function to designate the nonsymbolic aspect of the divine.

15. Schelling, *The Ages of the World,* p. 210.

16. *Ibid.,* p. 105.

17. Tillich, "Religious Symbols and Our Knowledge of God," *The Christian Scholar,* XXXVIII (Sept., 1955), p. 93.

18. "Epistemology and the Idea of Revelation," Kegley and Bretall, *Paul Tillich,* p. 209.

19. For Tillich's analysis of the personal, see his "The Idea and the Ideal of Personality," *Protestant Era,* pp. 63, 116–118 (originally *Religiöse Verwirklichung,* 1929); also, *Biblical Religion,* pp. 23, 28–29; *Systematic Theology,* I, pp. 176–177; and "The Christian Consummation: A Conversation," *The Chaplain,* XIII (April, 1956), p. 11.

20. Tillich, *Biblical Religion,* p. 83. Tillich's treatment of the personal God still contains an elusive feature. *What* is it that is personal in Tillich's view of self-determining freedom? Is God personal in the sense that as *ground* of being he is personal, even though sym-

bolically? Or is he personal in the sense that he "grounds" all personal beings who are thus somehow "in" him? It seems Tillich would deny that the ground of being-itself has self-determining freedom even symbolically, for he says in *Biblical Religion* (p. 24) that the personal applies not to the holy but to the bearers of the holy.

21. *Ibid.*, pp. 74–75.

22. Tillich, *Systematic Theology*, I, p. 263. See also II, pp. 7–8.

23. Some interpreters of Tillich who attempt to see his theology in terms of some sort of "synthesis" principle or in the framework of an "identity" ontology of the Hegelian type are the following: Hendrik Kraemer, *Religion and the Christian Faith* (The Westminster Press, 1957), pp. 427 ff.; Robert C. Johnson, *Authority in Protestant Theology* (The Westminster Press, 1959), Ch. 5; Hans Frei, "Niebuhr's Theological Background," *Faith and Ethics,* Ramsey, ed. pp. 34–35; and Arthur C. Cochrane, *The Existentialists and God* (The Westminster Press, 1956), pp. 79, 94, 98.

24. Tillich, *Die religionsgeschichtliche Konstruktion in Schellings positiver Philosophie* (1910) and *Mystik und Schuldbewusstsein in Schellings philosophischer Entwicklung* (1912).

25. Schelling, *Der transcendentale Idealismus* (1800) and *Darstellung meines Systems der Philosophie* (1801).

26. Hegel, *The Science of Logic* (The Macmillan Company, 1929), Vol. II, pp. 161–162.

27. Hegel, *The Phenomenology of Mind* (George Allen & Unwin Ltd., London, 1949), p. 79; "the night in which . . . all cows are black."

28. Hegel's term "transcend" (*Aufheben*) means to surpass by both canceling out and including. One might say that God, the Absolute, transcends in the sense of a reality that gathers up and includes all things.

29. For an excellent exposition of Hegel's philosophy of religion, see Karl Barth, *From Rousseau to Ritschl* (S.C.M. Press, Ltd., London, 1959), Ch. 7.

30. For an excellent account of how freedom became a central feature in Schelling's thought, see James Gutmann, translator and editor of Schelling's *Of Human Freedom* (The Open Court Publishing Company, 1936), Introduction.

31. Tillich, *Systematic Theology*, II, p. 14.

32. *Ibid.*, pp. 15–16.

33. One important qualification is due here. Tillich has distinguished between the *principle* of correlation and the way it is worked out in a particular theology. (*Systematic Theology,* II, p. 16.) And he has wisely said that there is no absolute safeguard that one side or the other may not be employed in such a way as to obscure revelation. But this merely stresses that theology itself has its being in existence, and will reflect estrangement. One might well find in Tillich's actual way of working this out eclecticism, synthesis, varieties of norms, etc. My own view is that Tillich's " hypertheism " is used by him to judge the given revelation. But this is not the intention or an inevitability in the method of correlation.

Chapter IV Karl Heim

1. For a good summary of the cult of German Faith, see Paul F. Douglass, *God Among the Germans* (University of Pennsylvania Press, 1936), especially Ch. V, and Walter Marshall Horton, *Contemporary Continental Theology* (Harper & Brothers, 1938), pp. 113–127.

2. For this material see Karl Heim, *The Transformation of the Scientific World View* (S.C.M. Press, Ltd., London, 1953), Chs. II, III, and IV.

3. See Heim, *God Transcendent* (James Nisbet & Co., Ltd., London, 1935), pp. 190–192. Quotations from this book are used by permission of the publisher.

4. For this more " personal " way of putting the problem, see Heim, *Christian Faith* and *Natural Science* (S.C.M. Press, Ltd., London, 1953), pp. 179 ff.

5. Heim, *Christian Faith,* pp. 160 ff. and 230 ff.; also his *Transformation,* p. 15.

6. For Heim's treatment of this problem, see *God Transcendent,* Chs. II–V; also *Christian Faith,* Ch. II.

7. It is true that Heim differs with Kant at several points: for compartmentalizing religious problems in his notion of the pure practical reason (Heim, *The New Divine Order* [S.C.M. Press, Ltd., London, 1930], p. 17), on the doctrine of the *Ding an sich* (Heim, *God Transcendent,* p. 47), and on his view of space and time as subjective conditions of our intuitions (Heim, *Christian Faith,* pp. 126–127). Nevertheless, Heim derives his view of the ego as an unre-

ducible subjective reality from Kant and Fichte, especially retaining Kant's epistemological conclusions, since Kant saw a great gulf fixed between the observing ego and the observable world (*ibid.*, pp. 112-113).

8. See Josiah Royce, *Lectures in Modern Idealism* (Yale University Press, 1919), Ch. II, where Royce traces the development of the doctrine of the Self in idealism out of problems within Kant's epistemology. When this was developed in Fichte and the early Schelling, it centered around two problems (Royce, *Lectures*, Ch. III), that of the significant Self rising above destiny, and the invisible realm of ideals and truths in which the Self was immersed. In Schelling, according to Royce, Nature is "the self taken as object," p. 104, but the Self was nonobjective.

9. Heim, *God Transcendent*, p. 86.

10. Bergson's way of putting this is that when the intellect attempts to grasp the world, it turns a fluid reality into a series of images; it breaks up the flow into discrete units for analysis and measurement. See Bergson, *Creative Mind* (Philosophical Library, Inc., 1946), pp. 190 ff. See also Oswald Spengler, *The Decline of the West* (Alfred A. Knopf, Inc., 1929), Vol. I, pp. 152-153.

11. Heim, *God Transcendent*, Ch. II.

12. These characteristics of "dimensional" differentiation are somewhat technical. They are (1) dimensional differentiation is between "spaces" not contents; (2) where there is unity and difference, such does not concern contents but "perspectives"; (3) whole-part relations take on a qualitative rather than merely quantitative change whenever a part is affected; (4) contact and separation differ between contents and "dimensions"; (5) the mode of knowing dimensional differentiations is different from knowing content differentiation. See Heim, *God Transcendent*, pp. 60 ff.

13. Heim, *God Transcendent*, p. 60. Other definitions of space Heim gives are: "an infinite continuum within which contents may find their place according to a principle of order inherent in the structure itself," *God Transcendent*, p. 125; also, "the form in which the whole of reality or else a part of it presents itself to a particular subject, or else a group of subjects, with which this reality enters a relation," *Christian Faith*, pp. 133-134.

14. See Heim, *Christian Faith*, Sec. 13.

15. Heim, *Christian Faith*, p. 140.

NOTES 235

16. Heim's panpsychist view of nature has one common root with that of Hartshorne's panpsychism, namely, the *Zendavesta* of Gustav Fechner.

17. Heim, *Christian Faith,* pp. 90–91. See also Heim, *Transformation,* pp. 62 ff., 174, and 229. The basis of positing this analogy of inner life at all levels is Heim's view that there is a principle of continuity, a wholeness-law (*Ganzheitstendenz*) running throughout nature.

18. In Heim, *God Transcendent* (p. 189), we find a less existentialist and more traditional version of this question, "Why does Reality have the character it has? Whence comes this universe? How may Reality be explained?"

19. Heim, *Christian Faith,* pp. 178–179.

20. See Heim, *God Transcendent,* pp. 207 ff., for a summary of this either-or.

21. See Heim, *God Transcendent,* Ch. VII.

22. Heim, *God Transcendent,* p. 16.

23. See Heim, *Christian Faith,* Ch. III.

24. Heim, *God Transcendent,* p. 217 (italics mine). See also pp. 77 and 211.

25. Dorothy Emmett, *The Nature of Metaphysical Thinking* (The Macmillan Company, London, 1953), p. 211.

26. Heim, *Christian Faith,* p. 205.

27. Heim, *God Transcendent,* p. 43.

28. Heim, *Christian Faith,* p. 152.

29. *Ibid.,* pp. 159 ff., and also Heim, *Transformation,* pp. 107–108 and 151.

30. Heim, *Transformation,* p. 107.

31. Maurice Friedman says that Heim turns Buber's doctrine into an "unqualified transcendence" of God. See *Martin Buber: The Life of Dialogue* (University of Chicago Press, 1955), p. 227. Harold Schulweiss also remarks that "the breach between man and God is complete in Heim." See "Crisis Theology and Martin Buber," *Review of Religion,* XIV (Nov., 1949), p. 39.

32. Heim, *Christian Faith,* p. 169.

33. *Ibid.,* p. 164.

34. Therefore one aspect of Heim's doctrine of transcendence is the traditional doctrine of *deus absconditus* especially applied to God's essence in *via negativa* fashion. Thus it is not surprising to

find Heim subscribing to the *nunc aeternum* doctrine of the relation between God and time. " The power that assigns this moment to me, as my ' now ', must itself transcend past, present, and future." (Heim, *Transformation,* p. 112.) A question might be raised, however, whether this is consistent with Heim's view that God is an all-embracing space, as well as a contemporaneous Thou. If even an aspect of God is a " space," in which all spaces and contents are gathered, one would think that their time would be real for God, and that he would not merely be transcendently related to their present.

35. Heim, *Transformation,* p. 155.
36. Heim, *God Transcendent,* p. 218.

Chapter V   Charles Hartshorne

1. For a recent study of this problem in the formative (patristic) period of Christian theology, with particular attention to the way the doctrine of the Trinity was meant to solve the problem, see Cyril C. Richardson, *The Doctrine of the Trinity* (Abingdon Press, 1958).

2. Hartshorne's historical analysis of orthodox theism is found in his *Man's Vision of God and the Logic of Theism* (Willett, Clark & Company, 1941), Ch. 3; *Reality as Social Process* (Free Press, 1953), pp. 23-24; and the commentary material in *Philosophers Speak of God,* William L. Reese, coeditor (University of Chicago Press, 1953).

3. Ontolatry is the worship of being over against becoming. (Hartshorne, *Philosophers Speak of God,* p. 24.) Etiolatry is " the worship of cause as against effect, sources rather than consummations, power rather than achievement." (Hartshorne, " Process as Inclusive Category: A Reply," *Journal of Philosophy,* LII [Feb. 17, 1955], p. 98.)

4. Hartshorne, *The Divine Relativity* (Yale University Press, 1948), p. 43.

5. Hartshorne's writings on humanism fall primarily in the 1930's and reflect the issues of the humanist controversy that was going on at the time. See Hartshorne, *Beyond Humanism* (Willett, Clark & Company, 1937), especially Part I. See also his *Reality,* Chs. 11, 12, and 13. Hartshorne uses the term " humanism " in a sense broad enough to include ancient traditions such as Greek skepticism and epicureanism, epoch makers such as Marx and Freud, and naturalists of the stripe of Dewey, Santayana, Russell, and G. E. Moore.

6. For Hartshorne's various attempts to find an exhaustive logical scheme by which to interpret theistic alternatives, see his *Man's Vision of God*, pp. 6 ff.; *Philosophers Speak of God,* pp. 13 ff.; and "Whitehead's Idea of God," *The Philosophy of Alfred North Whitehead*, Paul A. Schilpp, ed. (Tudor Publishing Company, 1951).

7. Such is Hartshorne's earlier and basic analysis (*Man's Vision of God*). Later versions of it (as in *Philosophers Speak of God*) are much more complex in that he extends the same threefold alternative to the doctrines of God as creative, temporal, eternal, conscious, ominiscient, etc.

8. Hartshorne's labels for his view have been many. In *Beyond Humanism* (1937), he spoke of a "new theism," a "naturalistic theism," and even a "theistic pantheism," p. 67. In *Divine Relativity*, he introduced the term "surrelativism" to stress his theism of a God who was supremely relative. The usual designation, however, is the term coined by Friedrich Krause (d. 1832), "panentheism."

9. Possibly the best introduction to Whitehead's metaphysics is his *Modes of Thought* (The Macmillan Company, 1938). Also relevant are *Adventures of Ideas* (New American Library of World Literature, Inc., 1955), Part III; *Science and the Modern World* (New American Library of World Literature, Inc., 1948), Chs. 10 and 11. Whitehead's mature statement is, of course, *Process and Reality*. A good and recent secondary source is William Christian, *An Interpretation of Whitehead's Metaphysics* (Yale University Press, 1959).

10. Whitehead, *Science and the Modern World*, p. 94.

11. Whitehead, *Religion in the Making* (The Macmillan Company, 1926), pp. 98–99.

12. *Ibid.,* p. 90.

13. Whitehead, *Process and Reality*, p. 522.

14. Hartshorne's metaphysics, his doctrine of nature, process, etc., are most fully set out in the articles in his *Reality as Social Process*. In addition see his *Beyond Humanism*, Chs. 8–12; *Man's Vision of God*, Chs. 5 and 7; and "Process as Inclusive Category: A Reply."

15. Hartshorne, "Time, Death, and Eternal Life," *Journal of Religion*, XXXII (April, 1952), p. 99; and "The Divine Relativity and Absoluteness: A Reply," *Review of Metaphysics*, IV (Sept., 1950), p. 32.

16. "Chance, Love, and Incompatibility," Ch. 5 of Hartshorne's *Reality*.
17. The main passages in Hartshorne showing forth his panpsychism are Ch. 8, "The Cosmic Variables," and Ch. 11, "Mind and Matter," *Beyond Humanism*. See also, *Reality*, Chs. 1, 2, and 4; *Man's Vision of God*, Ch. 6; and "Organic and Inorganic Wholes," *Philosophy and Phenomenological Research*, III (Dec., 1942).
18. Hartshorne, "The Idea of God — Literal or Analogical?" *The Christian Scholar*, XXXIX (June, 1956), pp. 135–136.
19. Hartshorne, "The Formal Validity and Real Significance of the Ontological Argument," *Philosophical Review*, LIII (May 1944), p. 240. See also Hartshorne, *Man's Vision of God*, p. 107.
20. Hartshorne, *Reality*, p. 160. See also his *Man's Vision of God*, p. 111.
21. Hartshorne, *Divine Relativity*, p. 7.
22. *Ibid.*, p. 71.
23. Hartshorne, *Reality*, p. 135.
24. Robert L. Calhoun, "How Far Beyond Humanism," *Christendom*, III (Autumn, 1938), p. 565.
25. John Wild, "A Review of *The Divine Relativity*," *Review of Metaphysics*, II (Dec., 1948), p. 76.
26. Hartshorne, *Reality*, p. 113. Other synonyms Hartshorne uses for superiority are supremacy, and also the verb, to surpass.
27. Hartshorne, *Man's Vision of God*, p. 47.
28. *Ibid.*, p. 221.
29. See Hartshorne, "Tillich's Doctrine of God," Kegley and Bretall, *Paul Tillich*, and Tillich's reply, *ibid.*, pp. 334 ff. Hartshorne's rebuttal is found in "Process as Inclusive Category: A Reply."
30. Hartshorne's unusual use of the term "literal" should be noted. He means by "literal," "a complete instance of," hence only God literally (perfectly, completely) loves, knows, creates, etc. (Hartshorne, *Divine Relativity*, p. 36.) Thus "literal" in Hartshorne is akin to an ideal instance or universal. Such certainly varies from the usual meaning of the term where concrete, spatial-temporal human experience is the controlling context.
31. Hartshorne, *Divine Relativity*, p. 125. See also his *Beyond Humanism*, p. 52.
32. This distinction comes from Whitehead who contrasted the Primordial Nature as the eternal with the Consequent Nature as the

NOTES 239

everlasting. (Whitehead, *Process and Reality*, p. 524.)

33. Hartshorne, "Whitehead and Berdyaev: Is There Tragedy in God?" *Journal of Religion*, XXXVII (April, 1957), p. 79.

34. Hartshorne, *Divine Relativity*, p. 76. See also his "The Divine Relativity and Absoluteness: A Reply," *loc. cit.*, p. 34.

35. Hartshorne, *Divine Relativity*, p. 66.

Chapter VI   Henry Nelson Wieman

1. See the writings of Shailer Mathews in this period: *The Gospel and Modern Man* (The Macmillan Company, 1910) and *The Faith of Modernism* (The Macmillan Company, 1924). Also, the writings of Gerald Birney Smith: *Social Idealism and the Changing Theology* (The Macmillan Company, 1913) and *A Guide to the Study of the Christian Religion* (University of Chicago Press, 1916), Ch. IX.

2. The "Chicago School" has connotations in several not unrelated contexts. The most inclusive is that group formed by Albion Small, Dewey, Tufts, Mead, and Veblen, all of whom applied democratic theory to various dimensions of society: economics, education, metaphysics, ethics, etc. In the context of philosophy of religion, however, the Chicago School comprised that group which championed both empirical and social interpretations of religion at Chicago from about 1921 on. Important in the early period were Walter Rauschenbusch, Shailer Mathews, Shirley Jackson Case, Gerald B. Smith, and Edward S. Ames. At a later stage, Wieman became the dominant figure in a group that included Eugene W. Meland and Bernard Loomer.

3. Gerald B. Smith, *Current Christian Thinking* (University of Chicago Press, 1928), p. 168.

4. Mathews, *The Faith of Modernism*, p. 115.

5. For biographical information on Wieman see the following: "Theocentric Religion," *Contemporary American Theology*, Vergilius Ferm, ed. (Round Table Press, Inc., 1932), I; "Some Blind Spots Removed," *The Christian Century*, LVI (Jan. 25, 1939); and the yet unpublished "Intellectual Autobiography" written for the Library of Living Theology.

6. The two teachers influential on Wieman at Park were Silas

Evans and Ernest McAfee. It was especially Evans who introduced Wieman to Royce's philosophy.

7. For a description of this "cultural" problem, see Henry Nelson Wieman, *Now We Must Choose* (The Macmillan Company, 1941); *The Source of Human Good* (University of Chicago Press, 1946), Ch. 2; and *Man's Ultimate Commitment* (Southern Illinois University Press, 1958), especially Chs. 1–3, and 14.

8. For Wieman's treatment of neo-supernaturalism, see *American Philosophies of Religion*, E. W. Meland, coauthor (Willett, Clark & Company, 1936), Ch. 5; "The Theology of Karl Barth," *The Christian Century*, LX (Feb. 7, 1934); "The New Supernaturalism," *Christendom*, III (Winter, 1938); and *The Growth of Religion*, W. M. Horton, coauthor (Willett, Clark & Company, 1938), Ch. 8.

9. "Theocentric Religion," *Contemporary American Theology*, Ferm, ed., p. 346.

10. Wieman's fullest treatment of the doctrine of knowledge and its related notions of truth, scientific method, etc., is found in his *Source of Human Good*, Ch. 8. See also Wieman's *The Wrestle of Religion with Truth* (The Macmillan Company, 1927), Introduction, Sec. 5; *Religious Experience and Scientific Method* (The Macmillan Company, 1927), Chs. 1, 2, 6, and 12; *Growth of Religion*, Ch. 13; and *The Issues of Life* (Abingdon Press, 1930), Ch. 7.

11. Wieman, *Source of Human Good*, p. 197.

12. Wieman, *Wrestle of Religion*, p. 213.

13. Wieman, "Can God Be Perceived?" *Journal of Religion*, XXIII (Jan., 1943), p. 26.

14. Wieman, *Source of Human Good*, p. 164.

15. *Ibid.*, p. 201.

16. For Wieman's concept of value, see his "Values: Primary Data for Religious Inquiry," *Journal of Religion*, XVI (Oct., 1936); "God and Value," *Religious Realism*, Macintosh, ed., pp. 155–179; *The Directive in History* (The Beacon Press, Inc., 1949), Ch. 1; *Source of Human Good*, Part I; and *Man's Ultimate Commitment*, Chs. 5 and 6.

17. Wieman, "Values: Primary Data," *loc. cit.*, pp. 392–398.

18. Wieman, *Source of Human Good*, p. 18.

19. Since *Source of Human Good* remains Wieman's most elab-

orate philosophical statement, his contextualist and operationalist metaphysics is to be found there. See also his *Man's Ultimate Commitment*, Ch. 4. For his earlier metaphysics see his *Wrestle of Religion*, Chs. 9–11; and the article, "What I Believe About the World," *Ventures in Belief*.

20. Like "new orthodoxy" the term "new naturalism" is not unambiguous. Negatively speaking, it refers to all nonreductive and nonmaterialistic naturalism; however, such criteria tend to be vague. The clearest manifesto of new naturalism is probably *Naturalism and the Human Spirit*, Y. H. Kirkorian, ed. (Columbia University Press, 1944). However, the new naturalism of Wieman seems to be a combination of two basic strands: (1) Process philosophy (Whitehead, Bergson, and Alexander) with its openness to metaphysics. Such would differentiate new naturalism from logical empiricism at least in temper. (2) Pragmatism or operationalism (especially Peirce, Dewey, and Mead), which tones down the speculative side of metaphysics.

21. In the sense Stephen C. Pepper uses it in *World Hypotheses* (University of California Press, 1942), Ch. 10.

22. This shift is especially illustrated in Wieman, *Man's Ultimate Commitment*, where Wieman makes his most explicit attempt to apply his philosophy of religion to society's institutions and their problems.

23. Wieman, *Source of Human Good*, pp. 105–106.

24. Wieman, "God Is More than We Can Think," *Christendom*, I (Spring, 1936), p. 440.

25. This analysis of an event into qualities and strands is found in Wieman, *The Directive in History*, pp. 15–16. Here Wieman defines quality as "the conjunction of all the strands necessary to the occurrence of the quality," p. 8.

26. *Ibid.*, pp. 14 and 21. See also Wieman, *Source of Human Good*, pp. 302–303.

27. Pepper, *World Hypotheses*, p. 238.

28. This would involve the detailed procedures Wieman outlines in *Methods of Private Religious Living* (The Macmillan Company, 1929) and in *Growth of Religion*. His contention is that God can be "perceived," but as in all refined perception, it is a matter of developing proper habits of sensitivity by which that elusive and

complex set of events which is God can be grasped. Thus God while perceivable is not immediately or easily available to everyone. Similarly, such processes as evolution or atomic energy were not perceived for centuries. See "Can God Be Perceived?"

29. See Wieman, "The Power and Goodness of God," *Journal of Religion*, XXIII (Oct., 1943), pp. 267 ff.

30. Wieman, *Wrestle of Religion*, p. 59.

31. Terminologically, various stages are apparent in Wieman's definitions of God, and the tendency is from a vocabulary of inclusiveness in the early Wieman (God as "total object," "total event") to a more specified type of event or process such as creative event or creative interchange.

32. Wieman, *Methods of Private Religious Living*, p. 22.

33. "God and Value," *Religious Realism*, Macintosh, ed., p. 159. See also Wieman, "Faith and Knowledge," *Christendom*, I (Autumn, 1936), p. 773.

34. Wieman, *Wrestle of Religion*, p. 194.

35. See Charles William Morris, *Foundations of the Theory of Signs* (University of Chicago Press, 1938).

36. See the Calhoun-Wieman debate in *Christendom*, 1936 and 1937, where Calhoun labels Wieman the "prophet of God's immanence." See also H. H. Farmer, "Some Reflections on Wieman's New Book," *Journal of Religion*, XXVII (April, 1947), pp. 117–119; and Charles Hartshorne, *Philosophers Speak of God*, p. 407. The harshest criticism came from Max Otto, who suspected Wieman of being an atheist (*Is There a God?* Cycle 2).

37. Wieman, *Source of Human Good*, pp. 144–145. Wieman is quoting approvingly an unpublished paper of one of his students.

38. Wieman, *Methods of Private Religious Living*, p. 147.

39. Wieman, *Issues of Life*, p. 163.

40. "God and Value," *Religious Realism*, Macintosh, ed., p. 175. See also Max Otto, *Is There a God?* p. 88.

41. Wieman, *Source of Human Good*, p. 77, n. 2, and p. 264.

42. *Ibid.*, pp. 195–196.

43. Max Otto, *Is There a God?* p. 243; also Wieman, *Issues of Life*, p. 173, and his *Growth of Religion*, p. 259.

44. Wieman, *Growth of Religion*, p. 261.

45. Wieman, "God Is More than We Can Think," *loc. cit.*, p. 436.

46. Wieman, *Growth of Religion*, p. 292.

47. *Ibid.*, p. 315.
48. Wieman, *Man's Ultimate Commitment*, p. 21.
49. *Ibid.*, pp. 26–27.

Chapter VII The Transcendence of God

1. See Paul Lehmann, " Barth and Brunner: The Dilemma of the Protestant Mind," *Journal of Religion,* XX (April, 1940). The actual controversy is found in *Natural Theology* (The Centenary Press, London, 1946).

2. The logical analysts feel that philosophy's task must be conceived not in terms of the question of being but in terms of the question of statements. Certainly this is a legitimate and valuable dimension of the philosophical task, but surely philosophy and logical analysis are not synonymous.

3. Dietrich Bonhoeffer, *Creation and Fall* (S.C.M. Press, Ltd., London, 1959), p. 10.

4. See the Neo-Thomist literature, especially the writings of Austin Farrer and Eric Mascall as well as those of Jacques Maritain. Contemporary versions of the teleological argument are found in in Lecomte du Noüy's *Human Destiny* (Signet Books, 1949) and P. A. Bertocci's *Introduction to the Philosophy of Religion* (Prentice-Hall, Inc., 1951). Charles Hartshorne is perhaps the most serious contemporary perpetuator of Anselm. See " The Formal Validity and Real Significance of the Ontological Argument." For the moral argument, see A. E. Taylor's classic, *The Faith of a Moralist* (The Macmillan Company, London, 1930).

5. See especially Martin Heidegger's *Sein und Zeit* in *Jahrbuch für Philosophie und Phaenomenologische Forschung,* Vol. 8, 1927; Albert Camus's *The Stranger* (Vintage Books, Inc., 1956); and Miguel de Unamuno's *The Tragic Sense of Life* (The Macmillan Company, 1921).

6. Martin Heidegger, *The Question of Being* (Twayne Publishers, Inc., 1958), pp. 55–57.

7. Rudolf Otto, *The Idea of the Holy,* Chs. III and IV.

8. Friedrich Schleiermacher, *On Religion: Speeches to Its Cultured Despisers* (Harper & Brothers, 1958), p. 69.

9. We are following Karl Jaspers here. See especially *Reason and Existenz,* Second Lecture.

10. Carl Michalson, "The Real Presence of the Hidden God," *Faith and Ethics*, Ramsey, ed., p. 257.

11. See Ch. I, pp. 37–40.

12. Rudolf Bultmann, *Primitive Christianity in Its Contemporary Setting* (Meridian Books, Inc., 1957), pp. 186, 166, 131.

13. John A. T. Robinson, *In the End God* (James Clarke & Company, Ltd., Publishers, London, 1950), p. 36, also pp. 124–125. Cf. Bonhoeffer, "The Church of Holy Scripture — and there is no other 'Church' — lives from the end. Therefore it reads all Holy Scripture as the book of the end . . ." (*Creation and Fall*, p. 8.)

14. See Rudolf Otto, *op. cit.*

15. See Gal. 3:6; Phil. 3:8–9; etc. See Martin Luther, *A Commentary on St. Paul's Epistle to the Galatians* (James Clarke & Company, Ltd., Publishers, London, 1953), pp. 223 ff., and 135.

16. See, for instance, Cyril C. Richardson, *The Doctrine of the Trinity*, pp. 35–37.

17. See Otto Piper's analysis of German theology of this period, *Recent Developments in German Protestantism* (S.C.M. Press, Ltd., London, 1934). Barth very early saw in Tillich a continuation of the basic principle of Schleiermacher's theology. *Church Dogmatics* (T. & T. Clark, Edinburgh, 1936), Vol. I, 1, pp. 52, 68–70.

18. Cushman, *loc. cit.*, pp. 210–211.

19. See Bultmann, "The Question of Natural Revelation," *Essays Philosophical and Theological* (S.C.M. Press, Ltd., London, 1955).

SOME SUGGESTIONS
FOR FURTHER READING

Chapter I   The New Temper and Its Background

Some of the key books and articles used to describe the transition in theology to the " realistic " temper are the following. For the general development of Protestant thought out of the Reformation see John Dillenberger and Claude Welch, *Protestant Christianity* (Charles Scribner's Sons, 1955), and A. C. McGiffert, *The Rise of Modern Religious Ideas* (The Macmillan Company, 1915). Especially good on the nineteenth century are Karl Barth, *From Rousseau to Ritschl* (S.C.M. Press, Ltd., London, 1959); Hans Frei, " Niebuhr's Theological Background," *Faith and Ethics,* Paul Ramsey, ed. (Harper & Brothers, 1957); and H. R. Macintosh, *Types of Modern Theology* (James Nisbet & Co., Ltd., London, 1937).

Some excellent monographs describing the rise of the contemporary theological situation are Daniel Day Williams, *What Present-Day Theologians Are Thinking* (Harper & Brothers, rev. ed., 1959); John Dillenberger, *God Hidden and Revealed* (Muhlenberg Press, 1953); Samuel McCrea Cavert and H. P. Van Dusen, eds., *The Church Through Half a Century* (Charles Scribner's Sons, 1936); and Paul Tillich, *The Religious Situation* (Meridian Books, Inc., 1956). Some key works describing the transition in American theology are George Hammar, *Christian Realism in Contemporary American Theology* (Lundequistska Bokhandeln, Uppsala, 1940); Walter Marshall Horton, *Realistic Theology* (Harper & Brothers, 1934); D. C. Macintosh, ed., *Religious Realism* (The Macmillan Company, 1931); and Mary Frances Thelen, *Man as Sinner in Contemporary American Realistic Theology* (King's Crown Press, 1946).

Chapter II   Reinhold Niebuhr

Since Niebuhr feels that his early works through *An Interpretation of Christian Ethics* (Harper & Brothers, 1935) are not indicative of his present thought, the most fruitful way to study Niebuhr is to begin with *Beyond Tragedy* (Charles Scribner's Sons, 1937), or works thereafter. Niebuhr has published several collections of his essays, any one of which would serve as a good introduction. They include *Beyond Tragedy; Christianity and Power Politics* (Charles Scribner's Sons, 1940); *Christian Realism and Political Problems* (Charles Scribner's Sons, 1953); and the recent *Pious and Secular America* (Charles Scribner's Sons, 1958). Niebuhr's great work, however, is his published Gifford Lectures *The Nature and Destiny of Man,* two volumes in one (Charles Scribner's Sons, 1951), while *Faith and History* (Charles Scribner's Sons, 1949) and *The Self and the Dramas of History* (Charles Scribner's Sons, 1955) vigorously extend the theological material of the Gifford Lectures.

Of Niebuhr's articles the most succinct statement of his total thought is " Christ vs. Socrates," *Saturday Review* (Dec. 18, 1954). Other key articles are his " Intellectual Autobiography " and " Reply " found in Charles W. Kegley and Robert W. Bretall, eds., *Reinhold Niebuhr: His Religious, Social, and Political Thought* (The Macmillan Company, 1956); " The Truth in Myths," J. S. Bixler, ed., *The Nature of Religious Experience* (Harper & Brothers, 1937); and " Ten Years That Shook My World," *The Christian Century,* LVI (April 26, 1939). The best secondary material on Niebuhr are the essays in the Kegley and Bretall volume. George Hammar's *Christian Realism,* mentioned previously, contains a classic study of Niebuhr's early development. An older analysis from a critical and conservative point of view is E. J. Carnell, *The Theology of Reinhold Niebuhr* (Wm. B. Eerdmans Publishing Company, 1951), while a recent summary is that of Hans Hoffman, *The Theology of Reinhold Niebuhr* (Charles Scribner's Sons, 1956).

Chapter III   Paul Tillich

Since the elusive character of Tillich's thought is mostly due to its rootage in nineteenth-century German philosophy, background reading is important for a serious study of Tillich. See especially Fried-

SOME SUGGESTIONS FOR FURTHER READING   247

rich Schelling, *The Ages of the World* (Columbia University Press, 1942), and *Of Human Freedom* (The Open Court Publishing Company, 1936); G. F. W. Hegel, *The Phenomenology of Mind* (The Macmillan Company, 1949), and *The Science of Logic*, 2 vols. (The Macmillan Company, 1929). See also Sören Kierkegaard, *Concluding Unscientific Postscript* (Princeton University Press, 1941).

A good way to begin reading Tillich is to start with his two books of sermons: *The Shaking of the Foundations* (Charles Scribner's Sons, 1948) and *The New Being* (Charles Scribner's Sons, 1955); and also his shorter monographs: *Biblical Religion and the Search for Ultimate Reality* (University of Chicago Press, 1955); *The Dynamics of Faith* (Harper & Brothers, 1957); and *Love, Power, and Justice* (Oxford University Press, 1954). Three books cover the most important of Tillich's works written while still in Germany, i.e., before 1933: *The Religious Situation* (Meridian Books, Inc., 1956); *The Interpretation of History* (Charles Scribner's Sons, 1936); and *The Protestant Era* (The University of Chicago Press, 1948). Tillich's "system" and his full philosophical theology is found in the two volumes (a third one still to come) of his *Systematic Theology* (University of Chicago Press, 1951, 1957), which cover three of the five parts of the system. Most of his key articles are now published in a volume *The Theology of Culture*, R. C. Kimball, ed. (Oxford University Press, 1959).

The best secondary studies are probably those found in Kegley and Bretall, *The Theology of Paul Tillich* (The Macmillan Company, 1952). The one full-length book on Tillich by one author is R. Allan Killen, *The Ontological Theology of Paul Tillich* (J. H. Kok, Kämpen, 1956); while good chapters and monographs on Tillich are found in Robert C. Johnson, *Authority in Protestant Theology* (The Westminster Press, 1959); and Sheldon Smith, *Changing Conceptions of Original Sin* (Charles Scribner's Sons, 1955).

Chapter IV   Karl Heim

Since Heim's thought reflects new currents in physics as well as philosophy (Buber and Bergson) and cultural analyses (Spengler), the following books would serve as good preludes to his work: Henri Bergson, *Creative Evolution* (Random House, Inc., 1944) and *Creative Mind* (Philosophical Library, Inc., 1946); Martin Buber,

I and Thou (Charles Scribner's Sons, 1937) and *Between Man and Man* (The Beacon Press, Inc., 1955); Oswald Spengler, *The Decline of the West,* 2 vols. (Alfred A. Knopf, Inc. 1929); and Louis de Broglie, *The Revolution in Physics* (Noonday Paperbacks, 1956).

Heim's writings are many and at least twelve of his books have been translated into English. Many of these are collections of sermons and essays. Possibly the most significant early work in English is *The New Divine Order* (S.C.M. Press, Ltd., London, 1930). However, the work that represents Heim's lifelong effort is the multi-volumed, *The Evangelical Faith and Modern Thought.* The first five volumes are now in English: *God Transcendent* (James Nisbet & Co., Ltd., London, 1935); *Jesus the Lord* (Oliver & Boyd, Ltd., Edinburgh, 1959); *Jesus the World-Ender* (Oliver & Boyd, Ltd., Edinburgh, 1959); *Christian Faith and Natural Science* (S.C.M. Press, Ltd., London, 1953); and *The Transformation of the Scientific World View* (S.C.M. Press, Ltd., London, 1953). The only secondary source on Heim so far is E. L. Allen's brief pamphlet, *Jesus Our Leader: A Guide to the Thought of Karl Heim* (Hodder & Stoughton, Ltd., London, 1948).

Chapter V   Charles Hartshorne

A. N. Whitehead and Charles S. Peirce are probably the two key figures behind Hartshorne's "revisionary theism." For Whitehead, see the works consulted in the text. For Peirce, see Charles Hartshorne and Paul Weiss, eds., *The Collected Papers of Charles Sanders Peirce,* 8 vols. (Harvard University Press, 1931–1958). Also illuminating would be Gustav Fechner's *Zendavesta* (Leipzig, 1851); and *Religion of a Scientist,* Walter Lowrie, ed. (Routledge & Kegan Paul, Ltd., London, 1947).

Possibly the best brief encounter with Hartshorne's thought is afforded by the short essays collected in *Reality as Social Process* (Free Press, 1953); and also Hartshorne's introductory essay to *Philosophers Speak of God,* William L. Reese, coeditor (University of Chicago Press, 1953). Hartshorne's early period is represented by the essays in *Beyond Humanism* (Willett, Clark & Company, 1937). The full statement of his theism, however, is to be found in two works written in the 1940s. The first and longer statement is *Man's Vision of God and the Logic of Theism* (Willett, Clark & Company,

1941); while the later elaboration is *The Divine Relativity* (Yale University Press, 1948). Hartshorne's articles are numerous. Among the more important are "The Divine Relativity and Absoluteness: A Reply," *Review of Metaphysics*, IV (Sept., 1950); "The Idea of God — Literal or Analogical?" *The Christian Scholar*, XXXIX (June, 1956); and "Whitehead and Berdyaev: Is There Tragedy in God?" *Journal of Religion*, XXXVII (April, 1957). Secondary works on Hartshorne are almost nonexistent.

Chapter VI   Henry Nelson Wieman

The writings of both Whitehead and Peirce would be helpful preparation for the study of Wieman. However, more relevant to his contextualism and operationalism would be: Stephen C. Pepper, *Aesthetic Quality* (Charles Scribner's Sons, 1938) and *World Hypotheses* (University of California Press, 1942); Charles William Morris, *Foundations of the Theory of Signs* (University of Chicago Press, 1938); and John Dewey, *Experience and Nature* (Dover Publications, Inc., 1958).

Wieman himself has written almost a dozen books. Examples of his early works are *Religious Experience and Scientific Method* (The Macmillan Company, 1927); *The Wrestle of Religion with Truth* (The Macmillan Company, 1927); and *The Issues of Life* (Abingdon Press, 1930). An example of Wieman's early practical religiousness is his *Methods of Private Religious Living* (The Macmillan Company, 1929). If the reader, however, wants to study Wieman in his most elaborate and mature statements, the following should be consulted. For his philosophy and value theory, *The Source of Human Good* (University of Chicago Press, 1946) remains definitive. Three books attempting to apply "naturalistic theism" to cultural problems are *The Directive in History* (The Beacon Press, Inc., 1949); *Now We Must Choose* (The Macmillan Company, 1941); and the recent *Man's Ultimate Commitment* (Southern Illinois University Press, 1958). The footnotes to Chapter VI will include references to many of Wieman's key articles and debates. Although no lengthy secondary work on Wieman has yet appeared, the reader should anticipate the publication of a Library of Living Theology volume on Wieman's thought. See also James Alfred Martin, Jr., *Empirical Philosophies of Religion* (King's Crown Press, 1945), pp. 86–110; and Huston

Smith, "An Operational View of God," *Journal of Religion*, XXXI (April, 1951).

Chapter VII The Transcendence of God

On the notion of the Transcendent as Limit (part 1), the following may be helpful: Dietrich Bonhoeffer, *Creation and Fall* (S.C.M. Press, Ltd., London, 1959); Edwyn Bevan, *Symbolism and Belief* (George Allen & Unwin, Ltd., London, 1938), Ch. 2; Martin Heidegger, *Existence and Being* (Vision Press, Ltd., London, 1949); and *The Question of Being* (Twayne Publishers, Inc., 1958); Karl Jaspers, *Reason and Existenz* (The Noonday Press, 1957); Rudolf Otto, *The Idea of the Holy* (Oxford University Press, London, 1923). For the Transcendent as God, Part 2, material from the writings of Bonhoeffer, Barth, Bultmann, Brunner, and Kierkegaard would all be relevant in addition to the writings of the five men considered in this study. Key articles and books on the theological impasse have been referred to in the notes. The "conversionism" represented in the analogy of grace might be further studied in H. Richard Niebuhr, *Christ and Culture* (Harper & Brothers, 1951), Ch. 6; and *The Meaning of Revelation* (The Macmillan Company, 1941).

Index

Absolute, the, 98, 102
Abstraction, 139, 143
Actualism, 40
Actus Purus, 131, 158
Agapē, 71 f., 203, 204
Alexander, Samuel, 46, 196
Ames, E. S., 24, 163
Analogia entis, 126
Analogia fidei, 213
Analogia gratiae, 217 ff.
Anselm, 195
Apologetics, 124
Aristotle, 83, 139
Atheism, 105
Augustine, 68
Autonomy, 18–20, 26, 55

Barth, Karl, 33, 36, 103, 104, 183, 191 ff., 210, 212 ff., 216
Becker, Carl, 19
Beginning, the, 194 ff., 205
Begriff, 99
Being, 142–143, 207
Being-itself, 86–87
Bergson, Henri, 78, 113, 143, 164, 206, 234 n. 10
Bernhardt, William, 180
Bevan, Edwyn, 103
Boccaccio, 15
Boehme, 33, 89, 98, 99
Bonhoeffer, D., 195, 208
Bourgeois culture, 19, 27 f., 55
Brunner, Emil, 26, 33, 36, 38, 192 f., 212 ff., 218

Bruno, 15, 105, 107
Buber, M., 30, 46, 114, 118, 225
Bultmann, Rudolf, 36, 192, 206, 212 ff., 214

Calhoun, Robert L., 30, 35, 153, 175, 181, 242 n. 36
Camus, A., 197
Capitalistic spirit, 76
Carnell, E. J., 71
Chicago School, 163, 165, 239 n. 2
Chronos, 80
Classicism, 61 f.
Cohen, Morris R., 155
Common sense, 67
Communism, 55, 103 f., 196
Contextualism, 173, 175, 179 f., 240 n. 19
Continuity, 16 ff., 38
Copernicus, 15, 105, 107
Correlation, method of, 97 ff., 213, 233 n. 33
Creatio ex nihilo, 50, 158
Creation, doctrine of, 68, 204 ff.
Cross, 49

Dante, 15
Darwin, Charles, 18
Dasein, 197, 203
Deism, 15, 17, 19
Demonic, the, 75 ff.
Demythologizing, 34
Depth, the, 198 f., 208
Determinism, 108

Deus absconditus, 46, 189, 208, 235 n. 34
Dewey, John, 132, 136, 164, 179
Dialectic, 70–71, 99
Dialogic philosophy, 43, 48, 114
Dickie, E. P., 103
Dillenberger, John, 33
Dimension, 116 ff., 234 n. 12
Ding an sich, 107

Eichrodt, Walther, 34
Élan vital, 78
Emmett, Dorothy, 88, 91, 92, 124
Encompassing, the, 29
Encyclopedists, 16, 107
Enlightenment, 17, 19
Ens realissimum, 41, 126, 159
Entropy, 185
Erasmus, 15
Erigena, 132
Erlebnis, 38
Eschatology, 70, 205 ff.
Essence and existence, 38–39
Essential being, 101
Eternity, 71
Event, 174
Evil, 188
Evolution, 18, 23
  emergent, 31, 196
Existentialism, 28–29, 100, 225
Explanation, nature of, 198

Fechner, G., 145, 235 n. 16
Ferré, Nels F. S., 93
Feuerbach, 14, 22
Fichte, 98
Finitude, 29, 69, 84, 201
  existentialist analysis of, 29
  and the infinite, 84
  and nonbeing, 84, 90
Forsyth, P. T., 22, 26
Freedom, 44, 48, 95
  and individuality, 48, 55 f.
  and nature, 63
  and structure, 47, 53
Freud, Sigmund, 27
Fundamentalism, 26 f., 225 n. 19

Galileo, 15
German Faith Movement, 20, 21, 75, 78, 104, 106, 109, 233 n. 1
Geworfenheit, 118, 120
God
  as absolute, 70, 132, 159 f., 189, 210 f.
  body of, 157 f.
  as creator, 65, 121 f., 134, 158, 186, 204 ff.
  as event, 180 ff.
  as free, 46, 206 f.
  as hidden, 46 f., 189
  as holy, 208 ff.
  as immanent, 72, 126
  as judge, 48, 188, 206
  as omniscient, 133, 152
  as organism, 149 ff.
  as personal, 45, 84, 92 f., 126 f., 153, 187, 231 nn. 19, 20
  " place " of, 13 f., 202 f.
  primordal and consequent natures of, 50, 140 f., 146 ff.
  as redeemer, 48, 205 ff.
  as suffering, 49, 72
  as transcendent self, 45 ff.

Hammar, George, 72
Hartshorne, Charles, 50, 72, 130–161, 206, 236–239, 248–249
Hebraism, 52, 59
Hegel, F., 22, 28, 29, 88, 89, 97–102, 200
Heidegger, Martin, 29, 118, 120, 199
Height, the, 199 f., 210
Heilsgeschichte, 33
Heim, Karl, 26, 30, 47, 73, 96, 103–

129, 138, 141, 155, 165, 233–236, 247–248
Hellenism, 52, 54, 69, 229 n. 37
Heteronomy, 78
History, 60 ff.
History of Religions School, 34
Hitler, A., 75, 104, 111
Hocking, W. E., 130, 164
Hodge, Charles, 26
Hulme, T. E., 31
Humanism, 15, 134 ff., 162, 236 n. 5
Husserl, E., 130
Hypertheism, 82, 84, 90 f., 147, 211, 230 n. 7

I and Thou, 114 ff., 119
Idealism, philosophy of, 22 f., 55 f.
Identity principle, 89, 97–100
Immanence, 16, 71, 223, 224
  cosmological, 16
  demonic, 76
  humanistic, 16
Immanentism, 20, 27, 80, 106, 138, 167
  epistemological, 38
  metaphysical, 108, 109
  methodological, 24, 182
Individuality, 48, 55 f.
  and nature, 63
  and personality, 84, 92 f.

Jaspers, Karl, 29, 202, 208
Jesus Christ, 52, 203, 207, 213, 217
Justitia originalis, 62

Kairos Circle, 75, 80, 212
Kant, 77, 107, 111, 117, 195, 216
Kerygma, 14, 37, 52, 212, 214, 219
Kierkegaard, Sören, 27 f., 36, 38, 89, 102
Knowledge, theory of, 168 ff., 240 n. 10
Kroner, Richard, 179

Lebensphilosophie, 75
Lehmann, Paul, 193
Leibniz, 140
Liberal theology, 20 ff., 52, 162, 166, 223 f., 226
  and dialectic, 71
  and humanism, 21, 22 f.
  and immanence, 21
  and supernaturalism, 21
Limit, the, 201 f., 250
Logos, 80
Lovejoy, Arthur, 16, 30
Luther, 138
Luther renaissance, 33

Macintosh, D. C., 178
Man
  as *homo religiosus,* 24
  as individual, 55, 57
  as self-transcendent, 43 ff., 55
Marx, Karl, 22, 27
Mathews, Shailer, 163
Meaning, 55 ff., 172 f., 187, 228 n. 21
Mechanism, 65
Meland, E. W., 162
Metaphysics, 31 f., 173 ff.
Montaigne, 15
Morgan, Lloyd, 31, 117
Morris, C. W., 181
Mysterium tremendum, 209
Mysticism, 32 f., 226
Myth, 54, 73, 184, 194

Naturalism, 61, 62, 65–66, 199
  naturalistic theism, 167
  new naturalism, 32, 37, 173, 241 n. 20
  reductive, 142
Nature, 63 ff., 67, 139, 141 ff., 176
Nazism, 76, 103
Néant, le, 197
Neo-orthodoxy, 102, 166, 212

Neo-supernaturalism, 10, 25, 37, 166, 212, 240 n. 8
Neo-Thomism, 9, 243 n. 4
New physics, 107 ff., 110, 115
New Theology controversy, 22
Newton, Isaac, 15, 106 ff.
Niebuhr, H. Richard, 20, 250
Niebuhr, Reinhold, 37, 42-74, 96, 138, 167, 226-229, 246
Nietzsche, Friedrich, 22, 27, 29 f.
Nihilism, 103-104
Nomos, 78, 81
Nonbeing, 82, 84, 90, 194

Obscurantism, 10, 20, 52 f.
Ontolatry, 131, 236 n. 3
Ontology, 228 n. 17
  Niebuhr on, 51 ff., 227 n. 10
  Tillich on, 82 ff., 230 n. 8
Operationalism, 174, 221
Ordo Cognoscendi, 29, 217
Ordo Essendi, 217
Organismic theism, 50 f., 139 ff.
Otto, Max, 135
Otto, Rudolf, 32, 200

Panentheism, 137, 149
Panpsychism, 65, 118, 142, 238 n. 17
Pantheism, 109, 142, 150
Parmenides, 69
Participation, 90, 93, 94, 96, 100-102
Pascal, Blaise, 41
Passibilitas Dei, 69, 71
Peirce, Charles, 131, 164
Pepper, Stephen, 165, 175, 179
Perfection, nature of, 137 f.
Perry, R. B., 25, 164 f.
Philosophy, nature of, 193-194, 243 n. 2
Philosophy of religion, 162-163, 167
Pietism, 17, 26
Plato, Platonism, 69 ff., 101, 140, 199
Plotinus, 69

Pluralism, 66 f.
Polarities, polar world, 94, 155, 118 ff., 201
Pragmatism, 165
Preservation, 208
Process, 142 ff., 175
Process philosophy, 139 ff., 226
Profane, the, 75 ff.
Protestant orthodoxy, 26
Protestant principle, 81

Realism, 25 ff.
  critical realism, 25, 31
  and existentialism, 29
  realistic theology, 25, 36, 224-225 n. 16
  religious realism, 25, 31, 224-225 n. 16
  and World War I, 35
Reason
  ecstatic, 91 f.
  and self-transcendence, 44
  technological, 76 f., 91
Religion, 177
  crisis of, 105 ff., 131 ff., 166
Renaissance, 15, 52, 55
Revelation, 91, 102, 213 ff.
Ritschlian school, 22, 33
Romantic movement, 16 f., 56
Royce, J., 164

Schelling, F.. 28 f., 79, 81, 85, 88, 89, 97-102, 230 n. 9, 232 n. 30
Schleiermacher, F., 17, 32, 40, 200, 215, 217
Scholasticism, 99, 126
Science, 165, 168 ff., 194 f.
Secularism, 105, 110
Sein des Seienden, 199
Self (Ego),
  and body, 49
  Heim on, 111 ff.
  in idealism, 234 n. 8

mystery of, 45, 47
self-consciousness, 44 f.
Smith, Gerald Birney, 163
Social Darwinians, 20
Social gospel, 21, 24
Sola gratia, 38
Sola scriptura, 15
Space, 117 ff., 125 f., 234 n. 13
Spencer, 20
Spengler, O., 104, 113
Spinoza, 16, 136, 142
Supernaturalism, 9 f., 18, 23, 77, 84, 88
   and immanentism, 81
   and liberalism, 21
Surrelativism, 160, 237 n. 8
Symbol, 84, 87, 92 f., 96, 231 n. 4

Theism, 131 ff., 163
Theologia naturalis, 193
Theological Discussion Group, 37, 42
Theological impasse, the, 40 f., 212 ff., 226 n. 37
Theological Renaissance, 13, 32, 40, 245
Theology, 53 f.
   Biblical, 33
   correlation (apologetic), 40, 213 ff.
   historical, 33
   kerygmatic (confessional), 192, 213 ff.
Theonomy, 78, 80 f.
Thomas Aquinas, 132, 195
Tillich, Paul, 10, 26, 47, 74, 75–102, 103, 111, 147, 155, 165, 167, 187, 192, 193 f., 211, 212 ff., 218, 230–233, 246 f.
Time, 43
   and eternity, 51, 69 ff.

Transcendence
   epistemological, 38 f., 189 ff.
   existential, 39, 127 ff.
   as freedom, 95 f.
   functional, 186 ff.
   and history, 62
   intramundane, 111 ff., 123 ff.
   kerygmatic, 37 ff., 51, 187 ff., 202 ff.
   and meaning, 59 f.
   nonsymbolic, 82 ff., 231 n. 14
   ontological, 55 ff., 183, 184 f.
   as superiority, 153 ff.
   supramundane, 123 ff.
   symbolic, 91 ff.
Troeltsch, E., 164
Truth, 38 f., 169

Unconditioned, the (*das Unbedingte*), 77 ff., 86, 91, 230 n. 4
Ungrund, 90
Unvordenkliche, 81, 100

Value, theory of, 170 ff., 240 n. 16
Van Dusen, H. P., 31
Via negativa, 88, 133, 221
Via Revelatus, 92

Weltanschauung, 15, 73, 105
Weltbild, 15, 34, 105
Wesley, John, 17
Whitehead, Alfred North, 50, 55, 130, 139–141, 143, 170, 173, 179, 180, 184 f., 199, 208, 237
Wieman, Henry Nelson, 31, 162–191, 239–243, 249–250
Wild, John, 153
Williams, Daniel Day, 13, 228 n. 21
World War I, 24, 35, 103
Wortmächtigkeit, 214

www.ingramcontent.com/pod-product-compliance
Lightning Source LLC
Chambersburg PA
CBHW050439240426
43661CB00055B/2444